MICHELLE FORD

OLYMPIC CHAMPION

For my sons, Michael and Bo.

MICHELLE FORD
OLYMPIC CHAMPION

turning the tide

with Craig Lord

FAIRPLAY
PUBLISHING

First published in 2024 by Fair Play Publishing
PO Box 4101, Balgowlah Heights, NSW 2093, Australia

www.fairplaypublishing.com.au

ISBN: 978-1-925914-92-4
ISBN: 978-1-925914-93-1 (ePub)

Cover design and typesetting by Leslie Priestley

Front cover photograph of Michelle Ford supplied by the author.

Back cover photograph by Sebastien Moret, Amarock.
All other photographs are from the personal collection of Michelle Ford Eriksson.

All inquiries should be made to the Publisher via hello@fairplaypublishing.com.au

NATIONAL
LIBRARY
OF AUSTRALIA

A catalogue record of this book is available from the National Library of Australia.

Contents

International
Olympic
Committee

The President

Foreword

Michelle Ford is a force of nature. Like so many Olympians her athletic journey is an inspiration. It is a story of how an individual's sporting perseverance and eventual triumph carries a much wider message for us all in how the human spirit can overcome adversity.

First and foremost, Michelle is a competitor in everything she does, and from the very first time we met more than forty years ago she has always held strong opinions, and never been afraid to express them. She was always a strong advocate in all the areas and issues that impact the lives of athletes, whether it be equal opportunities and access in sport for women, the fight against doping or our shared crusade for the central role for athletes in the management and administration of sport.

Michelle's sporting record speaks for itself, but her continued fight against the iniquities of doping, particularly her continuing fight to right the wrongs of the era in which she competed highlights her amazing tenacity and the fighting spirit, which was the foundation of her incredible sporting performances as a young athlete.

Those who know Michelle also know that aside from the campaigner and competitor is also a person who enjoys life and who is a loyal ally. This book of her life shows her battles and her Olympic triumphs, and it also shows a remarkable character whose Olympic journey did not end when she stopped competing.

Thomas Bach OLY

Part 1
Star Rising

Chapter 1
Water Leaves No Trace
of Sweat and Tears

I leave the launch pad bound for another world. For a fleeting moment, I see the lights, colours and crowd in the mirror of still water.

I'm flying through the air. The surface shatters into fragments, like a star exploding. And I plunge into another world. I'm in my element.

For a moment, everything's a blur. A galaxy of bubbles. The rush and rapid lap of liquid around me silences the roar.

It's been like that since I was a young child splashing in the spray off the beaches of Sydney, diving into waves and bodysurfing back to shore in a powerful surge.

Later, on the way to making my first Australian Olympic swimming team at 13, setting world records at 15 and claiming an Olympic gold medal in the month I turned 18, the blur was a sequence of streamline, kick, feel, catch the swell, pull, ride, repeat.

Long before I reached my teens, the fun had turned to dedication, determination, discipline and the daily pursuit of hyperfitness and the sharpening of skills that the swimmer calls a 'feel for water'. Swimming is a sport of racing swans. Much of the strain, gain and even pain is out of sight below the ripples.

In water, you see neither sweat nor tears, though plenty were shed by me and generations of female athletes whose fate it was to compete during an era when Cold-War politics spilled into sport like poison.

It was a time of boycott, death threats, doping and incredulity, a season of light and darkness, a spring of hope for some, and a winter of despair that's lasted a lifetime for others.

How to fathom it all 40 years on?

The Here, Now and Then

Legs crossed on the lambswool carpet, I sit opening the past with a keen sense of the present. I'm back in my childhood bedroom, echoes whispering from the walls. It's almost exactly as it was back then in its original glory: a museum of memorabilia, medals, trophies, letters. And boxes upon boxes of books and news articles, some of which I'd never opened.

These cuttings had not been interesting to me at the time and for decades since I'd avoided the joys and sorrows of what was and could never be changed.

The events of the past decade have drawn me back to what I regard as a timeless story. It's not locked in this room; it's not history on a shelf in a box. It's a living lesson and parallel of developments unfolding in world sport today.

As we approach the Paris 2024 Olympic Games, talk of boycott hangs heavy in the air following the Russian invasion of Ukraine.

Each year, countless athletes either decide to dope or are persuaded and even coerced into cheating. We know because technological advances in the past 20 years have made it possible to freeze blood and reanalyse samples whenever new methods of detecting banned substances are developed.

As a result of the International Olympic Committee's program of revisiting frozen samples, 65 athletes from the Beijing 2008 Olympics were retrospectively disqualified. A total of 51 medals were taken away, nine of them gold.

During the same exercise for London 2012, 139 doped athletes were taken out, 65 of them caught in the reanalysis program and retrospectively banned. Of those, 39 had to hand back medals, including 13 titles. Through the International Olympic Committee's medal reallocation program, doping performances have been struck from the record books and prizes have been handed to the next clean athlete on the result sheet.

The fallout from the Russian doping scandal from the 2014 Sochi Winter Olympics was still rumbling on when Tokyo hosted the COVID-delayed Summer Games. Memories came back to me. It was the biggest systematic cheating controversy since my era in the 1970s and '80s when East Germany plotted the most audacious systematic heist ever witnessed in world sport. The ghosts of a time when female athletes in particular were used and abused as pawns in a Cold War game of supremacy have not been laid to rest.

Generations of athletes, their families, coaches and communities continue to be haunted by that era. Some have passed away without ever having felt any sense of healing or seeing the guardians and governors of sport reach for reconciliation and justice.

Back to the Future

Driven by a keen sense of déjà vu, I finally found the reason and strength to go back to the boxes, books and folders that were now on the carpet in front of me.

Half a century ago. Where to start? My fingers flipped mechanically through the pages of the books on Australia's sporting greats. I'm there, woven into my country's tapestry. A flood of memories unleashed emotions I'd kept under lock and key for all too long.

Was it time? Courage replaced reluctance and I found myself standing on a chair heaving my archive out of high cupboards in search of answers.

As in my swimming days, once I'd made up my mind, nothing could stop me. It was time to celebrate and come to terms with what I had achieved and what I had endured along with generations of female athletes robbed of their dignity and just rewards.

It was daunting at first but as I rewound, I saw the battles and the many injustices that can shape an athlete for the rest of their life, and I felt obliged to dive deeper. The deception, the political games, manipulation in the media, the cynicism of armchair critics and arrogant amateur blazers, the egos; it all came flooding back.

For the first time, all these decades later, it dawned on me that the competition isn't just the person in the lane next to you; it's the unknown, the unexpected, the things that society throws at you.

Beyond the lights, cameras, action, medals, headlines and dramas played out in the media, a lot of opportunity flowed from the hard work. International travel and lifelong friendships were part of the sunny side of a life less ordinary as an Olympic athlete.

Yet as I browsed through all of that in the cuttings and scrapbooks and letters locked away for decades, the story behind the story was unavoidable. Decisive parts of my story remained untold.

By the time I arrived at my second Olympics in Moscow, I was already an old hand when it came to understanding that rivals were not only those you competed against but those who doped them, the East German architects of the sporting crime of the century.

I'd been coached to win and expectations of success were high for my debut at Montreal 1976 but the prize I took home was not the gold, silver or bronze that someone wins in all events once every four years. It was the gem of knowledge that there was much more to this game of Games than I could possibly have imagined in the innocence of my youth.

It seemed that the stirring and motivational 'Citius, Altius, Fortius' ('Faster, Higher, Stronger') Olympic motto was also a mantra of ambition for those attracted to sport by a gold rush of a different kind. One in which the athlete was a mere pawn in the bigger

Games in which democracy was in the blue corner, and communism in the red.

There's great aestheticism, beauty, grace and gratitude in a life dedicated to athletic pursuit and many of the lessons learned set you up for the long years ahead, providing you with thick skin helpful to survival. Resilience and an ability to keep moving forward no matter what are powerful tools in the kit of life.

At the same time, fair play, athlete welfare and justice were all too often trampled underfoot, not only by 'the other side', the rivals in the next lane and their controllers in the shadows, but by our very own guardians. They were always men and they were mostly amateurs with more blazers than knowledge and integrity. They were consistent: their self-interest and self-importance finished ahead of all athletes every time, and most especially if you happened to be a woman.

And here I sat more than four decades on, the same issues still playing out like a broken record.

Time to take the plunge. Time to write it down.

For a moment, everything's a blur ... the bubbles start to clear and I'm coming up for air with every passing box unturned.

This is my story.

Chapter 2
In the Beginning

"Hide not your talents, they for use were made, What's a sundial in the shade?"
– Benjamin Franklin

A 1976 study by a Cologne sports science team on German children and adolescents concluded that Olympic champions are born to excel in their sport. *Swimming World Magazine* highlighted its key findings: hereditary factors are vital and suggested that while the average adolescent absorbs 45 millilitres (ml) of oxygen per kilo of body weight, anything over 60ml indicated a potential champion.

On that and other measures, including attitude and a stubborn refusal to see size as a setback, I was born to compete—and swim fast. Make no mistake: there's also a lot of heavy lifting and sacrifice in the alchemy of potential to champion.

My junior years toughened me up for all that was to unfold. I was the girl with two black teeth, sustained when I fell off the back of the scooter. Tagged as freckle-faced, shy and modest, I was slight in stature, timid and would usually only speak when spoken to. Best to sit quietly in the classroom and not seek attention, I thought.

Out on the sports field, my true character blossomed. Shoulders back, head focused, eyes flaring with intent. Calculating and competitive, I was ready for any challenge.

My elder sister Suzanne and I were born in England. It was the end of the baby boom years and hospitals were full. Lacking space and medical practitioners, the British government decreed that those families with running hot water must have their second child at home with a midwife.

My parents set off into the world after graduating from Sydney University. Her physiotherapy diploma in hand, Jan left for Canada, while Ian, responding to a campaign to recruit medical practitioners to Britain's National Health Service, moved to England, along with a few of his dentistry mates.

It wasn't long before my mother crossed the high seas from Edmonton, where she'd been an intern at a hospital, to England to be reunited with my father. They got married, Jan secured work in one of London's hospitals and my sister was the first of the Ford children to arrive, in September 1960.

I was born in a Buckinghamshire maternity ward in July 1962 after my mother had been granted special permission to have her second child in a hospital despite the UK policy of encouraging women with experience of childbirth to opt for home delivery.

Just six months later, our young family was heading for a life back in Australia with my parents having had enough of the drab, rainy English weather. My sister and I were destined to grow up in the land of our nationality.

We settled in the southern suburbs of Sydney in Blakehurst on the shores of the Georges River, a tributary to Botany Bay, the birthplace of modern Australia, and close to the southern beaches. Our lives would be tied to the water's edge.

My father, a keen sailor, just missed out in his bid for a berth on the 1976 Olympic team but was a member of the training crew based at Kensington, Sydney. My mother played competitive hockey and tennis. Convinced that children should do all sports to develop and strengthen the mind and body, the Fords made sure their children grew up active.

Falling in

On a sweltering, sticky summer's day, we kids were in our swimsuits and our parents were standing around the barbecue in a neighbour's garden. Their house was special: it had a backyard pool. In the '60s, not many houses had pools in Australia, so this was going to be a real treat.

Sitting on the side of the pool, legs dangling aimlessly in the water, I watched as the other children splashed about. I still hadn't been taught to swim, but I was three and seeing the other kids in the water was just too tempting. I launched myself off the side, felt the rush of cool, refreshing water and headed for the other side.

I was perfectly happy in this early quest until some commotion sparked my curiosity and I hurried as fast as I could across the pool. As I reached for the wall, I felt a hand grasp my arm and tug me out of the pool.

What was all the fuss about? Everyone was staring at me as I sat quietly with a towel around me. Someone asked me if I was okay. Why wouldn't I be? In fact, I was as pleased as punch. I could swim! The worried faces turned to astonishment as it dawned on them that I'd actually swum several metres across the pool. Self-taught.

My sister started swimming lessons soon after so I pestered the instructor to let me join her until he finally caved in and allowed me to take a kick-board and kick next to her. My competitive spirit out, I tried with all my might to beat Suzanne, which probably annoyed her a fair bit.

The teacher, Ross Cornwell, spotted it and to my delight, he took me seriously and began teaching me to swim. It wasn't long before I was able to join the local swim squad at the Sans Souci club pool. I wasn't aware of the man who would become my first coach but he'd spotted me on my first day on the team and would later write a note to me: "Michelle, you didn't need much teaching, you swam across the pool the very first day!"

Sporting opportunities for females were limited, but that didn't stop me. What couldn't be played by a girl in the open, like football and cricket, was played in the backyard. Besides that and swimming, there was ballet, gymnastics, netball, tennis, squash and music lessons to fit in after school as well as horse riding with my sister some weekends and chores in our family-run kiosks.

Other than catching up on schoolwork, weekends were otherwise spent water skiing and competing in scheduled Sunday sailing races. Bed was just about the only place we were ever still.

Until the age of six, we were not entered in any formal competitions, but that did not deter us from being the creative children that we were. A forest reserve leading down to a small inlet beach was our playground, where we spent many hours inventing challenging and competitive games.

For me, sport was fun. I loved testing myself, comparing results and trying to do better. Some games ended in squabbles which taught us life lessons in compromise and negotiation. I also developed a sense of strategy and how to get an edge and sometimes win, always within the boundaries of fair play. The times when I lost were the most important: they made me keener to win!

There were no barriers, no signs to say 'don't do this or that', and often we would extend our games beyond the initial challenge by adding an extra degree of risk, speed or precision to the task. Some were more dangerous than others, like who could walk along a small beam two metres up without falling down onto the rocks. We were free and although I didn't know it at the time, I was learning coordination skills that would stand me in great stead for the Olympic life ahead of me.

Adventurous, energetic and notorious for returning home with an injury or a rip here, or a scrape and a gash there, we were often greeted at the door by quizzical grown-ups asking, "And what have you been up to?" It was tautological. Before we could answer, a command inevitably followed: "Go and get cleaned up!"

During most of those years, my two black teeth were a burden I was keen to get rid of. Each festive season I'd sing, "All I want for Christmas is 'me' two front teeth!" Many years passed, it seemed to me back then, before my second teeth pushed through, with nature and my father's tugging skills mercifully freeing me of the stain of one of my many childhood knocks. I was able to smile again.

When Swimming Took Off

It was spring 1969. I was seven years old, my sister nine and my brother Richard five. My younger brother William would not arrive until my 10th birthday in 1972.

October school holidays announced the beginning of the summer season and the opening of the council 'Olympic' pools—50 metres long—the only dimension recognised if you wanted to set records and qualify for competitions.

Those pools and miles of coastal beaches became Sydneysiders' refuges during the hot, searing summers. Learning to swim, an essential of Australian life, was a key reason why swimming became the nation's most popular participation sport. Today, it's estimated that more than six million Australians swim regularly.

Private lessons had helped me develop good basic skills on front crawl before I improved on the other strokes in the training squad. Years of pestering our parents led to an above-ground 'Clark' pool being installed in our backyard where we honed our skills. You might think that we would have had enough of the water, but this was pure fun on our terms. Seeing how many lengths we could do underwater was one of our favourite challenges. Little did I realise that I was developing an aerobic capacity biding its time.

The next level was just around the corner, at our local Sans Souci pool.

It all started when we moved houses to Sans Souci. "A couple of afternoons a week, just to get you ready for the school races," our parents told us. But it wasn't long before me and the rest of the Ford clan had swimming practice twice a day, once on Saturdays and then at our local club races on Sundays. That was our weekly schedule from the time I was seven in the spring until I was 12.

It was a military operation of sorts, with other sports packed in at least once a week in between all the swimming. Saturdays would often be an early swim, then ballet at 9 a.m., tennis and squash from 10 a.m., netball training and then swimming competitions in the afternoon.

Sundays began with swim club at 7 a.m., then off to Sunday school for 10 a.m., after which we'd refuel in time to rig up our *Manly Junior* boat for the sailing races in the afternoon. My brother Richard was captain and me a forehand who spent most of my time bailing out the boat!

Swimming topped the bill but nothing else was off the menu. Piano, 30 minutes per child before school each Monday, meant that our mother would dash back and forth to the pool carting each one of us in turn to our time slot with the teacher. We all wanted to be first to make an early escape from doing more lengths of the chilly pool.

In January 1970, the end of the school year was only weeks away, and for me, it was the end of infant school. A new universe was waiting for me. I would leave behind the less stimulating classes of cutting and colouring and enter the more exciting world of primary school in January 1970 and its sports program. I couldn't wait! Open to those in Years 3 to 6, the fun would begin with the school swimming carnival in January, which left me a couple of months to learn and perfect the four strokes.

Except for the ocean pools, Sans Souci was the coldest pool in Sydney. It was open-planned and exposed to the elements blowing across the mouth of the Georges River Bay. Cold winds swept through every afternoon during training. We called them 'southerly busters' because the temperature would drop suddenly by 10°. Gusts whipped up white-tipped waves down the pool and our tiny arms struggled to clear the surface. We all swallowed large amounts of water, especially doing butterfly as the swell washed into our faces.

In Sydney, all outdoor pools closed for winter. They were unheated, so the swimming season began in October and ran through to March. Water temperatures murmured around 16°C early in the season, rising to a more pleasant 23°C at the height of summer.

Chattering teeth, lips and hands in multiple shades of purple were common. I was able to handle the chill better than most, although by the end of sessions I'd be shivering just as much as the rest. There were no hot showers to appease our scrawny bodies in those days. Shaking and goose-pimpled, we could barely speak before the thaw started in the warm car on the way home, our hands and hearts warmed by a steaming portion of hot chips from the fish shop next to the pool if we were lucky. Anticipation of those salted chips, those thick, warm strips of potatoes fried in oil, kept me going in the pool. They were the best.

Come the annual school carnival, the goal was simply to make it down a length of the pool. There were 12 of us in the 'little squad', as they called us. The senior squad was mostly surf guys training for the surf life competition, a national sport for men back then. And the coach was Ken Wiles, who from my kid's perspective was the big intimidating bloke who ran the pool.

One day as we gathered in our nylon suits, giggling and chatting under the huge oak tree that towered above the cement steps around the pool, the senior squad coach wandered towards us with a much younger man by his side. I'd seen him about the pool lots of times before.

"Kids, this is your new coach, his name is Dick Caine," said the boss before walking away. Blond, dressed in a white, long-sleeved t-shirt, shorts and white socks to his knees, Mr Caine introduced himself as a 'garbo', or garbage collector. A wave of chuckles erupted. Nobody believed him, but he was telling it like it was.

Determined and wanting to please our new coach, I set out to show him what a quick learner I was in the chaos of swerve-swimming that was dictated by an absence of lane ropes to divide us from the senior lanes, into which we'd often wander. I knew that the fastest swimmers led the way in training—and that's where I wanted to be.

Years later when I raced for Australia, Dick Caine said, "I first thought Michelle had something special when she could learn strokes in a few weeks where others took months, and though being very young, she could handle big sessions and freezing water."

Freckle-Faced Kid Done Good

Entry into the Australian school year back then was determined by your age on the 1st of July in any given year. However, the parents of those born in July could request early enrolment and that's what my mother and father did for me, understanding that I would always be the youngest and possibly the smallest in my year.

The rules were different in sport: you were allocated to a group based on your age on the 1st of January in a given year. Age was arbitrary to my coach. One morning he said to this seven-year-old, "I want you to enter all the races at the school carnival. Even the open events—100m freestyle and 200 individual medley."

"No," I said in stubborn refusal. I'd only swim the 50m races in my age group. The others didn't have to swim the other races, so why should I?

However, come the day, I'd been entered in the two longest races at the school carnival. On the starting blocks, dwarfed by the older and taller girls, fury with my coach filled my mind. Then the whistle blew and I had nowhere to go but the blocks. Some of the girls stood to the side of their block for the start because the platform was nearly a metre high and towered above the water. But I climbed up the red-tiled steps to the top and took the ready position, proud that I could dive off the 'big block'. The gun fired.

Coming up for my first breath, my arms and legs fell into race rhythm on the way to the end wall. I took my last stroke and looked across the lanes. I didn't feel particularly challenged. I hadn't won but it didn't matter. Secretly satisfied, I walked back to my coach. "You did very well, Mich," he said as he patted me on the shoulder. "See, you can do it". I wasn't quick enough to qualify for school State Championships, but I won all my age group races and became the star of my class.

Back in school the next day, I was the centre of attention. The shy, freckled-faced girl was now someone.

Chapter 3
Carss Park Cannonball

"Success is no accident. It is hard work, perseverance, learning, studying, sacrifice and most of all, love of what you are doing or learning to do."
– Pélé

Our 'little squad' would soon learn that our coach was motivational and eccentric. One morning, we arrived at the pool with sleep still in our eyes. But they were wide open moments later when we thought we had walked onto the set of a Hollywood movie: the car parked in the middle of the pool was all too real. Coach was nowhere to be seen and our workout was cancelled.

The car belonged to Coach Caine. There was a funny side to his eccentricity, especially for us youngsters. We had never seen a car in a pool before. There was a serious side to it all, too, rooted in a truly tough upbringing. He left home at 12, worked on farms shearing sheep and never finished high school. However, he was a keen swimmer, the water a place of solace from all the hardship.

Sadly, at 14 he was even robbed of that outlet for his energy and talent when he was banned from taking part in 'amateur' sport because he'd taken a job as a lifeguard. Earning money from engagement in any aspect of 'sport' was not permitted under the then Rule 26 of the Olympic Charter, which these days has no mention of the word amateur. Swimming authorities declared him a professional and that was that for the rest of his youth.

Devastated, he began working at local pubs and nightclubs, and two mornings a week he would do the garbage run. Coaching was not on the radar until he was asked to take on our small group of kids at Sans Souci pool.

Dick Caine was a man of the '50s. He loved his cars and horses, with Friday nights reserved for the 'trots' and betting on the races. When he won, he was happy and sympathetic to us in our workouts. When he lost, we all took cover. Car-parking antic aside, he was reliable: at the end of his 4 a.m. garbage run, he would be at the pool by 6 a.m. ready to coach, after which he'd head back to the track to train horses. We'd see him again at 4 p.m. each day for afternoon practice.

Over the first two seasons with him, our race times improved and helped attract more children to our squad. He had a certain gift for teaching and motivating kids. Coach Caine was strict and demanded discipline.

With a growing team, it was time to find another pool so when the new council pool across the bay came up for tender the following year in 1971, my father took the initiative to apply and was awarded the lease with Dick who would head up the new swim program. Dick would later sign the lease to set himself up for a long career in coaching.

When the council approved the lease in 1971, everyone was excited. Our little squad that had grown considerably over the two years was to leave Sans Souci—its big oak tree, the stench of diesel fuel from the road and those blistering winds.

Carss Park was an oasis. Situated on the shores of Kogarah Bay, the 50m, seven-lane outdoor pool was slightly more protected from the weather. Like other facilities built around Sydney in the '50s, the complex was a red-brick structure with no heating, no hot showers, and just looking at the changing rooms with their grey cement floor and open roofing made you shiver. The council stipulated that the public must have the use of half the pool, and training squads were able to use the other half. On hot summer days, hundreds of little swimmers and bathers competed for space, with only a corked lane rope separating the two.

At times like that, there were so many of us that we snaked around lanes divided by bubble-corked ropes, and it was impossible to tell where one swimmer's hands ended and another's feet began. It was like squeezing thousands of fish into a small pond, all splashing around.

Dick's philosophy was 'have fun kids and you will win'. He was big on variety, too. As American magazine *Swimming World* reported in April 1976 under a headline 'A New Aussie Star': "*Once or twice a week, instead of the usual training in the morning, he takes his squad for an eight km (five-mile) run through bushland. 'Running helps develop leg muscles and stamina and gives the children a break away from the usual training,' Caine said. 'Children need variety, they become bored very quickly, and the run in winter warms them up before a swim'.*"

Few swimmers in Australia were doing weights or running as part of their program. In addition to Dick's diverse training methods, four-mile runs along the treacherous highway and gruelling weights sessions, he'd have us horse riding, water skiing, surfing, and having barbecues and outings to the movies. We would all pile into his purple car, all 14 of us! Proud of his team, he'd take us out for a Chinese supper after each championship meet. We'd bring our best wares to the final night of competition and get all dressed up for the dinner. Dick would have us sitting at the biggest table in the centre of the room.

"Variety is the spice of swimming [...] Caine believes in limited distance and feels young swimmers should enjoy the sport rather than missing out. We have BBQs, go horse riding, movies and dinners together. And the way I work it out, there need be no loss of application to school work."

(E.E. Christensen, "Have fun kids and you'll win", The Sun, 1976)

Although he had no formal education, Dick was conscientious and armed himself with the latest knowledge by reading all he could about swimming technique and science. To further his ideas, he would consult peers in Australia and the USA. He'd also often invite a sporting hero to the pool to talk with us.

He was young, smart and sensitive, and he showed sincere appreciation of everyone on the team. He had an amusing but stern manner and his work training horses had heightened his natural intuition: he could read his swimmers and adapt our training accordingly.

Having missed out on formal education himself, Dick appreciated the importance of schooling and adjusted our workouts accordingly, including setting a 6 a.m. start time to allow us to get as much sleep as we could. This was at a time when other squads would already be in the pool at 5:30 a.m. or even earlier. His ethos included winters away from the pool to allow his young squad to concentrate and catch up on school and the rest of life. His methods and patience, together with hard work and determination from swimmers, was a recipe for success.

The Workout

Chlorine-bleached hair dripping, and with an apple and a vegemite sandwich in my box for lunch, I would arrive in time for a 9a.m. school start, most days. It was a scramble: 90 minutes swimming; wrap a towel over wet swimsuit; jump in car; wipe windows constantly because dripping hair and wet 'cossies' fogged the windows; dress; breakfast; bus to school where I would arrive with the stench of chlorine oozing from me.

Afternoons were no less hectic: 3:30 p.m. pick up at the back gate, a wardrobe change in the back of the car with uniforms shed and swimsuits tugged on with one hand as the other fed us vanilla slices or homemade cake - our fuel for surviving the next training session at 4 p.m. after a detour to pick my brother up at his school.

Morning training tended to be calmer endurance sets, with the more dynamic, challenging and captivating workouts kept for the two-hour afternoon session. Compared with the higher mileage other teams were clocking up, Dick's programs emphasised shorter distances but higher quality. "It's not the kilometres that count, it's how you do them," he'd say. Each set came with a goal of its own. Everything we did was aimed at making us better all-round swimmers and so medleys (all four strokes) and butterfly were common practice.

With no lane ropes and more than 50 kids aged nine to 12 all doing backstroke, we'd be heading in all directions on a collision course. I think that's why Dick seemed to dislike backstroke and we did less of it than everything else.

He believed that you needed to train near race pace to succeed, something that's become a feature of training today. Accordingly, after a heavy pre-season endurance program and in readiness for the racing season, the workouts would turn from short-interval sets to more quality sets with increased recuperation time. A common set would be 8x400m freestyle, descending in time every one to four, then from five to eight.

Whenever he saw us settling into 'boring' mode, he'd stop us after the first 400m and have us climb out and sit behind the blocks to hear 'the deal': "Either you can do all 10" (... raised from eight), "... or you can do four under a time close to race pace". He'd then give each swimmer their target time to hit if the set was to end after 4x400. If our reply was too quick, he'd jump in with: "... or if you prefer, you can do 2x400m in an even faster time". That last option was only given days out from an important race, with the target time being close to the state or national record. And there was always a 'kicker': the whole lane had to agree and swim the set times, otherwise we'd all end up doing a bigger set than the original one. It taught us something about team and strategy.

Dick knew how we ticked and when we were capable of rising to the challenge even when we were exhausted. We did not have to say anything, he just knew. He was a master at getting the best out of us even when we didn't believe it was possible. His attitude could be summed up in Audrey Hepburn's classic line: "*Nothing is impossible, the word itself says 'I'm possible'!*"

I fell for Coach Caine's deal every time: I understood the consequence of falling shy on the shorter set but any chance of an early escape from the chill was worth taking. I rarely missed my target time, but if someone in the lane did, our shoal began again.

Winning

Swimming is an individual pursuit in a team environment. Dick made every swimmer feel important and insisted they gave their best. Some profited from the social aspects, but most were there to perform. The faster swimmers were put in the middle two lanes, others in the outside lanes, regardless of what type of swimmers you were. On national squads, distance, middle-distance and stroke specialists would be in separate lanes from the sprinters. This was one of the reasons why I resisted attempts to get me to be a distance swimmer in my early days.

Training was intense but entertaining with the sound of banter, jokes and laughter part of the daily chorus. I enjoyed the social side but it was the competition that inspired me. It was what I was there for.

Come race day, the routine became familiar but always thrilling. The heady mix of adrenaline and child's play made for frenetic and action-packed competitions. We drove our parents and coach crazy. Warm-up, racing suit on, focus. On the blocks, I would try to calculate how long each starter took to get from 'Take your marks' to 'bang!'. I would anticipate each start: hold, 1, 2, go! Dive: arms outstretched; body flexed; streamline and emerge into a strong stroke. Fast reflexes are natural but I had also trained and perfected the art. Races are won by 0.01 of a second. Everything counts.

The chicken handicap at the club championships was my favourite and most memorable yearly competition. A set of times from the season were averaged and each swimmer was given a handicap, with the slowest setting off first and the rest in turn according to their place in the pecking order of speed. Age didn't matter.

Everyone had a chance to win a race that should have come down to a blanket finish but for the fact that when the race is a chase, the natural racer thrives. Although I would start 10 or even 20 seconds behind others, I loved hunting them down, passing them and then touching the wall first for the prize. A dead chicken!

Many girls on my team were faster than me in training, but not when it came to competition. My first breakthrough came when I established the 10 years 100m freestyle NSW state record and qualified for my first National Championships in the youngest category, the under 12s. From there, the new standards and titles piled up and I raced the fastest age groupers in Australia.

"By the time Michelle was 10 years old, I knew I had a champion in the making."
– Coach Dick Caine

By 1974, now 12 and in high school, swimming was part of my daily routine. I still competed in other sports but my goals were all in the pool. In September that year with summer approaching, Caine spoke to my parents about my potential. He suggested I get back into training a couple of months earlier than usual to have enough conditioning in time for the peak racing season, December 1974 to March 1975.

I was 1.4m tall but had gained strength through winter weight training and the coach felt it was time to make my mark in senior races. The nod given, mornings were devoted to weights and running because there were no 50m pools open at that time of year and a lane was hired for afternoons in one of two heated 25m pools where there was room at the closest local surf club. We were a small group of five from the top squad.

I had imagined a steady build-up. How wrong I was. Vigorous and unrelenting. Weights, treacherous five-mile runs followed by six miles or more in the pool: my whole body ached. There was no let-up, no compromise allowed. It was one for all, all for one: one failed, we all started again. We were not used to the heat of indoor pools and emerged from training like beetroots glowing in the sun.

Fatigue set in and concentration at school became harder. My teachers would systematically note on my report cards that "I could do better if I devoted as much time to my studies …" as I was giving to swimming. I was at a selective high school, a government school that catered to more advanced students. Standards had to be maintained. It was hard to please everyone but somehow I managed to balance school and swimming and meet the expectations of my teachers, coach and parents.

I continued to flourish in the pool. By January 1975, I held 12 NSW state titles, each won in record time, including three national records in the 100m freestyle, 200m butterfly and the 400m freestyle, where I slashed nearly 13 seconds off the previous national mark. I also established the world's fastest ever time by a 12-year-old in the 100m freestyle and was compared to the greats of Australian swimming, Dawn Fraser and Shane Gould, both world-record holders in the 100m in their day.

Headlines had me down as the *'Carss Park Cannon Ball'*, *'Mini Torpedo'* and *'Michelle Super Fish – at 12'.*

My 100m swim featured in the gazette of the Department of Education, alerting my teachers to the pioneering effort. Although proud, they still insisted that my education should not be sacrificed.

Rising Star

I became aware of the word 'Olympic' in 1972. I remember sitting on the sofa with my father watching the Munich Games on TV and Shane Gould, the Australian heroine, winning one of her three gold medals and record five medals in individual events, a tally that remains unmatched to this day. As Shane climbed on to the podium to receive her medal, Dad turned to me and said, "Michelle, one day this could be you." I was nine and thought, if you say so, why not!

I had no concept of it being the ultimate goal in an athlete's career. The Olympics were only talked about when the Games were on. We watched on our new colour TV but for the most part anything outside Australia was a different planet. At nine, too young to make Nationals, little did I suspect that within four years I'd be an Australian medal hope heading into the next Olympics.

My maternal grandfather Oliver (Ollie) Alldis, who came to all our swim meets and kept a diary of all our times, suggested I might bring home a gold one day. I laughed but he looked me straight in the eye and said, "Michelle, here is what I will do. If you break a senior state record, I will give you $10; a national record, $15."

Interesting. But it would be a long time, if ever, before he would have to pay, I suggested. He ignored me and got back to his quest: "If you win the Australian titles, another $30, then a world record $100." I didn't know the value of money but I sensed that it was a ludicrous amount. But the challenge of the 'game' intrigued me!

I now thought he was joking but the spark caught hold. What if? He went on— Commonwealth record, Commonwealth medal, Olympic medal and then, out it came: Olympic gold gets $500. It seemed so far out of reach that it was insane, a fantasy of his aspiration for me.

I loved racing and just wanted to win. The elation of improvement drove my passion. It's the most amazing sensation to be tapered (meaning rested from heavy training and primed, ready for racing): you feel light and powerful, and you float high in the water. Swimming is an exact sport—the stroke, the distance, the time fixed and decisive— there's no room for wriggling, opinions or excuses. The result is what it is, whatever the weather—the rain and cold that's emblematic of many of our meets simply adds another layer of toughness.

If a race didn't work out, there were always lessons to be learnt. Some took time to understand, while others taught mental toughness and bore new energy, determination and belief. We cannot win every race but we can be the winner of our dreams.

My goals until now had been a progression of targets through club, regional and state competitions before the season ended with the National Age and Open Championships. The more races I swam, the tougher I became. My coach interpreted this as 'swimming every race possible on the program'. Or, if the program was too easy or there were not enough events to swim, he'd make me swim butterfly instead of freestyle for any distance, including the 400m or even the 800m.

Fortunately, there were no 1500m events at those competitions, but swimming butterfly and not freestyle for the 400 and 800m was enough to surprise the crowd and other competitors. Any stroke as well as crawl can be swum for those events, as long as you stick with the one stroke all the way.

The National Championships and grand finale of the season would see most swimmers limit their events to their special stroke and distance. Not me! Having established records in all strokes and distances except the breaststroke, I would swim almost every race on the program (free 100/200, 400/800, butterfly 100/200, backstroke 100/200 and 400 individual medley). I insisted on bypassing the longer distances only to be defeated by my own success, with my times endorsing my coach's view that my future rested in the endurance events.

"Michelle's a slim (1.4m) young star with a powerful stroke, is perfectly balanced as she cleaves through the water ... Michelle is a top class butterfly swimmer and

can cope with distances from 100 metres to 1500 metres in freestyle."
(Alan Clarkson, 'Girl Trio With a Golden Touch', Sun Herald, December 20, 1975)

I set more than 20 records in 1974 and 1975 and made my first international team. When the official letter arrived in the post, dated January 5, 1975, announcing my selection to represent NSW in my first international meeting in New Zealand, I was overjoyed.

By 12, I had clocked the fastest time in the world for my age. I was heralded the next great hope since Shane Gould. Dick Caine and my parents began imagining that I might make the Olympic team the following year. They hatched a plan for me to train through the winter and the next season's meets. The targets were the 200m and 400m freestyle, and my main event, the 200m butterfly.

I was now in the line-up for a 1976 showdown. I was 13 and more confident with each competition delivering more improvement and sweeping me into the limelight. Headlines declared: 'World Beater at Just 13' and 'New Swim Starlet Is Busy at 13'.

I had risen to my grandfather's challenge and was ready to prove that a 13-year-old could make the Olympic team and be a medal prospect.

"Michelle Ford, Australia's latest water baby... the slim 13-year-old swimming sensation likes cooking, sails a dinghy, plays the piano and excels at her school studies. On top of that, she manages to train for up to four and half hours a day. Michelle broke six NSW and three Australian records, and in her first test in open competition, she went even better with an Australian senior record. In a little over a week, she has set a total of 16 records. Swimming experts forecast a bright future for Michelle, including a place on the Australian team for the Montreal Games."
(Phil Scott, 'New Swim Starlet Is Busy at 13', Sun Herald, January 15, 1976)

"'In just over two weeks, Michelle has reset 16 state and Australian records... I think that Michelle should have more than satisfied the Olympic selectors ... I don't intend burning Michelle out and in the future she will compete in just four events at each meet but we will be training hard,' said her coach Dick Caine."
(Katrina Lee, 'Michelle Races Dad for a Place in the Olympics', Sunday Telegraph, January 25, 1976)

Swimming officials remained sceptical about taking a 13-year-old with no international experience but the 'best' team possible should go and there were no age limits for the Games in 1976. It was time to hit the selectors between the eyes. A win at trials would surely do the job.

Birth of Resilience

Talking through the work schedule and enduring it are two different things. The 1975–76 season had got off to a tough start but had become more arduous with my swim practices doubled to five miles a day. I made a wish for an easy workout every day. I needed to recuperate but instead I was pushed to my limits again and again. My body would bounce back, miraculously, but the mental toll started to show. I'd decompress in the car on the way home, tears flowing through my complaints about the insensitive nature of my coach and his drive to get us to do the impossible.

I swore I'd not be going back the next morning. But once home, a good dinner, homework and bed provided the change of mind and calm I needed, yet when the alarm went off at 5:50 a.m., I would pretend not to wake when my mother came to get me up. She would plead with me, then go and warm up the car because she knew that in the end, I always went back for more.

There's a point at which your body can go no further, your spirit is broken and your dreams start to fade. It's a testing time for everyone—the athlete, team, coach and parents too—when they have to contend with their child's emotional roller coaster.

Without the scientific feedback swimmers are used to these days, we were in the dark. My body rebelled, and my mind was drained. I was angry and in survival mode. My coach could see it in my eyes: productive sessions were out of the question. When I didn't make the times he'd set, he'd punish me with a 16x400m butterfly set and tell me I wouldn't be leaving the pool until I was done. To rebel, I'd swim the slowest 'fly I could so that he would have to either stay behind with me or, sooner or later, let me out. We had plenty of practice at mind games!

Ahead of me were the even more intense training days of summer break and December school holidays. Christmas Day dawned and we were scheduled to have morning training and then the rest of the day off. After opening our presents, we arrived at the pool in festive spirits and anticipating a fun and easy workout.

But the Grinch was on shift. Coach Caine gave us the most gruelling and longest workout ever. Our parents came to collect us and were told to go home and come back in an hour. Kids were waving their parents back to get them out of the water. Dick was deaf to it all. We arrived at Christmas lunch frazzled, tired and extremely hungry.

There was no mercy. The coach knew how to break in a horse. We were now tough and resilient.

Through it all, Carss Park team spirit flourished. We shouldered each other through the hard times and cheered for each other. Success for one was success for all and recognised by our coach. Every member of the team medalled at the 1976 State Championships. We took 50 titles.

"Carss Park squad of talented water babies [...] In the NSW state championships concluded last night where Michelle was the outstanding swimmer, Carss Park took over 40 medals and were top club. The highlight was Michelle's 13 years 400m freestyle swim, in which she broke Jenny Turrall's record. Michelle does not swim for records and Coach Dick Caine says that like all his protégés, she swims for the club. 'Michelle swims for the team, as do all our swimmers, and it is the collective effort that is making all the team do so well,' he said. 'She does her best every time she races and, by beating a Jenny Turrall record like she did last night, we all get a thrill.'"

(E.E. Christensen, 'Michelle Runs Swim Record', The Sun, January 12, 1976)

Dick sent me a personal thank-you card: "Dear Michelle, From your cranky old coach. Thank you."

That, I would come to realise, was code for 'time to get serious'. Halfway through my first year as a teen, the Olympic trials were on the horizon.

Chapter 4
The Olympic Dream

"I have had dreams and I have had nightmares,
but I have conquered my nightmares because of my dreams."
– attributed to Jonas Salk

History hangs heavy in the air at the iconic North Sydney Olympic Pool: its hallowed waters witnessed many of Australian swimming's greatest pioneering moments after it opened in 1936 on the cusp of World War II.

It was built to host the 1938 Empire Games. Heating wasn't added until 2000 when the city hosted the Sydney Olympic Games. A year later, it finally got a place for competitors to warm up in when a 25-metre indoor pool was added.

Long before then, 86 world records had been set at the pool; among the pioneers were Murray Rose, Dawn Fraser, Shane Gould, John Konrads, Ilsa Konrads, Lorraine Crapp, Frank O'Neill, Judy Joy Davies, John Devitt and Kevin Berry.

I would join the list one day but at 13 I had some yards to go. In February 1976, it was all about making the team at selection trials for the Games of the XXI Olympiad in Montreal, Canada.

I wasn't the favourite in any race but I qualified for evening finals in three events— the 200 and 400m freestyle and the 200m butterfly. The 'fly was my first final, my favourite race and my best shot at making the team. My target was Nira Stove, who had broken the Australian record in 2 minutes 17.71 that morning for a ticket to lane 4 in the showdown.

I'd listened to Coach Caine and others warning me of the 'mind games' rivals would play to tip me into self-doubt, throw me off my game, and take the edge off my spirit and growing confidence. A spree of record-breaking at the State Championships had drawn a lot of media attention. There'd been six NSW standards and I'd landed every title on every stroke barring my nemesis, breaststroke.

Could the 'Carss Park Cannonball' beat rivals three and more years older to become the youngest ever to make an Australian Olympic swim team?

My capacity to switch off and not fret about finals all day—having a midday nap and a juicy T-bone steak with fried eggs instead—were all part of my strategy. Those were our weapons back then. Today, Olympic swimmers use tents that simulate altitude conditions to boost red blood-cell counts, jump into ice pools to ease the impact of heavy work on their muscles, and they and their coaches work with an army of nutritionists, doctors and sports scientists flushed with knowledge.

In our day, research on the needs of athletes was thin on the ground and earning any money or receiving funding was not allowed under amateur rules. Vitamins were recommended but weren't for me. Steak and eggs filled my tank. My mother had read that protein was important, so steak it was, except the time she served up lambs' brains. As hungry as all we kids were, we couldn't stomach that!

I arrived at trials ready to swim faster than ever before. The physical work had been done. I was ready but my coach had a last-minute trick up his sleeve to get me to 'the ball'.

The warm-up before racing can make or break the day. It's where nerves are running high, adrenaline is pumping, skills are primed and reassurance is given. On this day, it's also where mind and body become one, partners for the fight to earn Olympic selection.

North Sydney had just the one seven-lane pool, so warm-up was a boiling bowl of fish flipping in different directions, swimming different strokes and speeds. Injuries in this scenario are not unknown. An ant-hive of coaches scurry about the drenched deck, calling out instructions, whistling and waiting for that rare clear stretch of water in which they could time their swimmers without traffic getting in the way.

The crush gets worse in the last 20 minutes when the outside lanes are cleared for sprints and everyone else is packed in the middle five lanes.

Coach Caine had a better idea in February 1976. There was another pool 15 minutes down the road. He spoke to my parents and told them to bring me there instead. He wanted me to be calm and focused.

So, there we were, on a sultry late February afternoon at the public pool that was closed for the day, except for me. I set off on a relaxed 400m freestyle, sending ripples out across the empty expanse of cool water. At some point during warm-up, Dick stopped me and asked me to join him and another man on the deck. "Do you know who this is?" he asked. Of course I did. I'd met him before at the Carss Park pool and he'd given me a 'fly set to do.

It was Kevin Berry, Olympic champion for Australia in the 200m butterfly at the

1964 Tokyo Olympic Games!

I'd rarely do any butterfly in warm-up but this day was different. I was told to do an easy 50m butterfly. Caine and Berry had known each other since they were boys on the same swim team. They set off walking down the side. "Set, go!" shouted Dick. It all felt so effortless. I wanted to see what time I'd done but they stood just out of earshot mumbling as they looked down at their stopwatches.

"Well?" I asked.

They smiled but it was clear they had no intention of telling me why. I was just told to go and get changed into my racing kit. The clock was already ticking.

The locker room was deserted. Wet stuff thrown into my duffle bag, I walked back to Coach and Olympic champion ready for finals in my blue tracksuit with a shiny, light-blue Lycra swimsuit underneath. Kevin, now a newspaper photographer, pulled me aside as we were leaving the pool. "I've never seen a more perfect butterfly swimmer before. I know you can win this final," he told me.

My chest puffed out as confidence surged through me. With his hand on my shoulder, the man who'd set two of his five world 200m records at the North Sydney Pool looked me in the eye and said, "I will be there when you touch the wall; I want to see your smile."

I was alive, switched on, raring to go! Teamwork and confidence helped flick the switch from 'race' to 'my race' and at 13, I was hungry for direction. I listened intently to their words on the way to the pool and never doubted them. Dick's belief was my strength. It was obvious he was nervous, too: he'd never had a swimmer who'd got this far. Years later, he would recall:

> *"Four weeks to go to the Olympic selection trials … both of us were stressed and in the press every day. It was '13-year-old from Carss Park trying for place on Olympic Team', 'youngest ever' and so on. The pressure was great. So to give us both a lift, I ask a training mate of mine, the great Olympic Champion Kevin Berry, to come out and talk to Michelle and perhaps give her a set and tell me what he thinks. They hit it off and he gave her a set of 4 broken 200 butterfly [4x50m butterfly]. All with full recovery, but all within three seconds of world-record time. Michelle does this. Kevin whispers to me that she will make the Olympic team and could even take the gold. Along comes the morning, the heats of the 200. I knew Kevin and his race plan for 200 'fly to perfection: first 50m, relax, second 'I am feeling great', third 'explode', fourth 'win'. For months I had worked this over and over in practice with little Mich. By then, Michelle had been nicknamed by the media 'the Carss Park Cannonball'."*

A Ticket to the Olympics

No one dressed up for the finals like Coach Caine did. He wore a large, white-collared shirt under his electric purple suit, with matching high-heeled shoes, John Travolta-style. Proud and otherwise reserved when it came to race day, he sought out his own space under the stands in an alcove where his swimmers could see him and get their last-minute pep talk, before going to the pre-race marshalling area. Dick was a master of that moment.

He was always more nervous than me. These were his first National Open Championships and Olympic trials but he'd worked hard, just like I had. He knew that the right words at the right moment could work wonders.

"Go down the first lap feeling really good and easy, you won't even feel it," he said. "Start building the second lap and stay just on the hips of the front-runner." He drew a line on his leg to indicate the place on my rival's leg I was to stick to like glue. "Stay just here!" he said. "This is your moment," he continued, pointing to the halfway wall. "This is where you come off that wall like a ball of fire into the third lap. Just keep your head down and GO! ... off the last wall, this is where you bring it home; your last lap will feel good. You have done all the training. You are ready."

And I was. The clock was irrelevant. This was about winning, though Coach Caine knew precisely what speed I was capable of. I walked out to centre stage in my first Olympic trials final knowing this was my best chance of a ticket to the Games. I knew that my family was up there in the stands cheering me on. I clocked the purple suit and took a last glance. Dick nodded. There were no more doubts; the tension melted away.

In my zone at the back of the blocks, I'd already reached the turn in my mind's eye. Deep breath, echoes of "light and easy, Michelle ... then give it all on the third", then stillness. Here we go. "Take your marks ..."

The gun fired.

The first two laps felt easy. Too easy, I thought. I was one of the last to the first turn. Down the second of four laps, latent energy was bubbling over. Hold back, it's not time. Halfway, hands on wall, flip round and ... GO!

I surged off the wall and had passed everyone except the favourite well before the last turn. Nira Stove and I were neck and neck, but momentum was with me, my body was high. I was gliding through the water. Time to "bring it home": my coach's words rang in my head.

Two big butterfly kicks off the final turn, I was unmatched down the last lap. My 2.16.55 victory set an Australian and Commonwealth record. It was inside Canadian Wendy Quirk's 2:17.07 from January 1975. I looked to see my coach jumping into the pool. We'd done it! At 13, I was the youngest winner at trials and on the way to my first Olympic Games!

I'd lived up to the faith of my father, my grandfather, and honoured the support of my mother and family, my coach and proved to myself that I was capable of anything. I was no longer that little girl on the sofa nodding to "That could be you one day" but not truly believing.

Coach's Perspective

Years later, Coach Caine would reflect on our trials campaign and the work we'd put in. This was his perspective:

> "My coaching time with Michelle would sometimes be a love/hate relationship. But always love and respect won out. The sessions became monstrous as the Olympic selection trials were coming up; 2 to 3-hour sessions, running, weights, and all in freezing water, with a cold shower to finish. Michelle when tired and upset would often look as if she had two black eyes and would often try to tell me off. When I saw this, I would not argue nor even say good morning.
>
> "On the morning [of the 1976 Olympic trials], I was sick with nerves. We scraped through to the finals and I wanted to be near Michelle until she stepped up onto the blocks. Just before the final, Kevin Berry came over. 'Dick keep calm, tell Michelle you love her no matter what. I will be ready to take her winning photo.' Off goes the gun. First lap, Michelle's almost last. Second lap, moving up but everyone giving her no chance, third lap, explodes off the wall. She turns together with the favourite. She wins by a body length. Youngest girl to make the Olympic team!"

A good coach is someone who stands by his or her swimmers, knows them and what they are capable of, and believes in them. They are the trainer, psychologist and to some extent, confidant. They have an influence on your character, your ethos and morals, especially among the young. They are protective, no matter what happens, and in Dick's case, he was an artist and an eccentric with a sixth sense.

Great Expectations—No Support

The swimming team was announced on March 1, a good five months before the Games and an eternity in swimming terms. The 28-strong squad of 13 men and 15 women would be guided by two coaches, a general manager and women's team manager. Our team was small in comparison to our rivals—the Americans, East

Germans and Russians chief among them.

Australia had long punched above its weight in the pool and expectations of a big haul were high. The *Sunday Telegraph*'s Olympics special on April 11 predicted 13 medals from the youngest Olympics squad ever: the girls had an average age of 16, the oldest an 18-year-old, while the oldest man was 23, a couple of years above the average.

Four years after Shane Gould's epic Games in Munich, speculation focused on who would be Australia's next golden child in the pool. I was among those named, with times not far from the world records in the 200m butterfly, and the 200 and 400m freestyle. *The Sun* newspaper said I was *"tipped to set a new world record before training camp ends"* ('Countdown on the Olympics', The Sun, May 24, 1976).

It all had a ring of certainty about it but the decision-makers were not singing to the same tune as athletes and coaches. All athletes had to have their selection ratified in April by the Australian Olympic Federation (AOF) before we could head off to the two-month training camp in May and June. At the time, that was longer than a traditional summer swim season.

Australia, like all countries in the Southern Hemisphere, was already at a disadvantage. Pool closures during our winter months meant that early trials in late summer were our only option. Americans, many of whom trained throughout the year, held their trials much later, within a few weeks of the Games. That schedule made much more sense.

As John Thirsk put it in the *Sunday Telegraph* Olympics Special of April 11:

"This year our athletes will have the following against them – competing out of season, little international competition, and competing against athletes who are virtually full-time at their respective sports."

Shortly after trials, our season was over. Teams disbanded and coaches faced serious logistical problems finding suitable 50m pools to train in, such as those that didn't come with a risk of frostbite!

At Carss Park, I fought to stay functional, the water at 17°C, my hands and feet purple and numb. Morning workouts were supplemented with running and weights but winter was closing in and cold southerlies ruled out training outdoors. The nearest 50m indoor heated facility was on the other side of Sydney and too far to get back in time for school, so it was 25m indoor training whenever we could for at least two months up to the official training camp in mid-May.

Other tensions surfaced: one-on-one coaching was intensive and we'd get to boiling point some days, so other swimmers were asked to join in and keep me company.

The other matter was heart-wrenching: all Coach Caine's hard work was just filling the gap before he'd lose me to another coach. In those days, most coaches with athletes on Olympic teams never got to finish the job of seeing their charges to the blocks for the big one, and in 1976 management specified that there would be no home coaches allowed near their athletes, either during training camp or at the Games. It was a hard pill to swallow for a man who had guided me from learning to swim to national champion and record holder on the cusp of world-record pace.

The Long Way Home

The Australian Olympic team across all sports was ratified and officially announced on April 9, 1976: 193 athletes and support staff. Days later, the postman delivered my first official letter from the AOF (Australian Olympic Federation) Secretary General, Mr Julius Patching. Headed *"Most Important Notice"* in stencilled lettering, it informed, itemised flights and Olympic kit, congratulated and lauded, then told us the honour would only *"be finally confirmed if the medical tests are completed to satisfaction"* and if we maintained form, which was to be tested at trials on June 20.

There was also a one-page competitor's agreement to sign and send back. Each agreement carried the athlete's number. I was 186 and that was the very impersonal reference on all of my subsequent communication and team gear. Even so, I cherished what became my favourite number for the rest of my career. It was special; it belonged to me and represented membership of a privileged and exclusive club that few ever get to join: representing my country at the Olympics.

The long wait had ended. It was time to pack. Mid-May and we were three months past my win at North Sydney. I'd now be away from home for the same length of time before I'd be back from Montreal.

It was the middle of a school year in Australia. I would be absent for a total of 66.5 days in my third year of high school (Year 9) and some of my teachers did not approve. In order to pass the year, I had to find a way to get the class notes: August holidays would be spent catching up on schoolwork. Before leaving for the Games, I left a pile of carbon paper sheets with friends so that I could get a copy of their notes.

On the last day of school, my schoolmates staged a big farewell and gave me the biggest card I'd ever seen with notes from the entire year wishing me success in Montreal. In sewing class, they made me a red dragon, symbolic of our 'St George and the Dragon' school motto, to take with me. Their support kept me going through the next couple of months of unexpected trouble and turmoil.

On my last night at home, I barely slept. A swim-club friend, Christine Jeffs, stayed over and we talked all night about the adventure ahead. I had never travelled overseas, never been away from my family and never been away from my coach. It didn't seem to matter. All I could see was racing the best in the world, wearing the green and gold, and standing on the podium.

What I didn't realise was just how bleak the landscape of sport in Australia had become.

Bumpy Road

It came down to this: there was not enough money to 'do it properly', to fund athletes and the preparation they needed. The solution of the Amateur Swimming Union of Australia (ASU, now known as Swimming Australia) was a seven-week camp in Perth, Western Australia, a five-hour flight from the east coast of Australia, and the furthermost city from Montreal.

Lack of funds meant that we would be housed by local families. Some of our provisions were sponsored by local businesses, including the butcher who gave us steak, the baker and the milkman.

Patriotic families put their hands up in good faith only to be faced with the realities of elite sport that they had no knowledge of and nor could they cater for it. There was the twice daily drop-off and pick-up at the pool; quadruple portions of food to feed ravenous, hard-working athletes; the provision and supervision of day-time sleep; and the need to understand the thoroughbred temperaments that can go hand in hand with 'world-class athletes', particularly when they're very far from home.

Normal family lives were heavily disrupted by tough, rigorous and demanding schedules for seven weeks. It all proved too much for many.

On arrival in Perth, we assembled at the Beatty Park Swimming Centre where we were introduced to our host families. My first was a family of five who lived in a little house not far from the pool. There were only two bedrooms in the house, one for the three children and one for the parents. No one had seemed to check the logistics nor had they asked if the hosts understood anything about the needs of elite athletes.

It was dinner time when we arrived at the house. I was famished after a hard workout and the long five-hour flight. I was shown a room with a bed in it. This would be home for the next seven weeks. Tears welled in my eyes. I'd never felt so far from home, family and friends.

My bed was to be the bottom bunk bed of a 3x3 room with a second bunk bed and a cupboard in it. I would be sharing the room with three children, all younger than me. I put a brave face on and headed for dinner: six plates of meat pies and frozen peas stared back at us. My face dropped. There was no one to call and no one to ask for help. I was 13 and I felt trapped.

I didn't unpack. I was determined to take my bags and leave there and then. But I had nowhere to go. I had never been to Perth before and didn't know anyone. Tired, I cried myself to sleep.

Our first training session was set for late morning. At the pool, I spoke to the team manager, explained my situation and asked to be moved. He told me that I should stay because they were nice enough to have taken me into their home and their feelings would be hurt if I moved.

I was confused. I'd heard from past teams that training camp was a great team-spirit kindler. No longer. The ASU's best for the best was this: let's save a quid and have the team billeted out!

I'd ridden my way through many painful training sessions before but this one was another level. I dreaded the end of training when the family would come and take me 'home'. The team manager tried to reassure me that things would get better but promised to look into alternatives.

Not long after, an offer of accommodation came from a family where two of my older teammates were already staying. It would mean a 40-minute drive back and forth to training mornings and afternoons, but I didn't mind. Staying in a self-contained granny flat out the back of the main house sounded appealing—and some of my teammates, girls who had already been on Australian teams, were already there.

My prayers were answered: the move was confirmed. The manager took me to collect my belongings and I was off to a new home and back with the team in a team spirit I was so longing for. Sharing, talking and living with people who understood the word Olympic, who knew what it was to go to training every morning and then go back for more hard work in the afternoon.

Letter to My Parents, May 17, 1976

Dear Mum, Dad and all,

… I don't know my new address, but I am glad I am leaving this house because there is no fruit and they all are heavy smokers and eat cakes and lollies all the time. The place where I am going to stay is good. It is a flat at the back of the house and has got all the things you need, e.g. stove, bathroom and TV. and the lady is really nice …

Love Michelle

PS. I will ring you on Friday at 1h30pm Perth time, 3h30pm Sydney time. Try and be home please.

PSS. Am I glad to be leaving this place; they don't have any meat either.

My new 'family' lived in the main house, so we didn't see them often. Although they had a young swimmer, they didn't really understand the intensity of an elite swimmer's life either, but it was better than where I had come from. We would eat with the family, and the mother would take us to the pool twice a day.

That was where I started my Olympic journey, but it was far from ideal. Competition, 'best practices' and even swimming were not topics of conversation at the dinner table. Getting us to training when a favourite TV show was on proved challenging. The solution? Easy! Just drop the swimmers off to afternoon training two hours in advance in order to get back in time. Perfect!

The family soon grew tired of our demanding schedules and the steaks and other food we were supposed to get drained away: we rarely saw steaks nor the other sponsored provisions. Daily bread and a bottle of milk were staples, however.

All in all, I felt incredibly lonely on camp. Cut off and separated by miles of Australian desert from the two foundations in my life—my parents and my coach were missing.

I missed them, the conversations we had, and the daily routine. Letters back home took days and use of the house telephone was difficult and expensive. A few weeks into camp, Telecom (now known as Telstra) organised for the team to use their closed offices on Sundays to call home. The weekends soon became a shining light at the end of a long tunnel.

Coach Caine's letters were a comfort. He wrote to say that he was missing me and was frustrated that the worksheets I was sending back each week "didn't show the times I would have expected from you". I could not let on that I had the same concerns.

"Mich," he wrote on June 8. "Have they given you a chance yet to swim any effort work? I was hoping that you might be able to ask them to cut your mileage down and give you more rest and effort work. I think if you can swim 2 to 3 x 400s in 4:16 and 'fly 200s in 2:17 you are better off than doing 10 miles a day."

My new coach was announced to me in a letter heading into camp: "*Your chief coach is Mr Terry Gathercole who will be assisted by Mr Terry Buck. I feel sure they can depend on your loyalty and cooperation*". Obliged to follow, I also knew that their type of training was useless for me. It was all quantity, no quality. There was no one to confide in.

Between the long hours at the pool, the travel back and forth, and my body crying out for rest, I usually only slept and wrote letters between workouts. But sometimes the girls went shopping and we'd have team cook-offs.

Weeks passed and training was the same each day—long, hard and boring! By the third week, we had swum 297 miles—9 kms (5.5 miles) in each morning session and 6 km (3.5 miles) in the evenings. It was the first time I was training seven days a week with only Sunday afternoon free. I had never done so many miles, nor workouts. My arms were heavy and sore.

I had to force myself to believe this was the training I needed to medal in Montreal.

Letter to My Parents, May 30, 1976

To Mum, Dad and all,

Training is really hard, but it is good over here. I am pleased with my times but keep thinking of those Germans. I pretend that the boys are the East German girls so if I get behind, I think I am in the race, and then I go harder. I feel really sore, but I keep on going harder. When I want to have a 'loaf', I can't help thinking of what you said, and so I don't get much rest in training! Also, I know that no one here is going to push me like Dick (Coach) does.

I'd been used to doing weights in between swim sessions. Not here—there was no weight room, no weight coach and no instruction. 'Team stretching' as they called it was the only dry-land exercise we did. We were six weeks out from competition and I should have been doing race-pace timed efforts from a dive with longer recovery times. No chance!

At least the June 20 fitness races were coming round and I'd get a competitive hit. My mother and three-year-old brother, William, were also coming over to Perth to see me swim. It was still weeks away, but I counted down the days.

Come the hour, the trials weren't really held in race conditions. We didn't even have a full line-up in each 'race'; it came down to a few teammates and some out-of-season local swimmers. I kept wondering, *"Is this the Olympic dream they talk about?»*

Dick must have been gnawing his fingernails to the bone when he saw my times. He was expecting me to break the 400m freestyle world record. I should have been clocking four minute-16s in training. Instead, I was four seconds slower in a race (4:20.30) than my time swum four months earlier. My 200 freestyle (2:08.97) was three seconds off, my 200 'fly (2:21.43) five seconds slower.

I was deeply disappointed, and frankly, I was embarrassed. I just wanted to go home. *I wrote in my logbook:*

"My times weren't very good this week because of my arms which were very sore and also we were told we were on a 'non-tapering taper'. I am not sure what a non-tapering taper was, I guess that we don't taper off any before the trials!"

As I explained earlier, a taper is an easing back from heavy work, a reduction in mileage, and a focus on shorter intervals and more speed. This allows the body to feel lighter and more energised. You get to race day rested and ready to blast at your best.

Oddly, the team coaches were pleased with me and my times. I was told I was doing well and would swim the 200 'fly, and the 200 and 400 freestyle in Montreal.

Then I learned that the team manager had changed the line-up for the 400 freestyle. No one bothered to tell me or explain why. At least the 200m butterfly was untouchable. The best in the world in February 1976, I'd set my sights on Olympic gold. My time would remain second fastest in the world that year until the month before the Olympic Games, when something extraordinary unfolded.

The Game Changer

Historically, Australian and American swimmers had dominated the record books. Two Australians on our team, Jenny Turrall (800m freestyle) and Stephen Holland (1500m freestyle) still held their world records. The achievements of Jenny and many others were about to be rolled over by the strongest female force our sport and several others had ever witnessed.

East German women had evolved as a dominant force in swimming since the last Olympics in 1972 when they claimed two gold, five silver and two bronze medals. At the first two World Championships in 1973 and 1975, they blasted the USA off the top spot in women's swimming. Rumours of doping were rife. We knew little about it, so hearsay and speculation fuelled our banter around the pool deck.

Our team managers were optimistic, insisting that the proposed introduction of testing at the Olympic Games would catch anyone on doping. That would prove to be the height of folly and naivety.

We knew that something untoward and off the chart was going on. It had never previously crossed my mind that anyone would be cheating.

But from our camp in Perth, we watched the news roll in: world records set in the USA were overshadowed the following week by events at the East German trials in Berlin, where an astonishing 12 world records fell in 11 events.

It was June and a game changer had rolled in like a tidal wave. Australian medal predictions were adjusted, discreetly at first and then with the force of an avalanche as the storm blew in.

Ian Heads noted in the *Sunday Telegraph* on June 6 under the headline 'Germans put cold water on our swim chances!':

"A shiver went through the swimming world this week with the news of the East Germans' rewrite of the record books. With frightening determination, the East German 'robots' headed by 5ft 10in Kornelia Ender, tore swim records to pieces [...] One of the most savage assaults ever seen on world record lists.[...] For years now it has been rumoured that the East Germans use anabolic steroids to build their athletes and swimmers. The rumours will strengthen after this fantastic blitz."

The bar had been raised by unprecedented margins. Shivers ran up my spine when one of our coaches said, "Take note, this will be your competition in Montreal." There was no further comment, nor any more talk of comparisons.

Given that each nation could have three swimmers per event, it was obvious to me that if we wanted medals of any colour in Montreal, we'd have to beat the East Germans.

Chapter 5
My Debut

"And then she understood the devilish cunning of the enemies' plan. By mixing a little truth with it they had made their lie far stronger."
– C. S. Lewis, The Chronicles of Narnia: The Last Battle

The coaches were obsessed with our weight. The ritual weigh-in for women was something to behold every morning. It travelled with us for nine weeks, from the Perth camp all the way to the Games in Montreal.

Protruding belly to the fore, Coach Buck stood by the upright physician scales and moved the small indicator along the top bar until the arm balanced and the exact ounce revealed itself. He yelled out the number so that everyone could hear.

Our male teammates were the spectators, female swimmers the target, the entertainment. The word 'fat' was part of the lexicon of our adult guardians. With no scientific data, no holistic approach to nutrition nor any guidance, each weigh-in became ever more depressing and damaging.

The humiliation got worse when our team manager declared to the media, "Disciplinary action will have to be taken against future overweight Australian swimmers."

I was just turning 14 and growing at an alarming rate. I'd never worried about my weight and I'd never needed to. We weren't 'fat' and we weren't blind either. It was obvious that other teams were working with physiotherapists and psychologists providing positive reinforcement.

Our rivals were being taught the power of visualising races; they were getting massages and management and coaching that seemed geared to feed them with feel-good stuff. On the Australian swim team, the fuss and focus were all about a few ounces. We'd brought our best swimmers to the battle but the best coaches and managers with the best knowledge were back home and far away.

The Olympics Get Real

We couldn't wait to leave Perth. It was July 2, the eve of departure for the Games, and packing was interrupted by the arrival of the boxes we'd been waiting for: our Olympic kit!

Swathes of torn plastic and cardboard carpeted the floor in moments. We moved from box to box trying on an array of outfits until we found the one that fit. There were two Lycra racing swimsuits with an imprint of a map of Australia, two t-shirts, a tracksuit (green with gold flares and a yellow top), one set of wet-weather gear, one towel, one pair of shoes, one travelling uniform, one marching uniform and one handbag. My two roommates and I paraded around like models taking photos. I'd never worn high heels and a handbag before.

The sprinters were true to their nature and got their stuff assembled before the rest of us had a chance!

Bags packed, my green duffle bag with my gold number '186' by my side, it was time to leave. The Games would begin on July 17. We left on July 3 bound for Montreal via Melbourne and a state send-off in the presence of Prime Minister Malcolm Fraser.

My parents would be at the Games so they sent my sister Suzanne and brother Richard to give me a hug before we left. Neither they nor the patriotic folk who came to wish us well and give us our first taste of celebrity status were aware of the conflict in all of us: we were thrilled at the prospect of representing our country at the Olympics but our hearts were heavy and a sense of foreboding was our constant companion.

We'd been let down on a number of levels on a seven-week camp that took us away from home coaches and the stability of home life in the critical last stage of preparation.

It felt like the Olympics was being treated like a local swim meet. We left for the Games with great expectations but with no idea what to expect.

It took another 24 hours to get to Canada via a short stop in Honolulu. We'd crossed the date line and our 9 p.m. arrival local time meant that we were about to live the same day all over again. A letter from J.F. Howson, Chef de Mission, dated June 21, 1976, told us to *"look very smart to give a good impression to the Canadians"*.

Prior to landing, we were told to change into our 'travelling uniform'—a brown skirt and striped shirt with a golden blazer for the girls, and pants and blazer for the boys. So, 250 athletes stood in the aisles of the special Qantas 747 flight, changing into the right uniform for landing.

Security had been increased in reaction to the 1972 Munich village shootings. In Australia, police never carried weapons, so I had never seen a gun or machine gun. From leaving the aircraft, our path was lined by soldiers dressed in black and armed.

It was daunting. From then on, they never left our side. We had a security escort at both the front and rear of the bus whenever we travelled. A total of 16,000 troops were employed to keep the Games safe.

First stop was the accreditation centre. We were now official and had our pass to the Olympic village where Australia was among the first teams to arrive. It was midnight but we were all famished and headed straight for the canteen. The few African athletes already there dispersed as they saw the gold and green army advancing!

After a late dinner, we were shown to the seventh floor in the women's quarters just above the team from Chinese Taipei. Hilariously, we were told that there could be no complaints or changes. That would have been impossible anyway: all 13 of us on the women's team and the manageress were bundled into a tiny two-bedroom apartment. My bed was one of seven in what would become a lounge when the flats were sold for housing after the Games.

There was no TV, no sofa, no place to relax apart from our beds, and no kitchen. A small cupboard, a personal chest at the end of each bed and a couple of tables filled the rest of the room. The manageress had one room to herself with a small fridge and a kettle, and the older girls were in the room of four.

It got very messy, especially after we were told we could not hang our wet things out on the balcony because it would look bad for those passing by.

Close to the central venues, our flat was part of two 19-storey buildings called the Twin Pyramids. There were 980 apartments, and 'Building A' was women only. The men and administration offices were housed in Buildings B, C and D. These were the most crowded living conditions ever for an Olympic village, with up to 14 per apartment sharing one shower, one wash basin and one toilet.

Apartment doors could not be locked so each resident had a storage chest with a key to lock up their valuables. With only one elevator, those living on the first three floors were asked to use the stairs to ease congestion.

Village life was a big distraction. The international zone had cinemas, open-air cafés and even a disco. We could meet visitors there with permission.

We felt like we were walking through a story book as tiny gymnasts like Olga Korbut passed us to the left and seven-foot female basketball players drifted by to the right. The diversity of shapes, sizes and cultures came together in one melting pot at around 6 p.m. each evening: as many as 500 athletes would show up for the trade in Olympic pins!

Dignitaries and politicians were constant visitors. Her Majesty the Queen of England, whose daughter Princess Anne would compete in equestrian events, invited some Commonwealth athletes to dine with her in the central cafeteria. She ate off paper plates, apparently.

My name was not pulled out of the hat and on the day Australia's Prime Minister

Malcolm Fraser visited the village, only 20 Australian athletes turned up. Many of the team were upset with the lack of government support and showed no interest in his visit. I really didn't know much about politics but I went along with a few other swimmers.

With the start of the Games fast approaching, there was a buzz in the air. The only time during the Games when all 250 Australian athletes came together was to observe the Olympic tradition of national flags being hoisted on poles in the village square. The burning question was: which anthem? The Labor Government had replaced 'God Save the Queen' with 'Advance Australia Fair' as Australia's national anthem in 1974 only for that decision to be overturned by Malcolm Fraser's coalition government in early 1976. However, Fraser also advised the Australian Olympic Federation to use 'Waltzing Matilda' for the Montreal Olympics because 'Advance Australia Fair' had the words "Britannia rules the waves" in its second verse at the time.

Regardless of the choice of music, it was a terrifically proud moment to be standing there watching the flag rise up the pole in the village and know that we were about to represent our country.

Our male teammates were housed in surprisingly more spacious quarters with fewer athletes per room, even though there were far more of them than females: of the 6,000 or so world athletes across all sports, 79.3% were men and 20.7% women.

Back in Montreal 1976, the Games were the first in Olympic history in which there was no fence between the men's and women's quarters. However, village rules stipulated that no male was to enter the women's quarters without special permission from village headquarters. This of course provided a challenge for some of the more industrious blokes who dressed up as women, but only a couple managed to get past security.

The separate living conditions and the restrictions placed on the female quarters presented a logistical nightmare and was at least part of the reason why team meetings and weigh-ins were held in the men's quarters.

Feeling Undermined and Overwhelmed

The weigh-ins just days out from the start of racing in Montreal left us feeling belittled.

On the cusp of the Games, we should all have been raring to go but the stress of such negative doctrine took its toll on the whole women's team. Our spirits were dampened and the mood on the squad sank when it should have been riding high.

By the time we arrived in Montreal, I hadn't seen my parents in months. I was delighted when they finally got tickets. They rented a little terraced house not far from the village. My grandfather, my biggest supporter, travelled with them. He was devoted to my career.

I had just turned 14 days earlier and was granted permission to leave the village to visit my family. My parents picked me up at the gates to the Olympic complex and took me back to their place for a tasty home-cooked meal. It was heaven. It felt like the first time I'd relaxed since arriving in Perth on camp two months before, but they knew something wasn't right.

I told them I was worried about my preparation. I felt flat and had no 'oomph' or excitement. There was no sense of build-up to the races. I'd been used to having Coach Caine by my side on big occasions. He always boosted my confidence. Now, he was restricted to sending telegrams with notes like, *"Pull your finger out Mich, don't let me down."* It was little help. Expectation doesn't dilute deflation.

Letters from family, cousins and friends were my only encouragement. They all knew, probably better than me, what I was capable of. But I knew my form was not what it had been; I knew that world records set by East Germans had changed the game and times that were a 'golden shot' a few months back were no longer likely to make the medals at all. My confidence was on the wane but I still wanted to win and, strangely, still thought I could.

I cherished the time with my parents and grandfather. It made me feel supported again, and able to rebuild and get my head in the right place for the job ahead. The trouble was that we were all rebuilding from such a low point that it felt we had to catch up from a long way back.

I watched the other teams with their entourage of support staff. They seemed catered to, cared for and psyched up for the biggest moment in the life of any elite swimmer who makes it to the Olympics.

Sadly, the whole experience of the training camp had taken the wind out of our sails. The continual harassment of our weigh-ins—the 'fat checks'—had taken the edge off us all. They were deeply demoralising.

An Intimidating Presence

The Games were about to begin and the mood became more serious. The Australian team had been in Montreal for nearly two weeks and we were familiar with the venues, travel times, security, village, protocol and the pool itself. It's important to get used to the blocks, the walls and timing pads, the lane ropes, the layout of the facility, and the places you can and can't go. On race day, you want no distractions; you want to feel comfortable, assured and confident.

We trained in the Olympic pool once a day, and either in the warm-up pool under the grandstand or at one of the seven designated training pools in Montreal the rest of the time. The racing pool was great. It would be my first competition indoors, which meant I didn't have to worry about the cold and rain. I could walk around the deck without wearing the UGG boots and beanies that I was used to having with me back home. Luxury!

There would be water polo matches in the main pool so the water was a uniform two metres deep and in that big tank I felt I was riding higher in the pool. The grandstands came down to the pool deck, encircling it on both sides to create a fantastic atmosphere. It was sold out and we couldn't wait to hear the roar of a 10,000-strong crowd.

Training was a chance to get a closer view of some of our rivals. The USA, the USSR and Canada (as the hosts) had the biggest squads but all eyes were on the East Germans. There were 51 of them, including a massive support staff of coaches, physiotherapists, a masseur, psychologist and weight trainers. They would arrive en masse decked out in their blue tracksuits with DDR written on the front in big bold white letters (representing Deutsche Demokratische Republik). Like the American team, they had presence— and if that was meant to be intimidating, it worked.

I watched them intently. They were focused, motivated and they yearned for Olympic glory. A well-oiled machine. Everyone was talking about them and their rise to the world's top female swimming force.

And force was just the right word for it. That really hit home one day in training when I looked up from the water and saw a hairy armpit and a massive arm of a swimmer holding on to the block. Australia had been allocated an early training slot and the East Germans were immediately after us. I was one of the Aussie stragglers still in the water when the clock ticked to GDR (German Democratic Republic) time. There was no interaction, just stern looks, so I left as fast as I could.

On my way along the deck, I stopped to watch another group stretching. Some of them were able to lock their thumbs together and rotate their arms in a full 360° circle. I was mesmerised. Like many swimmers, I was flexible in the shoulder girdle but there was no way I could get past half a circle before natural resistance called time during the exercise.

The next stop was even more alarming. Heading into the changing rooms, I heard male voices. Oops! Wrong door. I retraced my steps but the sign at the entrance told the truth: 'WOMEN'. Heart beating, I went back in and placed my kit bag on the bench, avoiding eye contact. The voices belonged to the GDR women.

Many other female swimmers commented on it and the media heard a whisper of the latest clue that something was amiss. When a reporter asked about the deep voices at a press conference with East German coach Ralf Gläser he replied, "We came here to swim, not sing."

The mantra and explanation for the East German superiority was that they trained harder and smarter: their cutting-edge sports science and systematic approach to talent selection and placing athletes in sports schools from a very young age was the 'secret' of their success.

While some of that held truth, it was what was not said that rivals from around the world pointed to. There was no evidence, but rumours were rife about how they might be cheating and getting away with it. Steroids seemed to be the logical explanation, going purely on the size of the girls and the depth of their voices. I'd seen and heard nothing like it before.

Blood doping was suggested but the most frightening rumour was abortion doping—the purported practice of purposely inducing pregnancy specifically for athletic performance-enhancing benefits, and then aborting the pregnancy.

A number of doctors and scientists have repeated claims of Soviet abortion-doping but nothing has been proven and Cold War rumours remain just that to this day. The suggested practice is not banned by the IOC, with the former head of their drug-testing policy Prince Alexandre de Merode having stated that the organisation does not "police motherhood". In a similar vein, the World Anti-Doping Agency (WADA) does not prohibit 'abortion doping' on the basis that there is no evidence that it is an effective way of cheating even if anyone has experimented with it.

In 2009, the *Journal of Intercollegiate Sport* (Issue 2, p.269–285) published a paper entitled 'Debunking the Myth of Pregnancy Doping' by Dr Elizabeth A. Sorensen of Wright State University. She concluded: *"Analysis of the scientific and popular literature on doping, blood doping, pregnancy and athletics revealed that the proposition that a female athlete can gain competitive advantage from pregnancy or abortion is unsupported by current science."*

Speculation centred on ways of increasing an athlete's red blood cell mass to allow the body to transport more oxygen to muscles and therefore increase stamina and performance. It was also suggested that if an athlete stopped taking a steroid six weeks out from competition, nothing would show up in testing. Methods to pump 'clean' urine into the test container from a rubber holder pressed in the armpit was another story doing the rounds, along with a story about a chemical that could be dropped in the sample to mask banned substances.

It was the height of the Cold War. Suspicion and conjecture ran high.

Few spoke up publicly about their suspicions but the media quoted American swimmer John Naber, on his way to winning four gold medals in Montreal, as saying,

"The East Germans are so big and strong that most of us are certain they have been on anabolic steroids (a masculine hormone drug banned from the Olympics but undetectable if not used within six weeks of competition)."

('American Girls Try the Old Cold War', The Sun Herald *Olympic Games Liftout, July 25, 1976)*

Tests for Drugs and Sex

Drug testing was simply a urine sample taken after the race in Montreal. The rules stipulated that all three medallists in each event and one other athlete/swimmer chosen at random would be tested.

Drinks were provided to stimulate the production of urine. When I was called on to provide a sample, I was ushered into a cubicle with just enough room to turn around and sit down. I was just about to close the door when a lady came in and said she had to watch. Nervous and slightly bewildered, I missed the small container that was provided but a little of it managed to make the target. "That will do," she said. I had no idea who she was, what qualifications she had or where my sample ended up.

All female athletes in the Olympic village were also called to the medical centre for a femininity 'sex test'. Cue jokes galore on the Aussie squad. How stupid to have a test to determine girls from boys! We were all naïve teenagers, of course, not to mention ill-informed in the seventies at a time long before the internet.

Every female participating in the Games was subject to a femininity test as part of their competition passport. The test was simple: a buccal smear test is a swab of the mouth and a hair follicle. They told me that my certificate would be sent to my team manager the next day. Data protection hadn't been dreamt of back then!

After my test, I hopped aboard an official transport bus and realised why the swab was not such a bad idea. One of the East German girls sat with her arm across the back of the seat. Her arm was thicker than my thigh. Someone said she was a 200m butterfly swimmer—direct opposition in my main event. There were lots of jokes about hairy armpits, deep voices and big muscles, but racing them in the pool was going to be no laughing matter.

Spies in the Camp

There was no interaction with the East German team. They were single-minded and robotic, it seemed to me. There was no tourism, no opening ceremony and no village life for them. What we were certain of on the eve of the Games was that Australia, in contrast, was not approaching competition with anything like the control and seriousness of the GDR.

It turned out that the GDR teams had agents recruited by the Stasi (East German State Security police). They were there to maintain a ring of steel around all East German athletes, coaches and officials. At the time, we suspected foul play but had no idea about the scale of the deception. All we knew was that their discipline was 100%, while ours and other teams were a very long way shy of that.

As a result of our independence and living apart in Perth, the team lacked cohesion and authority. There was no set routine at the pool or the village. Training times changed daily and mealtimes were never consistent. Never having lived away from home and having always been on a strict schedule, the lack of routine didn't work well for me.

Most of the time, it felt like being on holiday not being on an Olympic campaign. Others were saying the same. I was like a tourist—bright-eyed on the trail but flat in the pool. I felt like a visitor, not a performer. I kept telling myself that I was at the Olympics and I should get my head on straight, but after the first rush of village life, it didn't feel like I had convinced myself.

The Opening Ceremony—and Boycott!

More than 10,000 people lined the ropes outside the stadium. Most wanted to talk to us and wish us well, and some wanted to touch us. We were ushered into a big holding area and joined the rest of the Australian team when we spotted the gold shirts and blazers. Nations were seated on benches in alphabetical order but Greece was first as the country that started the ancient Olympic Games, and Canada was last as hosts.

Political tensions were running high after the Canadian Government refused entry to the 42 team members from Chinese Taipei (Taiwan). China, itself not a member of the Olympic movement since 1958, persuaded the Canadian Prime Minister, and later the IOC, that only it could compete as the Republic of China. The Taipei team flew home.

Hours before the opening ceremony on July 17, two days after my 14th birthday, 20 African nations announced a boycott of the ceremony and threatened to quit the Games if the New Zealand team did not withdraw. The New Zealand Government had allowed the South African Springboks to tour their country at the time of a widespread international ban over South Africa's racist apartheid system.

Opening ceremony organisers were caught by surprise. Athletes had been in the marshalling area with no food or drink for almost three hours and everyone was getting restless.

Some African delegates were also awaiting news on what they were to do.

African athletes were also a huge part of village life and were magnificently dressed in their national costumes but they never made it out onto the track. Their withdrawal at the last minute was in protest against the New Zealand All Blacks rugby team touring South Africa at the same time as the Games. As Nelson Mandela and others remained incarcerated in Robben Island for fighting apartheid, the Maori players in the All Blacks had been bestowed with honorary white status in South Africa.

Two days later, 29 countries left the village. There was a hole in the heart of the village with hundreds of rooms now empty, and the Africans and their athletic prowess and flamboyancy no longer a part of the Games. However, some individual athletes from those nations remained in the village with the intention of taking part nonetheless.

On the night of the opening ceremony, under the lights of the grand welcome Canada gave to all its visitors, 80 pigeons symbolising peace and brotherhood were released. We were young and the irony of that flew over our heads. We heard people saying it was brilliant but we missed it because we were part of the show and not on the stage when the birds flew the coop.

'A' for Australia meant we were among the first off the blocks when the parade began. There was a roar from the cheering crowd as we walked out. My heart was pounding. It was exhilarating. I was on cloud nine.

This, I thought, was what the Olympics is all about. We passed the Royal Box and I had forgotten that we were to look right, as instructed by our team manager, so I missed seeing our flag dip as per the official protocol. I can't say it mattered. There was so much else going on. It was a moment that I wanted to live to the fullest, to remember forever. As slowly as possible, we walked around the track waving and hearing a new roar from the crowd with each section we passed.

The loudest cheer was reserved for the hosts, of course. It was magical and I had to pinch myself to confirm I was there. It was really happening. I was about to face the best of the best in the world competing in the most prestigious multi-sports forum.

Back in the village, we headed to the canteen, all 10,000 of us—athletes, coaches and support staff. We were ravenous and needed to eat before bed. For us, swimming started the next morning. Fortunately, my event was on the second day and our coaches had given us the choice of marching or staying back in the village. Even if I was on the first day, I would never have given up this moment of walking into the Olympic Stadium of 80,000 voices in Montreal.

It was time to rest and get ready to race. Five months ago, our team had been pencilled in for a prospective 13 medals. Our worst predictions would be much closer to reality when the racing stopped.

Chapter 6
On the Blocks

"Learn from yesterday, live for today, hope for tomorrow.
The important thing is not to stop questioning."
– Albert Einstein

Montreal, July 18, 1976. Swimming is the first sport off the blocks. Over seven days of racing, we would witness the most dominant show of single-nation force ever seen in the Olympic pool for men and women respectively.

It was the closest swimming had ever come to a complete wipeout by the two tribes at the heart of the East vs West duel that was ramping up rapidly as global politics poured the propaganda of the Cold War into sport.

Between them, East German women and American men claimed 23 of the 26 titles, and all but two of the 29 world records set. Together they took home a total of 68% of all medals.

It took our breath away. We were blasted by a time-warp into the uncharted waters of a new era. The pace was not just driven by doping but also by sports science and a deeper understanding of what athletes and their coaches needed to get the very best out of themselves. Technical innovations also helped: Montreal marked the advent of goggles at the Games.

I was one of those who chose not to wear them because it was worse to have to race half-blinded by a cup of water washing about inside a goggle than sticking with the blur I was familiar with. The fitted black foam used to cause redness around my eyes and diving in was not a skill I had yet mastered with them. The risks of them falling off or filling up was too great. However, those who did use them could see underwater and were better able to judge the turns.

Goggles were also good for preventing the red-eye sting of chlorine but there was no avoiding the eye-watering numbers on the scoreboard.

The East Germans took 11 of the 13 women's golds and celebrated five gold-and-silver finishes in individual events, including one clean sweep of all three medals.

They also set nine of the 11 global marks by women at the Games.

The United States lost only one of the 13 men's finals and its dominance went beyond even that of the GDR women: the Americans crushed their opponents with nine 1–2 finishes, with four of those being clean sweeps in individual events. They also won both relay gold, and 17 of the 18 new world standards established by men at the Games had the US stars and stripes emblazoned beside them.

Britain's David Wilkie, based in the USA at the time, was the only man to stop the American gold rush and world-record bull run. Just one world record was left standing by the close of business: Mark Spitz's 100m butterfly was the last echo of his pioneering seven gold tally from the 1972 Games in Munich.

In a recollection of the greatest moments in swimming history, Mark Schubert, later to be head coach and team director of the USA, called the 1976 squad "the greatest male team we ever saw".

Australia was the last of the eight nations to take home at least one medal, a solitary bronze. Thank heavens for Brisbane's Stephen Holland! His bronze in the most epic three-way 1500m freestyle the Olympics had ever seen was our best performance and the only swim to send our flag up the pole in the pool. The dramatic fall from our previous Games was a talking point not only at home but around the world. The Australian media's high hopes of 13 medals when our trials had ended back in late February seemed like another lifetime ago.

But for coaching failures, amateur governance and a lack of will to fund athletes and make sure they had at least the basics for being competitive in a world on fast-forward, Steve might well have joined a great Australian 1500m tradition established by Andrew 'Boy' Charlton, Murray Rose, John Konrads and Robert Windle.

The 30-lap final had the crowd spellbound and on its feet as all three medallists came home inside the pre-race world record. Bobby Hackett from New York took the early lead and held it for 950m before Steve took over until there were three laps to go. Brian Goodell, coached by Schubert in California, then took the lead and out-sprinted the other contenders for victory.

Their speed was ahead of its time. When Americans took gold and silver eight years later at a home Games in Los Angeles, they swam slower than the three brawlers of Montreal.

Sadly, Steve hadn't just been battling Brian and Bobby. He'd been fighting through headwinds blown at us by our very own guides, guardians and political leadership.

He had done all he could to counter a system letting him down. He had arranged for his home coach Bill Sweetenham to be with him for the training camp, despite the rule that kept home coaches away. Bill travelled to Montreal and was there for the pep talk and the whole Australian team was there to cheer Steve on every stroke of the way.

Bronze had hurt Steve enough. Yet post-race verdicts in the media back home included "loser" and "failure". It was crushing for us all, and devastating for a man who was described as *"Superfish one day and a has-been the next"* in a column by Nancy Berryman under a banner headline: *'No medals for sore losers'.*

Later in the week, Steve finished fifth behind Goodell who set another world record in the 400m. After the Games, weighed down by the vile and unfair coverage in Australia and burdened by an outpouring of public disappointment, he said he was "washed up". A world champion at 15 and Commonwealth champion at 16, he retired at just 18 years of age. The loser was Australia—and teenage swimmers were not to blame.

As racing got under way in Montreal, I was 14 years and three days old and my eyes felt like they'd been wide open for weeks on end.

How It Began

Steve's swim followed my Olympic debut on the second day of racing. I had certainly gone the long and boring distance over the past nine weeks but I doubted I had done the right kind of work to be at my best. I knew something was wrong.

Intensive training periods end in 'taper'—an easing of work and more rest before racing. It leaves you feeling lighter in the water and helps you build up the big bank of energy needed for the last lap as much as the first. It's vital to get the timing right, like shifting gears in a car when you need to accelerate. Miss the mark, even by a day or two, and nothing fires as it should. You feel flat; you have no 'oomph'.

Heading into my first race, I had no idea how I would go. It was unusual. I had joined in the laughter in warm-up but with only two coaches to manage the chaos of a warm-up it became impossible for the swimmers to get a coach to time them.

The Olympics is like no other event. The scale of it and the elevated level of protocol draws the attention away from the focus on pure performance that I was used to back home. There was no Dick Caine and no Kevin Berry to manage this for me. Changing was a question of grabbing the first available spot on a bench for your bag and scrambling to get dry and changed before making your way to the team seating in the lower level of the stands and on the pool deck. The green and gold made us easy to spot in the stands. We were all there to cheer on our fellow team members.

Morning heats at any other competition lack atmosphere. Nothing is at stake and places in finals are filled by people you'd expect to make it at domestic level. That wasn't the case at the Games. The stands were full and vibrant and bigger than anything I'd experienced before. A cheer became a roar as the crowd noise reverberated off the high ceilings. Everything was different for me. I had to learn the protocol of being introduced before the race and having a box to put my clothes in instead of leaving them in a pile on the ground. The boxes were placed at the side of the pool for us to pick up after the race.

Thankfully, the start procedure was spelled out in all our rule books and was familiar to me. Even so, it was daunting to find that I was seeded in a lane next to the two-time world champion and record holder Rosemarie Köther-Gabriel in the fifth, final and fastest heat of the 200m butterfly.

It's at these moments that a swimmer must walk out to the blocks feeling on top of the world. But my body and mind spoke to each other: "You're not firing". I had to look past that and let the crowd build me. "You're good, Michelle," I kept telling myself. "These are the Olympic Games. This is what you have been working for."

It was as though I'd been preparing for a 1500 instead of a 200m sprint. I felt sluggish in the water. How had it come to this? I had left Australia with great hopes of winning, but any remaining confidence left over from questionable preparation drained away when I was confronted by the sheer size of the East German girls.

My warm-up was a tragedy. There was no meaning or objective. I just swam up and down aimlessly through a sea of arms and legs. I found myself in the changing rooms alone and feeling very small. Perhaps the coach would help lift me up like it was back home. Three Australian girls were entered in the 200m butterfly, but each of us was different and required a different send-off, yet we were given the same race instructions. Maybe I should have been prepared for this, but being my first Olympics, I wasn't. I certainly missed the personal touch of Coach Caine by my side, someone who maybe knew me better than I knew myself.

On the way to the marshalling area, I was missing that spark but held tight to the race tactics locked in memory. The scoreboard was at the end of the pool, so we could see what times were being swum in the previous heats. The fastest eight times were to make the final to be swum in the evening. The first race is always the most difficult as the nerves are high and the experience new. I watched the first heats and saw the girls from USA and Canada clocking high 2:14s and 2:15s. My Commonwealth record had been broken twice before it came to my heat. By that point, the first two East Germans had set a blistering pace of 2:11 and a 2:13.

I would have to slice more than a second off the Australian mark that I had set at trials to make the final but this was a 'fast' pool with deep, wave-breaker lane ropes and a fantastic atmosphere.

I felt psyched for a fleeting moment, despite walking out in the shadow of Köther-Gabriel's blue GDR tracksuit two steps ahead of me. But taking my tracksuit off, I felt indifferent. This wasn't me. I was usually so focused, so motivated, so pumped. As I stood on the blocks and looked down the pool, I heard Coach Caine's words of wisdom from trials: "Start building the second lap and stay just on the hips of the front-runner. You will come off that wall like a ball of fire into the third lap ... your last lap will feel good. You've done all the work."

But had I?

The gun fired. My 1.4-metre frame came up a shoulder length behind the blue swimsuit. I was racing without that relaxed-first-half feeling. Down the third of four laps when I would usually lift and gain on others, I found myself struggling. My arms were going through the motions but there was no vitality, force, flow or speed.

On the last lap, my arms felt heavy and the pain set in, both physical and emotional. The last heavy stroke taken, I looked up at the clock: 2:18.24, 5.5 seconds down on the East German and two seconds slower than my trials' times. I was out of the final. I felt I had let my family, coach and friends down.

I didn't want to hear what the coaches had to say. Instead, I went to the warm-down pool and swam a few laps with tears welling, then went in search of my parents and grandfather for comfort and support.

I was 16th overall and the third of the Australians in the heats. None of us came close to making the final. East Germany celebrated a sweep, Andrea Pollack won in an Olympic record of 2:11.41, Ulrike Tauber claimed silver in 2:12.50 and Köther-Gabriel bronze in 2:12.80. Even on an off-day, the winner of my heat (and still the world-record holder) had managed to knock Karen Moe, the USA's 1972 Olympic champion, out of the medals. Moe's time in the Montreal final was still an American record and the first sub-2-minute-13 second ever by a 200m butterfly swimmer from outside East Germany, and more than two and a half seconds faster than she swam when she won the 1972 Olympic gold medal.

Postcard Home From My Mother (July 20, 1976)

The Australian swim team is very slow. Michelle swam 2 seconds slower than 6 months ago. So did a lot of other swimmers. Everyone is asking why. It seems [coach Terry] Gathercole didn't taper them. The Australian team were doing 3 miles a session last week while yanks in the same pool did 1 mile – unbelievable but true. All the team must still get up at 5am even on the day of their races and Gathercole doesn't even go to the meet sometimes. Everyone disappointed and the parents are mad at Gathercole. Their morale is so low. Hope Steve Holland swims well tonight. Olympics are wonderful to experience but feel sorry for the team.

In a Lane Next to Ender

The next two days were a slaughter for the Australian team, especially the women: not one made a final, just four years after Shane Gould, Gail Neall and Bev Whitfield had all returned home victorious.

There were certainly extenuating circumstances, but things had clearly gone badly wrong. Our times across the board were slower than we had swum at trials. It was demoralising. We kept trying to pick ourselves up, but the downward spiral was difficult to reverse. Under pressure from the media, the coaches hid their responsibility behind the blame they placed on a lack of funding.

"We have talent in Australia, but we do not have the system to make them champions. We have been putting Olympic teams together on a shoestring."
(Ron Carter, 'Gathercole's Grim Forecast', The Age, *July 1976*)

There were two things that went largely unspoken. Our home coaches had been kept at bay and those who replaced them did not take our individual needs into account. And that had happened just as we were about to face the most formidable women's swimming force ever witnessed.

There were also other questions that the coaches hadn't answered. Three weeks before the start of racing, I had swum four minutes 20 in a 400m freestyle time trial. That made me the fastest Australian of the four on the team eligible for the event. Yet the coaches didn't put me in the race despite the fact that the training they had been giving me was more conducive to the longer distances.

No explanation was given. It just meant my morale took a hit.

The coaches seemed to be presenting themselves as powerless victims when they could have done more to engage with home coaches. They should also have challenged the Australian Swimming Union and its plans, and they should have raised more questions about the GDR.

The best women swimmers from all over the world were taking a drubbing from the muscled ranks of the East Germans. For us, however, it was not just a case of remove the GDR and we would not have looked quite so bad. We were also being thumped by swimmers from nations we had traditionally beaten.

On July 22, the fifth day of swimming and the last before a rest day would bring relief from the onslaught, it was also time for me to race the 200m freestyle. I convinced myself that I would do better. After a few days of less training, my body was starting to respond. I felt lighter in the water, and there was more lift in my stroke and more explosiveness in my muscle fibres.

I tried not to think about the East Germans and to focus on myself instead. That was easier said than done. I knew I had to be at my very best in heats just to make it through, so I went for it from the gun and had the ultimate hare to chase.

I was in lane 3 in the last of six heats. Next to me in lane 4 was Kornelia Ender, the world-record holder and the queen of the East German team.

That evening, she would win the 100m butterfly and 200m freestyle titles within 27 minutes of each other, the latter by the biggest margin in history, with both victories in world-record time. I would get to watch it unfold several hours later after an experience I've never forgotten.

Walking out to the starting blocks right behind Ender in the heats, I immediately noticed I was half her size in both height and mass. It was like playing Jack to the Giant in the storybook. I reached for courage, lifted my head, took in the crowd and looked down the pool. I needed to be in my zone, concentrating on my own race. I was in awe but not intimidated.

The gun fired. Back home, I was used to gaining an edge on the dive but Ender was something else. I came up halfway down her body. I sprinted to catch up as she paced herself. At the halfway turn I was closest to her in one minute 01 and came off the wall ready to attack. But there was no chance whatsoever. Her powerful legs had driven her off the wall with the kind of force I had seen my male training partners use when I had caught them up on the swim. She quickly established a two-second lead, a body length ahead of the field.

No matter, I told myself: make the final! I was still in second place at the last turn, with Jill Sterkel of the USA level with me. One lap to go. This is why you do sessions so hard they make your body scream but try as I might, my arms could turn no faster, my two-beat kick could not compete with the six-beat thunder in the legs around me and I faded to fourth. Ender cruised home in 2:02, while I touched the wall at 2:05. No final: 16th again.

Heartbroken, I felt that was it. My Olympic career was over at 14, I said to myself at the time.

Postcard Home From My Mother (July 22, 1976)

Michelle has just finished 200m and is very disappointed, but her taper was all wrong and we knew she would not go well. All the swimmers are very sad, and the parents mad. The other countries are very good, and it is good to see the races, each an Olympic and world record.

Later that evening, Ender claimed gold in the 100m butterfly and then set an astonishing world record as the first woman ever to race inside two minutes over 200m. Our jaws dropped with our spirits.

Of the 29 world records Ender established between 1973 and 1976, at the forefront was her stunning progress over the shortest distance on the program, the 100m freestyle: from 58.25 in 1975, it took her just one year to get down to 55.65 at the Montreal Games. That added up to an incredible 2.85- second gain since Shane Gould's 58.5 world record at the 1972 Munich Games.

Born in Halle, Ender won four world titles and a silver at each of the 1973 and 1975

World Championships. When in 1978 she wed Roland Matthes, the double Olympic backstroke champion for the GDR in 1968 and 1972, the event was described as "the world's fastest marriage". It was also rumoured as an arranged marriage so that their genes might provide the next generation of champions. The swimmers themselves later laughed at that suggestion.

The marriage lasted four years. Their daughter Francesca was the offspring of parents who boasted eight gold, six silver and two bronze medals at the 1968, '72 and '76 Olympic Games, 11 gold, three silver and one bronze medal at World Championships, and 49 world records. There was evidently a dark thread somewhere in the story.

Matthes ended his career in Montreal with a bronze in the 100m backstroke. His era as backstroke king was brought to an end by American John Naber, who, like Ender, claimed four gold medals as the best male swimmer at the event.

Meanwhile, just two women's titles went beyond the GDR. The first went to Marina Koshevaya from the Soviet Union in the most decisive 200m breaststroke victory in Olympic history. The second went to the USA in the biggest upset of the seven-day program.

Americans showed their upset more than most and began to question both the wave of success from a procession of big, powerful swimmers and the system that was making them superior. However, like Australia's media, the American media turned the questions and arguments back on their own instead of trying to seek explanations for events that were off the charts of expectation.

Shirley Babashoff was the most obvious case of an American swimmer who had her chances of joining the pantheon of greats in her sport dashed by the GDR, and then finding herself under attack in her own country.

When she questioned the East German dominance, she hit the headlines around the world but back home in the United States she was dubbed "Surly Shirley" because she was "shrill" and "angry". The tide turned the moment Shirley and her relay teammates (Wendy Boglioli, Jill Sterkel and Kim Peyton) brought the USA home and took the last gold of the competition from the GDR.

Arguably, that gold remains the greatest team victory by any American relay team in swimming history. Babashoff might have gone down in history as one of the golden greats of swimming with several titles in Montreal. Instead, she went home with one relay gold and several silvers and bronzes and was written up as a "sore loser", alongside anyone else who dared question the GDR 'success story'.

My Catharsis

My last day of racing in Montreal was also liberating. A weight lifted after the 200m freestyle heats. There was a kind of freedom, a release of the tension. No more training, no more weigh-ins, no more curfews. I now had time to explore Montreal, enjoy the village entertainment and spend time with my parents.

I continued going to the pool to support teammates who had become my family over the past two months. However, I felt a pang of frustration when, one by one, we didn't make finals. The press was critical of us, and the people of Australia didn't understand what had happened. Where, they asked, had the glory days of Australian swimming gone?

Australia ended the swimming with one bronze medal, the worst result in Australian Olympic history.

Coach Gathercole announced to the media:

"We were bitterly disappointed to finish up the way we have, but you can't do anything because of the power and strength of the other nations."
(Ron Carter, 'Gathercole's Grim Forecast', The Age, July 1976)

The flame had gone down, and the Games of the XXI Olympiad were officially declared closed. The village became a ghost town as teams left. Packing our bags, we were one of the last teams to leave. After six weeks in the village and a total of three months on the road, it was time to go home. Our special 747 Qantas charter flight was waiting at the Montreal-Mirabel International Airport.

We had come to Montreal with hopes of glory but were leaving with disappointment and betrayal. Those back in Australia said we had failed but considering the circumstances, we had done our best.

"Sport is a sweet and sour business. If you win you are a hero, if you lose, nobody wants to love you."
(John Landy, quoted in 'No Medals for Sour Losers' article, Nancy Berryman, Sydney Morning Herald, July 20, 1976)

For the swim team, our preparation had been riddled with flawed planning and poor organisation: our selection trials six months out from the Games; the Olympic squad billeted to families who, although trying to help, didn't understand what it took to compete at that level; the lack of an essential support team and only two coaches for the 28-member squad who had neither coached nor knew much about any individual athlete.

The administration only began thinking and planning for the Olympics scarcely one year out while the East Germans, Soviets and Americans were already working on four- to eight-year programs. And then there was the psychological effect of taking teenagers away from their homes with very little communication for three months.

Excuses were flying as reporters criticised and asked probing questions. What had happened to the golden era of Australian sport? Why had Australia not won gold? Why hadn't the athletes delivered?

It was perceived as a national crisis. The government came under fire from the media and athletes alike. Australia finished without a single gold medal and a dismal 32nd on the medal table for all sports, our worst-ever Olympic performance.

It was a giant embarrassment for the country and, suitably, pre-empted a full inquiry into the funding of sport that triggered a national opinion poll on the topic. Even the international press wanted to know: how did Australia, a nation of sporting heroes, sink so low?

We had been left behind. It was soul-destroying for athletes.

"Australia stood still while others turned amateur sport into a national promotion. We kept it at an individual level: the facilities, methods and amateur organisations remained pre-war; to win medals, to be competitive on the world stage, we had to have better management, facilities, and financial support.

Isolation and lack of finance meant no overseas tours were possible to gain international experience.

In Australia, we are still playing sport, but the rest of the world has made it a political business. Still we can at least lay claim to rugby league and cricket where good ole Mother England is an easy beat! Thank goodness the East Germans, Americans and Russians do not play footie or cricket!" (Rod Humphries, 'A Fading Sporting Image', Sydney Morning Herald, *July 1976)*

Our minds were a million miles from that as we boarded the plane in Montreal. We were just happy to be going home. We were out to let our hair down away from critics and happy to be in our own bubble for the last 30 hours of 'our Olympic experience'. There were special memories to savour: changing uniforms in the aisles of planes; the excitement of the village and its athletes from all around the world; racing the best in the world knowing that I'd been part of something special and had lived a dream; and the thrill of walking into the opening ceremony.

The last connecting flight from Melbourne to Sydney was the most solemn flight of our adventure. The media were waiting at the airport, primed for attack.

At 8:15 a.m., with smiles on our faces and dressed in our uniforms, we arrived at Sydney's Kingsford Smith Airport. Before we could see our families, the TV crews and print media were firing questions at us. The swimmers were hardest hit and we were not shy to share our feelings. A common refrain from those who had competed at their second Games was that Montreal marked "the unhappiest Games of my life". Retirements were announced in quick succession.

"I know we didn't get the medals, but the whole team felt downhearted. I have had enough of international swimming and that at least half the team will follow me and quit."

(Australian swimming team captain Graham Windeatt, quoted in 'Unhappiest Games of My Life' article, Gary Lester, The Sun, *August 8, 1976)*

Like Steve Holland at the age of 18, more than half the team did quit. I was 14 and watched and wondered.

All the good had been tainted by the things that let us down. For all our hard work and aspirations, the time and effort, and the financial burden on our families, mediocrity is what we ended up with. In the wave of judgement, the athletes and all the good parts were forgotten. It was all about the medals, the numbers, the 'success', without much understanding or respect for what we had done to get to the Games or what had inspired our journey.

That might have been more understandable had there been investment in sport, but we were rank amateurs compared with the highly organised East Germans.

Homecoming

My family and friends had skipped school to come and meet me at the airport. In their eyes, I was still a champion and I was grateful for their enthusiasm. I had missed three months of schooling and knew I had huge challenges ahead. But this homecoming was a celebration, regardless. They greeted me with balloons and a banner welcoming me back to Sydney. It was good to be home. I felt like I had been away forever.

It took me a while to settle down. I was back in school yet still away, reminded constantly of the Games by those who valued the very fact that at 13 I had qualified, and at 14 competed at my first Games. I was celebrated and happy. My attitude had changed. I was no longer the shy 13-year-old. I was now master of my own destiny, in my eyes. I was floating on a cloud.

It wasn't long, however, before I understood that my parents and teachers were not on the same cloud. I had fallen way behind in my schoolwork and although some teachers were excited to hear my story, they were not accommodating when it came to catching up on my schooling.

School holidays loomed and I was scheduled to spend the entire two weeks at my desk reading and working through the stencils and carbon copies that my friends had made for me. Concentrating was difficult as I wanted to be out and about with my friends but I knew I had to persevere. My maths teacher was the best. He came to our house and tutored me to get me up to speed for the final exam. With only weeks to go,

I was scrambling to get across the line.

Apprehension and tension were followed by relief and gratitude when my final marks came in. My friends had pulled me through, with a note that suggested I "should spend more time on your studies than in the pool"!

August is winter in Australia and outdoor 50-metre training pools would only open in October when the swimming season would commence. My coach began asking when I was coming back as pre-season training was under way.

I went along to the pool. We were a great group and my coach and squad were so keen to see me. They had all watched the Games on TV, and it was the first time that the Olympics were telecast live in Australia. They were thrilled for me and said they were proud of me. It was good to share my stories.

My eyes had been opened to the big, wide world but I craved normality, home and its comforts. The training had all been too hard, the sacrifices too great for the outcome, and doubts over the East Germans still gnawed. The racing in Montreal had ended with the USA topping the medals, the GDR a close second and the Soviet Union third. Australia was eighth with Steve's bronze.

There was already a lot of talk about what went wrong and how we could put it right next time. That didn't feel relevant to me. I was 14. The Games had come and gone and I didn't feel like it was something that I would be doing all over again.

I didn't go back to my home pool that day to tell Coach Caine I wanted back in. In fact, I told him I was done with swimming.

Part 2
Rivalry

Chapter 7
The Way It Was

"When two tribes go to war, a point is all you can score."
– 'Two Tribes', Frankie Goes To Hollywood

We had all returned to Australia despondent. More than half the Olympic swimming team had quit and the rest of us were in limbo: swim on or move on?

We had lived through a Games of two systems that left questions hanging. How had the GDR managed to achieve what it had? What to do about our own nation's shortcomings? As athletes we were just fodder for media and armchair critics who were not asking questions of the grown-ups in charge of the system.

Debate about both sides of the troubled story rumbled on. It was all too much. In my mind, swimming and the Olympics were in my past, even though my parents and coach tried to convince me that water was still my north and south.

It was the East vs West that the whole nation seemed to be talking about: how could a country like ours with a fine sporting heritage and tradition have fallen so far behind in just one Olympic cycle?

There was deep irony in that development. Rather than the capitalist world sounding the death knell for the amateur rules of Olympic sport, it was the communist world and its heavily subsidised sports systems that would send Olympic sport headlong into a capitalist era for athletes.

The response of the West was to find ways of funding athletes and with all the pressure going in one direction, the clock was ticking on Olympic Charter Rule 26, the amateur rule that prevented athletes from accepting financial payment for anything related to sport.

Within a decade, Olympic athletes would have the ability to earn money from what would come to be seen as their workplace, not their hobby. The roots of today's marketplace of grants, pay, prize money, sponsorships and partnerships go back to our era and attempts to match the professionalisation of sport in the Soviet Bloc.

In the 1970s, the athletes from the East were full-time professionals. The GDR system was set up to place athletes on that pathway between the ages of six and 10, when physical tests, including muscle biopsies and projections on height and build, determined which sport an athlete was best suited for. Sprinters and endurance athletes were filtered into their categories from a very early age and in a sport like mine, many of those who returned home from major competitions to state rewards were teenagers.

East Germany's rise had been meteoric across a spectrum of sports. The GDR won nine golds and 25 medals in all sports in 1968; then 20 golds and 66 medals in 1972; and in Montreal, it had knocked the mighty United States down to third place on overall medals with 40 golds and 90 podium visits in all. It was second only to its political master, the Soviet Union.

While we arrived in Sydney to a barrage of brutal judgements and hurtful headlines, a hero's welcome awaited the likes of Kornelia Ender and her teammates when they got home.

Heads of state, honours, prize money for their medals, and perks that extended to flats and cars: it was all part of what the communist world felt was fair under their understanding of the amateur rules.

Those rules had robbed teenage American Jim Thorpe of his decathlon gold in 1912 because he had accepted a small fee for playing baseball in a mini league before becoming an Olympian; and the rules were still in force in the 1980s when Sharron Davies, the British Olympic swimming silver medallist behind an East German, was barred from our sport after she appeared on a TV quiz show!

Her appearance was unrelated to sport and she was paid a small fee to cover her costs. But the sports authorities in the UK followed the Olympic rule to the letter and judged that she had been "capitalising on her sporting fame". Many others in the West, including my first coach in his youth, fell on the same Rule 26 sword and were forced to quit doing the sports they loved.

If Forbes Carlile, Shane Gould's coach and known as an innovator who embraced sports science, was credited with being the 'father' of the pace clock, the East Germans used the first pace-makers. Motorised pulley systems drove ropes dotted with markers on a loop that hovered over the lanes in the pool and ran down the side of tracks. The motor was set to travel at a specific time and the swimmer had to keep up with their marker. We relied on instinct and feel in our pace sets; they had an assistant guiding them to the world-record pace that the doping fast-tracked them towards.

The East Germans also had the first flumes—tanks in which they had to sprint against the tide until the point of exhaustion. The GDR girls would later describe how gruesome and frightening that was: they wore headgear adapted from gas masks, with one tube to carry the air in, and another to carry it out as they swam. The in-tube also had a tap that could be closed off, reducing or cutting their oxygen supply.

The data the East German coaches collected was fed back to physiologists, human-development biologists, chemists and other scientists who would instruct them on where improvements could be made using specific types of work. Some of that improvement was only possible because of drugs that allowed the athletes to recover from heavy workloads more quickly than we could on a juicy steak.

The books and scientific papers behind the GDR research into elite performance were later used by many countries, including Australia, to improve their own sports institutes.

Back in 1976, the East German Olympic team had clearly been getting a lot of help that left us looking as though we belonged to a bygone era. Moreover, they had not been asked to lodge for seven weeks with complete strangers with no knowledge of performance sport heading into an Olympic Games.

The GDR was busy leaving no stone unturned at a time when we were throwing rocks in the path of our own progress.

The Dark Side

In 1973, journalist Jean Pierre LaCour noted in a Paris journal that a *"vaccine against fatigue"* made up of *"toxic substances"* designed to hasten recovery was behind the sudden surge in GDR success in the pool.

The women claimed 10 gold medals to knock spots off the rest at the inaugural World Swimming Championships that same year. LaCour noted accusations that male hormones were being given to female athletes.

It all came to the fore in Montreal because the stage was much bigger than a single sport. The world was tuning in and for the first time at an Olympics, questions included: "What are they really doing to the girls to make them so big, so strong and so fast? And if they are doping, how are they getting away with it?»

No East German athlete tested positive in Montreal. Three other athletes fell foul of the tests: a weightlifter from Czechoslovakia, another from the United States and a Polish women's discus thrower.

> *"When asked about the rumours of support, financial and otherwise, Ender replied: 'Swimming is just a hobby for me, we work harder. We earn our results through dedicated hard work [...] Americans deal with group swimming instead of concentrating on the individual [...] It's silly to suggest that some machine is churning out East German champions'. Laughing, she says: 'passed the femininity test'."*
>
> *('American Girls Try the Old Cold War',* The Sun Herald *Olympic Games Liftout, July 25, 1976)*

In 1991 in her first interview with Western media since the Berlin Wall fell, Ender told Craig Lord in a report for *The Times* that she recalled being given "little blue pills" (Oral Turinabol) and grew out of her t-shirts in the three months leading up to the summer of 1976. She said: *"There were also injections to help us to recover and recuperate so the athletes could get back to hard training session after session without breaking down or being in need of a day off."*

We trusted the system. We had to assume everyone was adhering to the rules. They told us it was so. I believed that anti-doping testing was going to make things equal. However, by the time I left the Games, I too had become sceptical. An article in the *Sunday Telegraph* by John Moore seemed to confirm my doubts that we'd been competing on a level playing field:

> *"With a population of 17 million, the East Germans established itself as one of the world's three most powerful sporting nations. Winning an incredible 40 Gold medals including 11 in swimming ... The rest of the world, particularly the US and Australia was left wondering what they had to do to catch up and match the East German machine. Because that is what it is – a machine whose objective is to turn out a master race of sportsmen using chemicals, steroids and other drugs to build up the human body. Even in Montreal with the Olympics still on, they are working on the 1980 Moscow Olympics ...*
>
> *... The East Germans know the prestige that comes from champions and their entire social program is geared to it. There are special schools and colleges for talented youngsters. In this society, they are always looking for kids with talent – they would have been watched closely until about 10 years old, then if there were a top swimming prospect, they would have approached the parents. They might have decided that they should go to one of their elite sporting colleges, miles from home, in which case the parents would be offered a new job and other fringe benefits. The swimmer would have a muscle biopsy to determine whether their future was sprint or distance, bone measurements taken, blood tested, and the back of the hand x-rayed to determine possible growth in teenage years. Steroids would be used each day to build up muscle with an hour each day on flexibility exercises."*
>
> *(John Moore, 'Had Steve Holland Been an East German', Sunday Telegraph, August 1, 1976)*

Such reports were slammed by the GDR at the time, but John Moore was not speculating. In time, the truth would reveal that the 'rumours' were not blowing things out of proportion but were actually shy of the true depth of cheating that was driving the GDR medals' machin machine.

Flashback
GDR athlete Renate Neufeld, 1977–78

The first athlete to turn whistleblower on the East German sports systems was a woman, Renate Neufeld. She was one of East Germany's best track sprinters. In 1977, she fled to the West with the Bulgarian man she would later marry. She lay low for more than a year for the sake of her family's safety back home. But when she heard that her father had lost his job and her sister had been thrown out of her handball club, Renate decided to hold back no more.

In December 1978, she told the Sport Information Dienst (SID) news agency in West Germany:

> *"At 17, I joined the East Berlin Sports Institute. My speciality was the 80m hurdles. We swore that we would never speak to anyone about our training methods, including our parents. The training was very hard. We were all watched. We signed a register each time we left the dormitory and we had to say where we were going and what time we would return.*
>
> *One day, my trainer, Günter Clam, advised me to take pills to improve my performance: I was running 200m in 24 seconds. My trainer told me the pills were vitamins, but I soon had cramps in my legs, my voice became gruff and sometimes I couldn't talk any more. Then I started to grow a moustache and my periods stopped. I then refused to take these pills. One morning in October 1977, the secret police took me at 7am and questioned me about my refusal to take pills prescribed by the trainer. I then decided to flee, with my fiancé."*

At the time she defected, she carried a packet of grey tablets and a pot of green powder with her that she said she and her teammates had been told to take. West German doping analyst Manfred Donike identified them as anabolic steroids.

Professor Gary Bruce – 2009

In the course of his academic research in Germanic studies, Gary Bruce, a history professor at Canada's University of Waterloo, was researching documents in the Berlin archives of the notorious Stasi, the East German state police, when he came across a 95-page file relating directly to the Montreal 1976 Olympics. Two headings screamed back at him: *'Operation Finale'* and *'Destruction of the Rest of the Special Medicine'.*

It had long been known that the Stasi had recruited athletes, coaches and officials to spy on their teammates as part of the GDR's efforts to guard its dark secret. Spy leaders were also present in Montreal and exercising tight controls; the GDR girls were not staying in the village but were housed on boats in the harbour.

Professor Bruce had unearthed dynamite and in 2009 he shared the story with *The Canadian Press* news agency, which reported:

> *"After injecting athletes with performance-boosting drugs at the Montreal Olympics, East German officials dumped the leftover serum and syringes in the St. Lawrence River, newly uncovered documents indicate. A Stasi officer's final report on the Games contains a none-too-subtle reference to the drug program under the subheading, 'Destruction of the Rest of the Special Medicine'. About 10 suitcases of medical packaging, needles, tubular instruments, etc. were sunk in the St. Lawrence River."*
>
> Bruce explained: *"The documents make it clear that Stasi chief Erich Mielke saw the Games as a means to improve East Germany's standing in the world by ensuring all went well on the athletic field and that nothing went wrong away from it. He put the fabled Markus Wolf, head of the Stasi's foreign espionage wing, in charge of Operation Finale, a tightly controlled effort to monitor East German athletes in the years leading up to the '76 Olympics as well as during the 16-day sporting festival."*

The Seismic Shift

To the GDR, sport was about business, power and political preening. The nation was locked behind a wall in a closed system that put guards on its borders with shoot-to-kill orders from the state.

East Germany didn't like the idea of a world in which it was the poor cousin of West Germany. While famous car brands such as Porsche, Mercedes and Volkswagen were known for their progressive technologies and thriving markets, East Germans had the one-model-fits-all Trabant and a 10-year waiting list for the keys.

How then would it show the world that its system was thriving, its citizens healthy, smarter and more successful than those in the West? Sport would be the stage to display its communist might.

Markus Wolf and his fellow spies had done a masterful job of infiltrating every corner of the Olympic world and when the likes of Renate Neufeld raised red flags, federation insiders were always on hand to rip them down again. It was all rumour and speculation, they suggested. The truth, they said, was all about above-board breakthroughs in sports medicine, cutting-edge science and a systematic system of talent scouting.

Reuters' Olympic correspondent Derek Parr, who was based in East Berlin, reported:

> *"The East Germans pay painstaking attention to detail, and all the help that science and medicine can provide. The combination of German meticulousness and communist centralised control has produced what the West knows as the East German sports machine. Quoting Dr Edgar Waldner, acting college director, "Nowadays you will not find top sporting performances anywhere in the world without the collaboration of the medical side. We have not developed any miracle methods but we have made many important discoveries in areas such as blood circulation and the recovery of athletes after high-pressure efforts. The strength of sports medicine is not in any way world-breaking discovery but is the systematic application of experiences, and their translation into coaching – doping of any kind is forbidden in East Germany."*
>
> *('Saturation Screening Is East Germany's Recipe', Reuters, August 1976)*

Before the dust had settled on the 1976 Games, we were told that we'd meet an even bigger, stronger 'machine' in Moscow at the 1980 Olympics.

It was hard to get an accurate picture of what was really happening behind the Iron Curtain. Access was by invitation only. And even then, those who did gain access were shown the bits of the GDR puzzle that didn't reveal any evidence of the state secret underpinning their 'systematic' approach to sport.

Australia's Dilemma

That two standards were being applied to amateur status was a hard pill to swallow, especially for Australians. Sport was a pastime for Australians and natural talent was honed by desire, dedication, discipline and determination. In its purest form, sport was noble and aesthetic.

It was a love of sport that drove us to the pool or the track. Blessed with open spaces, good climate and the strong will of our people, Australia built its sporting heritage on talent and hard work.

> *"The East Germans have reached the heights at great cost to the individual's freedom [...] That kind of system wouldn't work in Australia, and I'd hate to see us try – I don't think we want that kind of sport."*

TURNING THE TIDE

('American Girls Try the Old Cold War', The Sun Herald *Olympic Games Liftout, July 25, 1976)*

We didn't suffer the destruction of World Wars like so many other countries and, on the back of massive post-war migration, the 1950s and '60s became a golden era for Australian sport. Australians topped the medals in the pool at the home 1956 Melbourne Olympics, finished third overall and then spent the next four Olympics in the top 10 of nations across all sports.

However, in 1976, we found ourselves 32nd. It was time to make crucial decisions. We'd been living in a bubble, content with punching well above our weight in sport. Montreal was a brusque wake-up call. The government, federations, coaches and athletes were forced to ask blunt questions. How can we compete in a world that's left us behind? What value do we place on Olympic gold? What can we do to revive our status in world sport?

There were no easy answers but it was obvious that unless we took a professional stance, we were destined to be little leaguers. Tradition and culture presented an obstacle: we were not a 'machine'. We were proud and courageous fighters—and that's what sport was about to us. Our diet was steak, veggies and the odd vitamin pill. Our then 14 million population was known as the folk from 'the land down under', and Australia was seen as a land of opportunity and home of 'the great Aussie battler'.

Our pride in all of that had taken a battering on our Olympic tour. Five medals from 613 athletes in Montreal had led to headlines that stretched from *'Australia's Golden Days Are Gone'* to *'A Fading Sporting Image'* and *'Our Swimming Team's A World Joke'.* Even *The Guardian* in Britain had a go: *"The country had stumbled into a national identity crisis ... brought on by the sudden collapse of Australia's greatest claim to world esteem – their athletes ...".*

The future looked bleak, too. *"Olympics – What now? We've missed Moscow already"* declared the Sunday Mirror on August 8, 1976. It opined: *"APATHETIC Australia has already relinquished any chance of medal success in the 1980 Moscow Olympic Games".* David McKenzie, IOC member for Australia and an Olympian, suggested it would take at least eight years to recover. He told *The Mirror:*

"The days when we could afford the luxury of attending the Games for the sake of simply competing are gone forever, as recognised by the IOC ... We need a scientific approach to training and coaching, facilities to launch a complete new program preferably guided by a central revamped administration. A world record does not ensure success."

The federal government commissioned an inquiry into the funding of sport and a due-diligence study for the development of an Australian Institute of Sport. It was new hope—but it didn't last long.

A U-turn was on the cards the moment Prime Minister Fraser told The Australian:

"Public concern over the dismal Olympic performances will be short lived ... and the injection of significant funds into sport would go against every economic principle expressed by the coalition government."

By the end of 1976, the Ministry of Tourism and Recreation (which included sport) was disbanded, and a 60% funding cut ordered. This left sport without a ministry or a portfolio in government, and only $A1.6 million in funding for all sport and recreation programs across the board.

Meanwhile, other nations and Games' organisers were publishing medal tables that had become a symbol of power and status overshadowing individual performances, in contradiction of the Olympic Charter.

Rule 6 of the Olympic Charter states: *"The Olympic Games are a competition between athletes in individual or team events and not between countries."*

However, Rule 6 didn't make the slightest bit of difference in the East vs West Cold War in sport or at any other time where nations and the world media pay keen attention to medal tables and use them to boast of their status in global sport. Medal tables have also become a key measure when it comes to the distribution of funding in many of the world's leading sports nations at the national level.

In our era, the status the Eastern Bloc craved was underpinned by a big bill that included a vast sports science and medicine machinery, sports schools and sports universities. Within that system, qualified professional coaches well versed in physiology and even psychology worked hand in hand with nutritionists and doctors. It was not commercial, but it was big business.

In the GDR, those professionals either agreed to be part of the state plan and all of its aspects, or they went back to a life more ordinary. Choice was seriously relative compared to our freedoms.

The biggest challenge for the West was, as Stu Isaac put it in *Swimming World Magazine* in 1977, *"to determine to what extent we can fund our amateur athletes under the current International Olympic Committee and FINA regulations"*.

The Amateur Rule—Australia-Style

The Australian public loves its sport and its sporting heroes. When media reports suggested we athletes were a lost cause, letters of support came flooding in from the fans.

We had been criticised for our lack of medals yet there was no mention of the fact that we'd been playing under different rules to the East. Where the West had interpreted Rule 26 with an iron fist and threatened athletes with lifetime bans, the countries behind the Iron Curtain had acted as if there were no impediment to the heavy subsidisation of athletes, including school and training costs, as well as performance rewards in money and kind.

It wasn't the IOC that was on our case, but our own sports administration. Their dictatorial approach was to bar direct funding of athletes as the only way to protect their 'amateur' status.

Questions were raised about what was or wasn't allowed, but it was up to each National Olympic Committee to sign a declaration confirming that athletes met all the criteria required and had a legal right to compete. Western nations enforced the amateur rule. The Eastern Bloc nations interpreted it differently and this was not challenged by the system.

When it became clear that Western nations would also have to start subsidising sport if they were to remain competitive with the East, Australian authorities opted for a funding program that directed the money through national federations that would take a share before any support was distributed to athletes.

The scheme didn't fly because industry and private donors didn't support a scheme where there was no guarantee that the money would make it to the athletes. They had no faith in it, so it was a stalemate.

The word 'amateur' stuck in the throats of many but the IOC had dug its heels in and persisted with the tone of a 1955 speech by then IOC president, American Avery Brundage, in which he stated, "We can only rely on the support of those who believe in the principles of fair play and sportsmanship embodied in the amateur code in our efforts to prevent the Games from being used by individuals, organisations or nations for ulterior motives."

There was a change of guard in 1972 when the IOC presidency passed to Irishman Lord Killanin who brought a softening of attitudes. Rule 26 remained a distinct part of the Olympic Charter but National Olympic Committees (NOCs) were given more leeway when interpreting the restrictions and any previous uniformity in applying 'amateur status' was lost from nation to nation and sport to sport.

The NOCs were faithful to the prevailing IOC line, while International Federations for each sport felt able to interpret the rule at their whim, sometimes on the basis of national laws where a federation was based. As a result, some athletes were able to maintain 'amateur status' while earning money from their sport.

Track athletes, for example, were able to accept 'trust funds' several years before the same facility was available to swimmers because of the different way in which the International Amateur Athletics Federation (now known as World Athletics), the International Swimming Federation (FINA, now known as World Aquatics) and their affiliated national federations handled the matter.

The USA responded to the East's system by spending millions on their collegiate system, with scholarships allowing athletes to study and train without their sports authorities being able to claim they were being funded in sport. To reinforce that, the National Collegiate Athletic Association (NCAA) imposed rules that still exist to this day: no student on a scholarship can accept prize money or sponsorship during their time at college.

In Australia, the hardline of 'amateurs only' continued to be enforced until the rule was tweaked in 1985. Rule 26 was enforced with an iron fist by the Australian Swimming Union, which was perceived to rule the sport in the interests of governors not swimmers.

Between Montreal and Moscow, the Soviet Bloc sports machine cranked up as the Australian system found itself stuck in first gear.

Swimming Against the Tide

The US Olympic Committee (USOC) set a course for swimming. In 1977, it declared that it was "set to establish a program for US swimming resulting in the highest medal production for 1980, consistent with American ideals".

There would be training camps for the "discovery of new talent"; an intense national and international competition program; and a learning curve for advanced coaching through seminars and sports medicine clinics. That would go hand in hand with the new commitment to funding athletes through college sports, with women among the beneficiaries for the first time in the 1970s after Title IX legislation guaranteeing 'equality' was passed in 1973.

A war of superpower sports nations was well under way, with the United States committed to sinking millions into hitting back at the communist challenge.

The ideology of the East was illustrated in a 1977 article by A.J. Cichoke in *Swimming World Magazine*. Under a headline *'The GDR's planned Dominance of the Moscow Olympics'*, he noted that success was not based on amateur sports *"as we know them, but on how the athlete can contribute his abilities for the betterment of the state ... There is no room in the GDR system for the amateur athlete ... it is for the elite only; there are no average athletes, the stakes are too high."*

Success was incentivised, though there was a catastrophic health consequence for many athletes after their sports careers ended. Meanwhile, athletes in the West battled with regulators, pleading for funding and access to quality training in conditions that did not include competing for space with the public.

As journalist Rod Humphries noted in his July 1976 feature entitled *'A Fading Sporting Image'*: *"Whilst others turned amateur sport into a national promotion, Australia stood still."*

In swimming, there was a desperate need to address governance issues at a time when self-protection and self-preservation were the focus of the leadership.

Our Montreal head coach Terry Gathercole penned a report, *'Montreal Olympics: Wake up Australia'*, in which he noted: *"We're still so far and away amateurs in every way in Australia. In other countries you're dealing with dedicated athletes and officials. We have to do the same, we have to find the right kind of officials, not people who are just seeking kudos, and we have to develop a system."*

And it needed a budget far bigger than Australian Olympic sport had ever known. There was no sign of that happening as we entered 1977 with the dim prospect of Australia sending only six swimmers to the two international meets planned. Swimmers and coaches were left scrambling to find their own solutions for training and competition. The US collegiate system offered our men scholarship opportunities, but they were not available to women at the time and home was our only option.

Coach Bill Sweetenham penned a June 1977 column for *International Swimmer*, our sport's national magazine, in which he asserted: *"Our doomsday fight is only a product of our system."*

Michael Wenden, the 1968 double Olympic champion, had set the tone of debate in October 1976, the month I made a steady return to swimming. His column in *International Swimmer* on the subject of *'Australian swimming and the ASU'* noted:

"Swimming administration is a subtle, internal power game; that the politics of swimming are the manipulations that occur to ensure maximum ego benefit to the sport of swimming and; that in a lot of cases the swimming administrators are those people who have an aptitude for political survival rather than those people with progressive ideas and the ability to implement them.

You will find that the powerful people are surrounded by 'yes men' – the people who don't really understand the implications of the decisions that they are to make and who simply go along with the leader.

The approach should be to develop the most desirable objectives, then see what changes have to be made to achieve those objectives.

So the Montreal results were not unexpected, in fact the trend has been there for years. The point being that our constitution has restricted the changes necessary to meet the prevailing conditions.

Gradual face-saving changes in the system will not do – you do not cure the disease by relieving the symptoms!"

After the Fraser Government reneged on its promise to fund athletes and closed down the Ministry of Tourism and Recreation (which included sport), the Australian Olympic Foundation (AOF) set up office, the first of its kind, in September 1977. Five months later, the new organisation, chaired by IOC Member David McKenzie, secured funding of $3.5 million for the preparation of the 1980 Olympic team.

However, the grassroots went thirsty. Associations and institutions below elite Olympic level but responsible for the birthing pools of Australian talent had to go cap in hand asking, "What about us?" The Confederation of Australian Sport (CAS), representing 67 national sporting associations and 5.5 million active sports people, successfully lobbied the federal government for a further $3 million over the next three years. However, it was spread very thinly.

Meanwhile, our competitors were already on the road to Moscow. In a feature headed *Comparisons 1956–1977, Sink or Swim'*, Jim O'Doherty told readers of *International Swimmer* on November 1, 1977:

"East Germany, USA, Canada and the USSR emerged as real powers for Moscow in 1980. The factors which these countries have in common are: 1. Organized programs, 2. Back up support in psychology and physiology, 3. Financial support, 4. National pride and the desire to be successful at the Olympic Games."

That echoed what Forbes Carlile told *Swimming World* soon after the last stroke had been swum in Montreal:

> *"First, the Swimming Union must have a PLAN. It is no good just asking for 'money for sport'. We have to know and spell out exactly how and where we want money spent, and this is where the Australian Swimming Union must come in and start acting quickly … I believe that even if money was forthcoming it would be largely wasted in terms of results. Our urgent need is facilities."*

Caught in the middle of a debate stacked with more blame than self-reflection and genuine interest in athlete welfare, swimmers faced Hobson's choice: we could either quit or bear the brunt and take the strain of a broken system.

Chapter 8
Metamorphosis

"Courage is the power to let go of the familiar."
– Raymond Lindquist

A broken heart was among my own challenges soon after returning to Australia. My beloved grandfather, who had made it all the way to Montreal just months prior to cheer me on at my first Olympics, tragically passed away. He suffered a fatal heart attack while as a passenger driving over the Sydney Harbour Bridge. I received the devastating news from my uncle on the phone when I walked in from training that day.

I would forever cherish the door my grandfather had opened in my heart and mind. He was the one who told me I could be right up there with the best. I carried his belief, strength and spirit with me into the next chapters of my swimming story.

Time moves on, and with the end of the school year, which I had successfully completed, summer was on the horizon. It was a luxury to have had the time to give my schoolwork singular attention, but I heard the water whispering to me.

Everything heals in time and a genuine love of sport can shine through the darkest moments and deepest disappointments. My coach and parents had formed an alliance: they were determined to convince me to get back to the pool.

There was no urgency as far as I was concerned. My full year of training up until my break would sustain me if I chose to return. The urge was stronger than I wanted to admit. Somewhat reluctantly, I agreed to swim casually with the team and keep my fitness levels ticking over and reacquaint myself with what swimmers call their 'feel for water'. Beyond that, I had no goal.

As the exams period drew to an end, coach Dick Caine tempted me with a "little race" at a local competition. "Just to get a swim in ... the time's not important," he said.

Great pressure is placed on you to perform when you return from the Olympics, so it was a smart move by Coach Caine to go for an event in which I had no official times. There would be no comparison, making it a tougher exercise for critics.

This would be my first 800m freestyle race. I disliked the longer distance events but as the laps unfolded, something innate took over, something latent, something I'd been trying to avoid. Fun got overtaken by the ambition deep within me. Like the young girl who had refused to do the whole school carnival program but ended up doing it anyway, here I was again: the wall I had built between me and the 800m was crumbling with every passing stroke. My competitive spirit was alive and kicking.

This was the kind of off-the-radar local event that drew little attention but a meet record of nine minutes, 16.5 seconds opened my 800m account and gave me one of eight wins that weekend. My swimming career was far from over. I was back, we were back—athlete, coach and team. It meant the world to me.

The summer of 1977 was an awakening for me just as much as it was for Australian sport in the debate about funding and how to respond to the game-changer Games of Montreal that were driven not just by the communist bloc but the United States too, with its men having produced the most dominant thumping of the rest of the world that swimming had ever seen.

All of that was in the headlines—and so were we once more after my return to championship racing: *"Dick Caine and Michelle Ford are out to prove Australia's swimming critics wrong ..."* opined *The Leader* on January 12 after the *Daily Telegraph* had noted three days before:

> *"Carss Park Swimming sensation Michelle Ford, 14, won 11 gold medals in the NSW Age Championships held last week at North Sydney Olympic Pool.*
>
> *These were: Freestyle 14 years, 100m, 200m, 400m, (Aust. Open record); Individual medley 14 years, 200m, 400m (record); Backstroke, 100m, 200m, Freestyle Open, 200m (14 years record) 100m, 800m (Open record); Butterfly 200m."*

Two months after my debut 800m, January 19 marked the day when I could say I held a senior and/or age record in every event barring my nemesis, breaststroke. It was a feat no other swimmer had ever accomplished. I was back in the world rankings as the first Australian woman to make that grade since the Olympic selection trials almost a year earlier.

I used the records as stepping stones and marker pins on the road to progress and self-improvement. I would sit for hours with my father dissecting each event's world record, analysing the pros and cons of each distance and stroke, and rating my chances event against event. The world record in my favourite, the 200m butterfly, was considered 'highly attainable', even though it was five seconds ahead of my best. The journey begins with optimism and steely determination, otherwise you're on the wrong road.

The 200m and 400m freestyle world records we had down as 'probable' even though the 200m was actually 'unlikely' given Ender's sub-two-minute victory in Montreal. It would be another two Olympic cycles before the first Australian woman would break that barrier.

Then there was the 800m. I had swum it twice but my father pinpointed it as my best chance. I wasn't sure I wanted to go there. I didn't like the training sets required but I also understood the logic in his calculation.

East Germany's double Olympic freestyle champion Petra Thümer had set the global standard at 8:37.14 in Montreal. In my second ever 800m, on January 8 at the NSW Age Championships, I had axed almost half a minute off my debut best in 8:47.54, the second-fastest time by an Australian after Jenny Turrall's 1975 Commonwealth standard. I worked out that I would need to improve 1.25 seconds each 100m to get past Thümer.

I was still far off—but from that point, each passing swim was no longer a quiet challenge but a headline with the question, "Can she do it?" Some thrive on that kind of attention. I preferred to shrug it off, bypass the game and play my cards close to my chest. It was an era where we had no managers and there was no such thing as media training. Coach and parents handled that side of things and that suited me just fine.

The headlines spurned a fan club of spectators. There were occasions when thousands would come to watch and cheer me on to the next record, from local age to senior national. Their passion left me elated. It was amazing to know I had touched so many people. This was genuine sport without the politics, corruption and scandals that nearly destroyed my love for swimming but that had all helped to make me wiser, stronger and faster.

Highs and Lows

My coach caught the wave too. He put me through the toughest two months of training I had ever endured, convinced the best was yet to come. Exhausted but satisfied, I was back with my team and what I knew, my passion and belief reignited.

I was buoyed by timed sets in training that indicated I could be the best in the world in the 800m one day. Later, Caine would recall:

"The greatest moment I had seen is when one day, in walks Michelle. We had been doing hard effort sets. I could see Michelle was not happy and I was tired and nervous about the upcoming championships and did not want a fight.

So not meaning it, I said, 'Look Michelle, you can do 800-metre session tonight, 16 laps, instead of six miles but you have to break the world record for 800 metres. If you do, you and all the team can go home.' 'Ok,' she says, glaring at me. So, I get on the PA system and call all the 500 public and rest of the team out of the pool and

announced that Michelle Ford is going to break the world record for 800 metres.
Up she gets and makes it, smiles at me, and walks out with the whole team."

Talk of doom and gloom in Australian sport continued, but it didn't worry us. We were the hope that all was not lost.

"Following recriminations over Australia's performances in the Montreal Olympics, it is refreshing to see someone with a positive attitude. Carss Park swim coach Dick Caine and his protégé, Montreal Olympian Michelle Ford, are proving the critics wrong ... He says determination and hard work can overcome the debacle Australian swimming suffered at Montreal. Australia, once regarded as a top Olympic nation, failed to win a gold medal last year. Full of confidence over Michelle's ability, Caine is sure he has another local swimming world champion."
('Michelle Answers Swim Critics', The Leader, January 12, 1977)

It was high summer and the competition season was in full swing. Training was tense and intensive. The coach was gearing up to have us in prime shape for the 1977 Australian Nationals that were just weeks away.

The press homed in on a developing rivalry—the imminent 'clash' between the two new darlings of Australian swimming, Tracey Wickham and me. At 13, we had both made the team for Montreal and we both swam 200m to 800m freestyle. By 1977 we represented hope in a rebirth of Australia's status as a sporting nation.

The 'duel' was pumped up in the media, daily at times it seemed. My parents told me to steer clear and be wary and aware of who I was talking to. My flamboyant coach was the one who engaged with reporters. I wasn't interested. I kept my head down and my eyes on the job. All the while, Dick's endorsement of me and my potential got bigger and louder with each passing article. He had confidence in me and told them so.

However, behind the show, he was jumpier than usual. My mind went back to the first day I had seen him on return from Montreal. I had walked up to him on the pool deck after being away all those months and noticed something had changed in him. He looked at me differently, there was a distance. He had been locked out of the whole Olympic experience, and I understood for the first time how deeply he had been hurt by that.

The ways of the Swimming Union had hit us both. He could not come to terms with, nor understand how a young 13-year-old swimmer could be taken from her home coach. He was simply asked to deliver the goods, no questions asked, and no prospect of reward or even involvement when the biggest lights were turned on.

We were now six months on from the lost northern summer that was our winter. The panorama of Australian swimming remained unchanged—the same policies and people were anchored in the federation. The criteria to be selected as a national coach were never advertised and the question remained: would my coach ever be invited into the inner circle, the chosen few?

Weeks before the National Championships and the moment when merit should have been taken into consideration, the Swimming Union announced the coaches for the upcoming touring teams.

Coach Caine was not part of the touring team, but he remained committed and repeated his conviction and belief in me. Yet it felt like the latest rejection had planted a seed of doubt when it came to whether he would continue to be my coach in future.

The Split

The Carss Park pool was divided by the nylon lane ropes keeping the training squad apart from hundreds of members of the public jumping in and splashing about as they enjoyed the last balmy weather before the onset of autumn.

Our lanes were filled with young teenage swimmers getting ready for the season grand finale, the National Championships, the most important event on the Australian swimming calendar. We were days away and the coach demanded rigorous discipline. Tensions were running high and that was always a signal that one of us could be kicked out of the workout at the drop of a hat.

That's just how our coach was before a major competition. The main set was often the spark and we tried to tick every box on his list of instructions, but the sessions were getting less strenuous as we tapered ahead of racing and when teenagers have extra energy, their capacity for mischief rises accordingly. The quality sets remained intense but there was a lot of joking in the rest between swims. It was a period in our preparation that we all looked forward to, but one where the coach would be more on edge.

We would feel sorry for those who took the brunt. "Here he goes again," we murmured to each other. An explosion of temper and show of spirit is entertaining for onlookers but no fun when you're in the crossfire.

I could see it coming but hadn't guessed that today it would be my turn. We had been together for 10 years. The coach/athlete synergy that had stemmed from mutual understanding fell apart in one snap moment. Just days before Nationals, the glue that had held us together came unstuck.

I had been kicked out of training before, told to "get out of the pool", and to "go home and think about it". It was part of the DNA of training at Carss Park. We all accepted that it happened from time to time but this particular day felt more severe, more final. Dick Caine kept telling me to "find another team"; he told me to "train with the other coaches, those who'll take you to the blocks".

I was lost. Maybe he no longer thought he was good enough or more likely he felt that the 'chosen' coaches who got the places on national teams would be better for me. Whatever the reason, I was out.

Carss Park had been my home, my team and my friendships in sport. My coach knew how I ticked and when it came to the alchemy of talent and hard work, my mentor was more familiar with me than my own parents.

All the effort, hype and thrill of my return to the pool back in October took on a different hue. At 14, I was on my own without a coach and not fully understanding what had happened, just days out from the season highlight.

1977 Australian Nationals

The media picked up the story. Questions were being asked of me that I had no answer for. I had lost focus on the competition. I managed to win the 200m and 800m freestyle and the 200m butterfly but I was confused and small things that wouldn't have affected me before began to niggle. I had no coach and no team. The stress may have contributed to it, but illness forced me to withdraw from the last day of action.

As I recovered over the coming days, I came to a decision: it was time to move on. But where to? I was high in the world rankings but maybe it was time to throw in the towel after all.

My father came to the rescue. At a critical moment, he picked up the slack and began coaching me. Being an elite sportsman himself, a sailor who made the trip to Montreal as part of the training crew, he knew the kind of work I needed. He and his programs were tough.

I was back at Sans Souci pool where my swimming career had begun, but this time on my own. Grateful that my father organised his workday around my training sessions, I would be at the pool at six every morning and back at four every afternoon. My father would stand on deck and deliver the workout he conscientiously wrote each day. If he couldn't make it back to the pool, my mother would stand in and she was the saint who coped with my bad moods on most occasions.

It was hard to stay motivated and I felt lonely, but my new coach accepted my cries of not wanting to do what was asked. It wasn't easy. There was no one to speak to, no one to spur me on or share the pain with. But Mum and Dad were the constant. They never gave up on me. My younger brother Richard kept me company in training even though he wasn't doing the same level of workouts.

World-Record Rattling

A month into this new routine, I lined up for my fourth 800m race. It was the last event of the three-day program at the New Zealand National Championships, and everyone was packing up to go home. I felt like that, too. A touch fatigued, I had no expectations, but that's what it's like sometimes. There's no sense of being pumped and primed for a special swim; it just happens. I surprised everyone, including myself, by giving the world record a rattle. In just a few months I'd taken 40 seconds off my time and now held state, national and commonwealth records for a distance I used to steer well clear of.

On March 19, the local *Weekend Star* reported: *"Mighty Michelle Ford gave the world 800m freestyle record a fright. The petite 14-year-old sped through the water to clock 8:40.3, only 3 seconds outside the world mark set by East Germany's Petra Thümer, which stands at 8 min 37.14. No electronic touch pads are in the pool and so no world mark could have been set ... and her goggles filled up giving her trouble on the way."*

My father's training methods must have been spot on. I needed to find another 800-metre swim in a pool equipped with electronic timing. I had been selected to represent Australia at the London Invitational at Crystal Palace in England, the land of my birth. That would do.

In early April, the international event got to the last day with Australia holding a small lead over the rest on points. The 800m freestyle and the 200m butterfly, my top two and toughest events, were back-to-back. I told the coach/manager, Jim O'Doherty, that I would withdraw from the butterfly to give the 800m my best shot at the world record.

However, at the team meeting that evening, the coach asked if I could swim the double to help Australia win the team trophy. My heart sank. The butterfly was just before the freestyle race, which meant that I would forgo my chance to join the ranks of world-record holders. Everything was in place: the electronic timing; I felt light and fast in the water; previous races that indicated I was on target form.

I looked around the room at the faces of my teammates. It was me and my world record or them and the team trophy. It was a tough call but the choice was obvious. The team report read:

"It was at this point in the competition that I felt Australia could win. We all realised that, to achieve this, Michelle would have to swim in events that were not planned ... yet she still competed in the 200 'fly and in doing so, sacrificed a better personal time in the 800."
(Jim O'Doherty, May 2, 1977)

Australia lifted the team trophy.

'Team' mattered. Wearing the letters AUSTRALIA on your back really meant something to me. I was representing my country. We took pride in wearing the green and gold wherever we walked on tour. Neither suited my complexion, but then I wasn't into fashion and looks. My hair was chlorine-bleached white with a green tinge from the copper in pool treatments in those days. We were swimmers with strong shoulders and svelte bodies. No one wore make-up. No time; no interest. We were a unit, a team and a family.

These smaller teams like that one in London were my favourites. We had a lot of respect for each other as we changed and drove each other to new heights. Bigger teams somehow got caught up in concerns over the rules at the heart of conflicts between management and the swimmers. Those things could be a drain on energy and a distraction from the joy of representing your country and being a cohesive force— one for all, all for one.

Finding the Right Team

Buoyed by team spirit on returning to Australia, I realised that doing it all alone was neither sustainable nor enjoyable. I desperately needed to find a team that would provide that fun factor, the daily challenge, and the motivation and stimulation that any athlete needs.

The right choice depended on so many factors. Which was more important: was it the coach, the pool, the team, the travel time to and from workouts and its impact on schooling, or the quality or quantity of work?

There was no substitute for quality but this was an era when many coaches were pushing for longer miles to improve performance. Training in a 25-metre pool when competitions are in a 50-metre one was not ideal either. Then there was the question of the right training partners, who were scarcer the further you moved up the tree.

One of the best men's teams in Australia was on the other side of town: a 40-minute drive each way. I would be back in time for school after the morning workout and be able to return for afternoon workouts. So, after a long and tumultuous year, it was decided that in September 1977, the new season would get under way with my new team at Heffron Park with coach John Rodgers.

When the new regime began, I found it tough to clock up to 17 km a day in the pool. It was far from my days at Carss Park where quality reigned over quantity, but I had to make the most of it. I knew that I needed the 'quality work' so I set out creating my own: every practice I would chase the boys. They probably disliked me beating them on occasion but we joked and teased each other and it worked. My times improved— and the team became one of the best in Australia.

Chapter 9
World-Record Club

*"Many of life's failures are people who did not realise
how close they were to success when they gave up."*
– Thomas Edison

It was January 1978 and, in their efforts to find a response to the communist challenge, event organisers, coaches and administrators had identified one of the drawbacks of remote Australia: we were starved of essential international competition.

The KB Invitational, sponsored by the beer company of the same name, was staged to address the problem. For the first time since the 1956 Melbourne Olympics, Australia rolled out the red carpet for elite swimmers. We got to race Americans and Europeans in our home waters.

The visitors got a taste of what it was like to be Australian with our upside-down seasons in 'the land down under' and a geography that dictated 30 hours of travel each way to and from Europe and 20 hours to and from the West Coast of the USA.

Under the amateur rules being applied more rigorously in the West than the East, the hand-picked elite swimmers would receive no payment nor be allowed sponsorship, but they could benefit from a more professional competition format with corporate dollars behind it.

The promotional campaign that came with the KB Games was something we hadn't seen in Australian amateur sport until then, though the Coca-Cola International in London had become an annual fixture since the early 1970s.

Goodwill was the only asset we had: we got the meet, and in return the organisers got us to promote the event they'd invested in. I agreed to be the 'face', or the poster girl for the event. Nowadays, that would come with a hefty fee and/or a sizeable prize pot. Back then, the only reward for being the drawcard was honour.

The whole event was to be held on one evening in January like a few hours at the opera or theatre, not over the days and long hours of a traditional swimming competition. I was up for two races: 800m freestyle followed by the 200m butterfly. There were no heats, just straight finals, which suited this 'get-in-and-do-it' girl.

I had flown into Brisbane earlier in the day after a well-earned sleep-in, a rare luxury I cherished. The fly-in-fly-out nature of the event made it the first competition where my parents were not present for my races. It was going to be a tough challenge: my international opponents included Montreal Olympic finalists. I had no idea where they were in their preparation, but I knew I was in a phase of heavy training off the back of a 1977 season of disruption, stress and apprehension.

There were lessons, too. A year of change that included a split with my old coach, my father taking up the strain, and the search for a settling into a new club with John Rodgers as my new coach had taught me that not everything goes to plan. I had learned that taking whatever comes in your stride is more fruitful than being blown off course by every unexpected drama or passing setback. The KB Games would be what it would be.

I arrived relaxed, positive and with an open mind, even though the 800m remained not only new but something of a mystery to me. The longest event on the Olympic program for women until the Tokyo Games in 2021, the 800m was the hardest event to train for and deal with mentally, at least for me. It tests your strategy and tenacity.

So why do it? Why listen to my father's logic when he suggested I could take 16 laps of pain and own it and make it mine? I was just about to find out.

The key is to have a goal. My late grandfather and my father had instilled that in me. I'd been working to see how far I could take the 800m. Here was the next test.

Joining the Club of Pioneers

The Valley Pool was charged by a buzz of anticipation as the stands filled and swimming officials dressed in their whites took their place on the pool deck. Everyone was curious to see how this new vision would pan out.

Music resonated around the venue, adding to the party mood. We were the entertainers and it felt like that as we marshalled for the first race of the evening, the 800m. I was thinking about how old the pool was. You could see it in the tiles and the skimpy lane ropes that looked barely able to withstand a ripple, let alone a wave, and in the pool's solid, stable and unforgiving build. The 'baths' had been here since 1925, with its original status and purpose still on the sign above the entrance: Municipal Swimming Bath.

The old wooden stands that lined both sides of the pool deck were creaking with enthusiastic spectators. My cousin was among them, courtesy of permission to leave her boarding school to come and cheer me on. Kay was my biggest fan and cheerleader.

Centre stage in a line-up of seven girls, I was next to Brisbane's Tracey Wickham, my age-peer rival since we were both 10, and Annelies Maas, who had taken silver for the Netherlands behind GDR Olympic champion and world-record holder Petra

Thümer in the 400 and 800m at the 1977 European Championships. The Dutchwoman was the girl to beat. She had swum an 8:39, just a second behind Thümer and almost a second better than the Commonwealth record I had set in New Zealand earlier that year.

As we took to our blocks, I felt the warmth of the evening sun setting slowly behind us. The final dance of my pre-race routine included shaking my arms and wobbling my legs to get the blood flowing faster.

My focus was laser sharp as I stared down the pool. "In Lane 1 …" the announcer began. When my turn came, I soaked up "Michelle Ford, 1976 Olympian, Australian record holder" with a sense of pride and a puffed-out chest. Olympian. I felt I could own it. I'd been there and done it and that was all that mattered.

My thoughts and the cackle and crackle of the crowd and the speakers were brought to a sudden halt when the whistle blew in the breeze. Silence.

"Take your marks …" Boom! We were off! Impact always triggers instinct at the moment: streamline, kick, surface, pull. Arms turning, breathing every three strokes, a powerful two-beat flutter in tow to propel my metronomic rhythm. First lap, tumble, second lap and repeat, never looking sideways, peripheral vision enough; in my lane, in the zone.

After the 200m turn, my mind sprang a surprise. A song, just two lines of it, came into my head and guided me for the rest of the race. It was as if I were in a trance, only partially aware of what was going on around me. I took a fleeting glance across the lanes to confirm that I held a slight lead over Annelies and Tracey.

The song still had me in its grip, so much so that two laps later, I'd lost count. Was it 300m, 400m or even 500m? I'd have to wait for the whistle, which always blew to alert us with 100 to go. Lap after lap … no whistle. Had I missed it? Had the others already stopped? How embarrassing if I did extra laps! My thoughts blocked everything else. I had no sense of pain.

Then, there it was: five metres off the wall, a loud, shrill peep. It woke me from the trance; the song vanished and I was back in the race. Time to sprint! My stroke rate quickened, I nailed my last turn, exploded off the wall and headed for the finish, oblivious to where the rest of the race had got to.

Halfway down the last lap, I could hear the muffled noise of the crowd cheering, including what sounded like the odd scream in the mix. Maybe it was for me. Or someone else? Was someone catching me? With 20 metres to go, I put my head down and channelled every last ounce of energy into bringing 'this wretched 800' home.

My hand reached out and hit the electronic timing pad with a thump as I'd been told that pads sometimes don't register a touch too soft. I pulled myself up on the backstroke bar to see what the commotion was about. There was a lot of fuss behind the blocks; the timekeepers and swimmers lined up for the next race were shouting and signalling something. I was confused. Were they talking to me? What was wrong? I looked right and left to see where I'd placed. There was no one there.

The crowd was still standing. The ovation was for me but there was no scoreboard and I was none the wiser until a chorus of voices from behind the blocks shouted out the letters "WR" on repeat.

Not DQ? WR? I sank below the water to rip my cap off, trying to work out what was going on. Then it hit me. I leapt up almost clear out of the water and screamed, "World record!"

Impossible. Insane. Stunned, I could barely believe it. Eight minutes 34.86! This was not just any world record, but East German Petra Thümer's eight-minute-35.04 record. I had never been one to show emotion but this was different. It came out of the blue, like those two lines from the song that I cannot to this day recall. Perhaps it was the shock. My 8:40 Commonwealth and Australia standards had been blown away.

I had joined the club of world-record holders, an achievement no one can ever take away. It felt epic, amazing and so cool. I was 15 years old, a mere 163 cm and 58 kg. I'd done it! My father was right and my grandfather spot on. They had said it was possible and now I had proved it. I floated somewhere between heaven and earth on my way to my next race, the 200m butterfly. I had a bit of time so I went up into the stands to find my cousin. We hugged as happy folk swirled around and showered me with plaudits.

An hour later, back on the blocks under floodlights as midnight approached, I was still on a high. I had no sense of being tired and it showed on the clock, which I stopped at 2:14.66, an Australian record. The crowd erupted and I remember feeling, "This is what it's about; what all the hard training is for."

Just over six hours later, I was on a flight heading down to Melbourne for the second leg of the KB Games. In the 400m freestyle on January 10, I topped Tracey's Australian record with a 4:14.19 victory. It would have won bronze 18 months earlier at the Montreal Olympics behind two East Germans. I was living a dream.

Who would have thought that just 18 months after the Australian meltdown in Montreal I would be the best in the world? I had ticked a lot of boxes on my late grandfather's list. I thanked him silently. His quest and mine lived on. His last gift to me was an opal bracelet with gold-plated trimmings. He had handed it to me with gentle pride and a sneaky conviction that I would keep going. It meant the world to me.

After the visitors had gone home, we had just over a week to go before we were back at the North Sydney Pool for the New South Wales State Championships.

In the days leading up to racing, a letter addressed to "Michelle Ford, 800m Freestyle World-Record Holder, Australia" arrived in the post with an intriguing stamp on it: DDR. From behind the Iron Curtain in East Germany, Petra Thümer had written to congratulate me on my new record.

I have no idea to this day whether Petra put pen to paper or whether it was arranged through the embassy. After German reunification in 1990, some former East German swimmers revealed that letters sent to the International Hall of Fame thanking them for an invitation to an induction ceremony but confirming that they were unable to attend for a variety of reasons were organised by the GDR Ministry of Sport, with the swimmers simply told to sign.

Record-Breaking Run Rolls On

I knew nothing of the GDR's Ministry of Sport in 1978 but I did know that I was on the crest of a wave and the record books were on notice.

Back to the grind in the days after the KB Games tour, I was confronted by flocks of media milling around the pool deck on arrival at afternoon practice. My coach John Rodgers was being interviewed by a TV crew. When it was my turn, talking to reporters felt like fun for a change.

It was quick fire and felt like all the sentences ran into one: "How does it feel to be Australia's first world-record holder in two years? *It feels great;* How long will you keep going? *I'll retire when I get sick of it, just like everyone else—if you don't enjoy it, you won't win, and in the end, you just give up."*

On it went from one reporter to the next until my coach broke it up, and sent me off to the pool and the media packing. I jumped in at the back of the lane of swimmers already well into their set, ready for an easy, light and enjoyable afternoon workout. After several days of intense competition and with a world record, I was ready for some fun.

I was in a playful mood and started to pull the legs of those swimming in front of me in the lane, going under water and making faces at those swimming above me and making jokes between sets. I was bubbling over. We'd been swimming 16 to 17 km a day. It had been unrelenting, exhausting and mentally draining. Surely I deserved a moment off the treadmill?

Coach Rodgers spotted the mood and called a halt in a way that took our breath away: the main set was a 16x400 individual medley. Brutal! When we'd done, I clambered out of the water exhausted, disheartened and mad at my coach. We all were. The 40-minute drive home was filled with a torrent of complaints about the coach and how we disliked him and his training.

At least there was something to look forward to. The next series of races were on the horizon and we'd surely get some rest soon.

During a taper, we would ease back on the long endurance work and concentrate more on race pace and recuperation. The most important part of racing, the taper is something relatively few coaches got right. The body needs to be trained at race pace to know what will be asked of it during a race. It is about testing your limits and pushing your system to create a higher threshold so that when asked, your body responds.

The mind is powerful, but it can only take the athlete as far as their body allows them to go. The balance of the two can make the difference between a good or an excellent performance. A taper can be a full 10 to 14 days, with high mileage replaced by quality, race-pace broken swims (in which a 200m event is mimicked in four lots of 50m swims with a short rest in between to test pace). Or it can be a one- or two-day taper where the emphasis is on complete rest.

"We'll start the taper soon," promised Coach Rodgers. Except we didn't, at least not nearly soon enough for my liking.

As the days rolled on, so did my frustration and the incessant fatigue that consumed every muscle of my body. Taper is also about recovery. I recalled what that had meant at Carss Park and how good it had felt but it seemed we were not going to follow the same pattern.

I hoped that swimming some 50 races over the last two weeks had given me enough sense of quality and race pace to pull me through.

One day out from the meet, the taper must be today, I thought. I was mistaken. The coach continued to pile on the work. Maybe he just didn't know me, I thought. This was my first major meet under his tutelage and he was probably nervous that I would lose conditioning, so he didn't want to let up on my workload.

The 800m was scheduled for the second of three days of racing but on the opening morning of the championships, I woke up with a pounding headache and an upset stomach. When I got to the North Sydney Pool, I wasn't feeling well at all. My parents were concerned but Coach Rodgers suggested I swim heats so that at least if I felt better later in the day, I'd have a spot in finals.

However, after watching me struggle through, he finally agreed to scratch me from finals. Relieved, I went home and slept for the rest of the day.

It was just what I needed. The next morning, I bounced back and set my mind on the plan I had since my world record in Brisbane: I would attempt to lower the record that I had set just two weeks before. That was important because the rule obliged world-record attempts to be announced so that organisers could make sure the required electronic timing was available.

The equipment was relatively new to swimming and was added to the rule books in 1976. No electronic timing, no world record. In 1978, NSW had only one set of electronic timing pads and few pools that were of conforming length once the equipment was placed at the ends of the pool. Since the 1960s, all competition pools had to be built to the metric system.

My coach had taken charge and made sure organisers were informed well in time. Everything was back on track—until I got an unexpected tap on the shoulder as I was leaving the changing room. It was the president of the State Swimming Union, Roger Pegram.

"Michelle, I was told you are attempting the record this evening but I have to tell you that we are not sure that the electronic timing is working properly."

Much drama ensued but just after the evening session was declared open, the president came to inform us that "all's in order ... I hope!"

Two False Starts!

I had to convince myself he was right and put it out of my mind but I was edgy and it showed when I false started. In those days, you got a second shot; the race was recalled and you started again. An official came to whisper the obligatory warning in my ear: a second false start would mean disqualification. Nodding, I fixed my goggles and got set.

With arms stretched out and toes holding tight to the edge of the block, I listened for the starter's gun. The wait was long. Too long. I heard a click, took the chance and launched myself into the pool. The false start rope, placed 10 metres out, stopped me and all the others who had also dived in. We were called back and assembled behind lane 1 near the starter's podium.

The seven of us looked at each other wondering what had happened. Who'd jumped the gun this time? I imagined it was me. Known for my quick starts, it would be just my luck that today I would be called out. The starter spoke: "I'm sorry, girls, but I had trouble with the starting gun, so nobody is disqualified". Shaken but relieved, we were back on the blocks.

Third time lucky. Off we went. With my adrenaline pumping because of the false starts, I felt I had set off too fast and might have sapped vital reserves critical to the end of the race and the plan. I had been trained to swim the back half of the race, the last 400m, at the same time as the first half. The goal was a set of even 100m splits at 1:04. That adds up to 8:32, which would have broken my world record by more than two seconds.

However, as the race unfolded, I didn't feel right. Nothing was flowing; my feel for the water was off. I wasn't 'catching' and 'holding' it. My hands felt like they were slipping through the water as if it were air. Later, it was confirmed that I had gone out too fast—by two seconds over the first 200m.

The third 100m felt much slower. My coach must have been wondering what was happening. But then on the fifth lap, it clicked and by the halfway mark I'd settled down into a better rhythm. There was a roar from the crowd at the 400m mark: flipping over at the turn, my feet touched the timing pad at four minutes 13.25, inside my own Australian record!

I had no idea I was swimming that fast but took the cheer to mean I was on course for the 800m record. In fact, the crowd carried me home from there. I sailed on the noise of them with long strokes, my head high and breathing regularly.

I was nearly a lap in front. This really was a world-record attempt and not a race. I was at that make-or-break moment when my body was screaming and my head kicked in to push through when the president's words came niggling: what if the timing doesn't work? I fought hard to cast momentary distraction aside and battled on.

After touching the wall, I knew the record had been broken: the officials were jumping up and down on the poolside, knowing that their manual clocks confirmed the great news. It took longer to confirm whether the electronic system had stacked up. Thumbs up! Eight minutes 31.30!

The papers could be summed up by this line in one of them: *"Michelle got out of her sick bed to slash 3.56 seconds off the mark set in a meet in Brisbane 10 days ago."*

The roar of thousands echoed under the Harbour Bridge. There was not a seat taken; thousands of spectators were on their feet. I put an arm in the air to acknowledge them and thank them for lifting me up when I thought I had got it wrong and felt like pulling the plug. The energy in the will of a crowd is real. It was thrilling.

By the time the other lanes were coming home, the president was leaning over the block with a glint in his eye: "Michelle, we're in luck: the timing system worked!"

I had joined the list of legends of Australian swimming as the 86th swimmer to set a world record at North Sydney. It was also the last one as new pools were subsequently built when competitions had to be held in eight-lane facilities.

My parents rarely showed emotion but they let me know how proud they were of what I had achieved. My siblings were amazed and thrilled, my friends overjoyed and my school finally able to see why my absenteeism was worth it! At the first assembly of 1978, I was brought up on stage so the world marks could be celebrated. Later, the School Board awarded me a 'Sporting Blue', the highest accolade for combining high standards in sport and academics.

It was a whirlwind of a start to 1978! Now I was on the radar for the GDR and everyone else.

Media Coverage
Ford's World Time. Wonder Girl Beats Virus

Miss Ford, 15, from Carss Park, clipped 3.56 sec off the world mark she set at the KB Games in Brisbane only 10 days ago. She won the State title in 8 min, 31.30 second.

She had spent most of the day in bed after the virus attack which forced her out of three finals on Friday night. She said she had a headache and felt really down before the race. "When I heard the crowd cheering, I thought I must have been close to the record and it made me go all the harder," Miss Ford said.

(John Blanch, Sydney Morning Herald, January 22, 1978)

Swim Coach Blazes a Tough Trail to Success

"I've seen them hiccup and vomit at the end of training," Rodgers said matter-of-factly. "That doesn't worry me one little bit. It means they're mentally tough. Training has to hurt to do any good. No kid's going to die." The words seem callous, but they are not. They simply convey the Rodgers formula for churning out successful swimmers – a formula with results which defy criticism. Headed by world-record holder Michelle Ford, Olympic finalist Max Metzker and the towering teenager Ron McKeon in his care, Rodgers has the most powerful swim "stable" in Australia and the main hopes for gold medals at this year's Commonwealth Games in Edmonton, Canada. How, I asked, had his swimmers become so good? ... "Mentally, physically and emotionally their whole life must be geared to swimming." A Rodgers-prepared distance swimmer at the height of midseason training will cover 120 km per week. Even a sprinter gets through more than 70 km. All this on top of a rigorous 40-minute circuit training program of weights and exercises. There's no mollycoddling at Heffron Park!

(Richard Sleeman, 'Rodger's Gold Formula', Sydney Morning Herald, January, 1978)

Michelle Ford Is Setting Herself Up for Gold

It's a wonder Michelle Ford isn't water-logged. The 15-year-old Olympian swims 16 kms a day – eight before breakfast, and another eight after school. But the dedication has paid off. She is one of the fastest middle-distance women swimmers in the world, and a red-hot prospect to bring home some Moscow gold in 1980. Michelle's career has taken a dramatic turn for the better since she switched events ... The decision to concentrate on the 800 metres was reached at a family conclave. A study of the record books indicated this was an event looking for a new champion, so in December 1976, Michelle moved into the long-haul league. Barely a year later she had become the world-record holder. Getting there has not been easy. Disagreement with coaches saw three of them come and go in the space of a year. Her present mentor is John Rodgers … She trains with a couple of young up-and-coming male swimmers, Ron McKeon and Max Metzker, the theory being that anything they can do she should do better. And it works. Her times for the 800 metres have eclipsed those set by the swimming greats of yesteryear, John Konrads and Murray Rose.

(People Magazine, *March 23, 1978*)

Chapter 10
New Lessons

"Education is the most powerful weapon which you can use to change the world."
– Nelson Mandela

Two world records, three Commonwealth records, Australian records in all my major events, accolades and being made Sporting Personality of the Year: the summer of 1978 ended on a high.

It was a fairy tale in which diligence, hard work and sacrifice had paid dividends. My grandfather would surely have been smiling down on me. I had ticked a lot of those boxes he'd suggested to his 10-year-old granddaughter as we stood in front of the trophy cabinet in my room.

Success empowers. My confidence had soared. At the end of my record-breaking summer of 1977/1978, I received a letter from a supporter and an old coach offering some perspective:

> *"Hearty congratulations on your outstanding efforts. [...] The proof of the pudding is in the eating, so you can readily realise continued efforts and family support, as well as dedication, is necessary to reach the top of the tree, but a little extra has to be pulled out of the cable locker to enable one to stay on top. [...] From my own personal observations, you have now developed in all directions and will most certainly achieve your ambition of gaining the world record for the 200 'fly, which I consider to be your best chance at the next Olympics."*
>
> *(Letter to Michelle and family from Jack Stutsell, swim coach, January 7, 1978)*

Getting there is one thing, staying there is another. I understood. I also realised that world records are there to be broken, only a gold medal lasts forever.

My quest was not yet over. "An Olympic medal, or why not, a gold medal for good measure," my grandfather had said. I had giggled at the thought. Potential had turned to podium prospect and now the big prize on his list was no longer something to laugh at.

In a quiet moment aside, I found myself calculating. It was exactly two years to finish high school, and two and a half years until the Games. Perfect timing. I would have eight months to prepare for the Games and be 100% dedicated to my goal. But for the plan to work, I would need to graduate.

The plan was in place, the struggle clear: how was I going to manage the rest of 1978? A European tour in April, the Commonwealth Games and World Championships back-to-back in July and August added up to 57 days of absence from school. That would be a third of the year. It was a tightrope; a delicate balancing act and my teachers were sure to be circumspect.

Back to School

It was January 28th and the first day back at school after the six weeks of summer break. The schoolyard was buzzing with the chatter of holidays, the beach, new boyfriends, movies and various escapades. I listened intently but couldn't add much to the chat about life outside the pool. My whole summer had been about training and competing.

Dressed in my new uniform, a blue pinafore measured to the regulation length of 6 cm above the knee, no more, with white-rounded collar, short white socks and black shoes, I was ready for the start of my senior years of high school.

I found my friends gathered in our new seating area: the spot reserved for the senior girls. This is where we would spend our morning breaks and lunches for the next year. Most of us had been mates since our arrival at the school four years earlier and our surnames began with the letters F to J. We were a diverse bunch with different talents and interests.

St George Girls High School, an all-girls school in the southern suburbs of Sydney, was built in 1916 in colonial double red brick that kept the classrooms to a cool 19°C, insulating us from the hot summer months. The school had its own tennis courts and the gymnasium doubled up as the school canteen. Some playing fields were situated on the outer perimeter.

Opportunities for women in those days were limited. We were told that having a tertiary education would enable us to get a better job, but the choice was ours: either leave in Year 10 or continue through the last two years of high school with the hope of securing a place at university.

Year 11 was important preparation for the Higher School Certificate the following year. Teachers were keen to show us the steeper learning curve we could expect in the coming year. It wasn't going to be easy for anyone, and particularly not for me with those 57 days away, and I had no idea which 57 days because my swimming schedule for the year hadn't been set.

On March 2, a letter from the Swimming Union informed eight swimmers that on March 11 we would be setting off on a competition tour to Leeds in England, Bremen in Germany and, after a last-minute invitation, Japan. We wouldn't return home until April 4.

The 40-hour flight out would help *"prepare us for the Commonwealth Games and World Championships later in the year",* we were told. Our coach and manager would be Terry Buck from the troubled Montreal Olympics. The good news was there would be no training camp because there was no time!

The trip was organised out of desperation in response to the incessant calls from the swimming community for more international competition. Money was scarce but in a show of goodwill, the ASU had sought some invitational competitions where the event's organising committee would pay part of the expenses. The deal only left scope for a few swimmers and one coach/manager.

The selection criteria were questionable: you had to be fast and talented across an array of events. The versatile were given priority over the specialists. We were six girls and two boys aged 15–17.

I wrote a note to hand in at school and sat outside the headmistress's office waiting to ask for permission. After a last tug of my uniform to make sure it complied with dress code regulations, I was called in. Mrs Woyde sat behind a large wooden bureau.

Always impeccable, with greying hair and her stern regard fixed in place, she flicked a hand to indicate that I should sit down. Instead, I walked towards her with my hand outstretched, my note clasped between my fingers, averted her gaze and sat down.

She read, sighed, lifted her head and looked me straight in the eye. "This year is an important year for all our students," she began. "You have new electives with new teachers ... You cannot afford to be behind in your studies if you wish to do well in next year's exam, especially as it will determine your entrance into university ... You have already missed so much school over the past years."

I nodded and promised once more to catch up on any work missed. She fixed me with a steely glare. My thoughts raced with the very different reaction of my friends, only one of whom had ever travelled outside Australia. "How cool," they said, "to be off to see the Eiffel Tower, Buckingham Palace and Big Ben." In my mind's eye, I had my bags packed and was heading for the plane ...

"Okay," she said, crashing into my daydream with a clear and stern voice. "On condition that upon your return, your swimming falls in line with your studies and not the other way around!"

There'd be a lot of catching up to do but the prospect of an adventure far outweighed the obligation and daily routine of schoolwork. My Easter 'holiday' was booked: Europe and Japan.

Explorers

There was just one week to prepare and get visas. I also had to find someone in each of my new classes to keep notes for me. Carbon copies awaited me on my return but until then I was off to see the real thing.

We were young explorers in 1978. We didn't just get to see swimming pools. Sport is an amazing passport to the wider world. At the end of northern winter and our summer, we were on top of the world, welcomed as visitors and treated to the sights, sounds, smells and tastes of faraway places.

The last stop of the tour was Tokyo, where we had been invited to race at the Japanese National Championships. There were no other foreigners there, just eight Australian kids and we were treated as dignitaries—assigned black limousines with a little Australian flag on the front. We finished our Easter break in style with a supper hosted by Japanese government officials—sipping saké, relishing the food and learning about Japanese culture, just over 30 years since a time of war and deep division.

Our bags laden with medals, we headed home feeling proud of our modest contribution to the rehabilitation of Australian sport after the drubbing of Montreal. The Aussies were back!

Or were we?

An Education Lasts a Lifetime —Sport Does Not

Anxious parents met us at Sydney Airport on our return on April 4. They were upset over the swimming federation's program for the upcoming Commonwealth Games team.

Selection trials would be all straight finals, the head coach would be the same as in Montreal and, worse still, another long and unnecessary four-week training camp was being planned.

Parents called for that idea to be scrapped. Not only would it repeat the mistakes of Montreal but wipe out schooling for most of us, including a wave of 15- and 16-year-olds. The camp would add even more time on to the two months we were already scheduled to be away for. "Leave our kids with their home coaches and keep them in school doing their mid-term exams," mums and dads insisted. They also noted that no other sport was asking this of their athletes.

The debate had started several weeks before our tour. In a letter to Syd Grange, ASU president, in February, Glenda Robertson's father wrote on behalf of the swimming parents: *"Parents of younger swimmers play an important role in their success through accepting a long period of disruption to family life to fit in with training programs. As one of those parents, I have become completely disillusioned with swimming though seeing the efforts of the swimmer, coach and parents wrecked in prolonged training camps."*

As the row erupted, more letters were dispatched to the ASU. They were forwarded to the Commonwealth Games Association, which sent them back to the Swimming Union in turn.

In a subsequent letter on behalf of parents on March 28, 1978, Mr Robertson further noted:

"Notwithstanding the controversy which surrounded the holding of the training camp in Perth prior to the Montreal Olympics in 1976, the Amateur Swimming Union of Australia at its conference in Brisbane in February resolved to accept the dictates of the Australian Swimming Coaches Association in approving a similar training camp in Honolulu prior to the Commonwealth Games this year. This camp is the concept of the chief coach appointed by that association, who, on present indications, will not have a swimmer from his own squad in the team.

It is understood that this approval has been given on the basis that officials of the ASU of Australia are still smarting under the criticism which was levelled at them following the Olympics and are now prepared to stand aside to allow the Coaches Association to receive the full brunt of the criticism which will flow from the inevitable fiasco resulting from the proposed camp.

We object to our children being used as pawns in the manner and to the apparent careless disregard given to their welfare. We do not believe our views as parents should be similarly dismissed. As we see it, the only function now required of us by the ASU or the Commonwealth Games Association will be to sign an indemnity absolving them of all responsibility so far as our children are concerned.

It appears that the Amateur Swimming Union of Australia has abdicated its responsibility to our young swimmers (age 15–17) as they are fully aware, as we are, of the personal pressures with which our young female swimming representatives will be required to cope as well as the damaging effect such a camp will have on their education.

[...] In our view there appear to be only two ways of ensuring that the welfare of our children is protected, and they are:

- *The camp is cancelled*
- *Our swimmers be not available for selection*

An editorial in The Sunday Mail gave credence to the argument:

"I have always felt that the competitors are the most important single part of any sport, but the people running Australian Swimming obviously don't agree.

Once again, they have decided the young kids to carry our banner at the Commonwealth Games in Edmonton will go overseas for a final training camp. Now either I have a very bad memory, or swimming officials have very short memories [...] after the Montreal Olympics, swimmers, parents, and coaches were complaining about the pre-Games training camp in Perth. Steve Holland and several others made it clear that being away from their own coaches and particularly family and friends, left a mental "low" that didn't help training or performances in the Games.

These are usually very young kids, and they often need a friendly shoulder to gripe on or some moral support when things aren't going the best. It is bad enough for an adult to feel alone in a strange city. It must be something again for a school kid feeling "down" in a foreign country.

When rumours started a few months ago that the swimming team could be sent for a lengthy training camp in Honolulu before the Games, there were quite a few people complaining. A couple of parents even rang me – asking that their names not be used for fear of reprisals against the kids – saying that if the overseas training camp was on they would not allow their children to be in the team. But despite the protest, the swimming officials have categorically stated last week that the camp will be in Hawaii, only the length of time in Honolulu is left to be decided."

(Brian Johnston, Sports Editor, 'Swim Kids Unhappy "Campers" Again?', The Sunday Mail, *March 26, 1978*)

Stonewalled

The stage was set for the next bout: in the red corner, the federation seeking sympathy and applause for their efforts to help the sport out of the doldrums; in the blue corner, the media and public as judge and jury. The swimmers were caught in the middle once more just as we needed to focus on the highlights of the season—the Commonwealth Games in Edmonton, Canada from July 27 to August 12; and the World Championships in West Berlin from August 19 to 31.

The federation rejected a call from parents for it to hire tutors to travel with us so that our schoolwork wouldn't suffer. My own school was among those that wrote in support of the parents' position. Parents all lobbied to raise funds to pay for tutors but the federation refused to budge, so an ultimatum was given in a joint threat: *"Either the federation accept to take tutors to the training camp, or the swimmers withdraw from the team!"*

On June 13, the national team was announced. Fifteen of the 27 swimmers selected were school kids. The money had been raised to send tutors with us but the ears of the ASU remained tone deaf. To add insult to injury, it dictated that all team members had to take part in a training camp in Hawaii. And that was that. A line had been drawn and none of the parents' requests had been met: there would be no extra chaperones and no tutors. We were there to swim, not study.

I was torn. My education was vital to my future but there would be no help or encouragement for it for almost three months. On the other hand, I had no appetite to miss out on representing Australia and the chance to excel on the international stage.

I found myself sitting in the headmistress's office with a begging letter in hand once more.

On June 26, 11 boys, 13 girls and six officials flew out of Sydney and would not be home for 12 weeks. Three members of the men's team would be joining us in Hawaii, direct from their US colleges.

The Training Camp

I explained the Hawaii training camp rules in a letter to my parents on June 30:

- Early arrival at training otherwise you would miss workout
  (workouts 5.45–7.45am and 3.30–5.45pm with stretching 15 minutes prior).
- Any weight gain – you would have to miss the workout.
- Nobody outside after 7.30pm. Lights out 9.30pm.
- No girl is allowed in a boy's room or vice-versa.
- Leaving the complex must be accompanied by a manager.
- Have to sit with a coach at all meals.

These are just a few. I know Terry has to do his job, but he may have gone too far. It feels like we're in jail here. I am hoping they will ease off in a few days. As for the meals, they have steak once a week and that is supposed to be tonight, then they cook stews.

P.S. I am still doing my homework, but I am very tired, so I sleep for 2 hours in the day.

It was going to be a long four weeks!

I trained with two groups. One was in the 'distance lane' with the 400 and 800m swimmers and the other was in the 'middle-distance lane' for my 200m freestyle and butterfly swims.

My home coach was permitted to join the team as an ex officio. It made sense. After all, John Rodgers had six swimmers on the team. But he had to pay his own way across the world, an infuriating situation picked up by reporter Dick Tucker in *The Mirror* under a headline *'Top Coach Blasts Games Penny Pinching'.*

A university lecturer studying heart rate and performance was also brought on board. The wake-up call in Montreal from the East Germans and Americans dominating there had had some effect. Mentors Forbes Carlile and Bill Sweetenham were paving the way for other Australian coaches by embracing a more scientific approach to preparation and competition, biomechanics, physiology and psychology.

The initiative was a good one. Knowing an athlete's threshold is valuable data. Every athlete has a point at which working just a little bit harder means having to stop a lot sooner. It's a sort of point of no return and knowing it can be a tremendous support to a coach in understanding their swimmer's capacity as well as their recovery time. It can be used to modify the intensity of not just one training set, but all. Only a few on our tour took full advantage of that knowledge.

And it showed.

Chapter 11
A Tale of Two Cities

"Life will throw everything but the kitchen sink. It is your job to avoid the obstacles.
If you let them stop or distract you,
you're not doing your job and failure will cause regrets that paralyze you."
– André Agassi

The nature of learning curves is that you can't always see around the bend to understand the purpose of the lesson. The Northern Hemisphere summer of 1978 would be a season of instruction that changed my life forever.

We were bronzed Aussies, fit and fast after four weeks of gruelling workouts in the Hawaiian sun, when we left for Edmonton in Alberta, Canada, host to the newly branded Commonwealth Games.

It was a similar gathering of nations to those that had come together every four years since the British Empire Games got under way in 1930. By 1954, the name had been changed to the British Empire and Commonwealth Games and then to the British Commonwealth Games in 1970.

By 1978, declarations of independence from the Empire were so widespread that 'Commonwealth' was what remained of the union of former colonies under English reign. There were 49 countries, including teams from Africa, the Caribbean and Pacific Islands, Australia, Canada and New Zealand, several states in southern Asia and the home nations of Great Britain—England, Ireland (later just the North), Scotland and Wales—having competed apart since the beginning of the Games in 1930.

Boycotts by Nigeria over apartheid and New Zealand's continued contact with South African sport, and Uganda, in protest at alleged Canadian 'hostility' towards the government of Idi Amin, were the main reasons why we were down to 46 nations and 1500 athletes.

In swimming, Commonwealth competition came down to a battle between Australia, Canada, England, Scotland and in a few events, New Zealand and Wales. The rest of planet swimming awaited us at the World Championships in Berlin two weeks beyond Edmonton.

Fuelled with more mileage in training over the last six months than ever before, I knew I was fit and in shape to race at my best. Physically, at least. At just 16, I was already one of the older girls on the team. I was now considered 'experienced', with two years of international competition behind me.

The boxes all appeared to be ticked: fit, focused, determined, trained hard, done everything asked of me, freestyle and 'fly feeling good, two world records in the vault. Ready. Or was I? You never know until you stand on the blocks and the form guide means nothing: the only thing that counts are the laps in front of you.

Rivalry

"Sport thrives on rivalry especially when two of the world's best come from the same country, both different physically and in attitude but with mental toughness beyond most," said British track ace Seb Coe about his domestic rivalry with Steve Ovett.

So, there we were, lining up for our first race, the 800m freestyle final in Edmonton. Alongside me was teammate Tracey Wickham, by then world-record holder. We were both just outside the 8:30 barrier for the 800 and Australia was poised to make history. I'd had a fine Australian summer, taking down East German Olympic champion Petra Thümer's global 800m standard in 8:34, then crunching that back down to 8:31 two weeks later in less-than-ideal conditions. I knew I could be much faster.

But I couldn't help wondering where a niggling line in the Australian *Daily Mirror* had come from before the Games. After I'd wiped nine seconds off my best in the course of setting two world records, why had reporter Dick Tucker written: *"Wickham ... is the only female prospective world record breaker who potentially would take 5 seconds off the current 800-metre record".* The other girl (me), he opined, would swim only one-tenth of a second faster than my best.

Not only did I know his opinion was nonsense, but it was unfair. A teenage swimmer should not have to be subjected to such speculation; it begged the question of who put it out there?

It could have been anyone in my rival camp. Swimmers and coaches can and do use the media to get a psychological edge on an opponent. In this case, yes, it hit home, but I never took such things to the blocks with me. Strong mindset and conviction, not fear, are your best friends in such moments—and that attitude is what accompanied me to the start of all my big battles.

The whistle blew. The only thing that mattered was the next 16 laps. The race was like a national title fight. It was Tracey and me, stroke for stroke, neck and neck, the rest dispatched in the first 200m. In the end, Tracey had the edge and pressed on for gold in a world record of 8:24.62, my 8:25.78 granting Australia a 1–2 punch and the honour of having not just the first but the first two women ever to get inside the 8:30 mark.

Or rather, shatter the 8:30 mark. The closest to us, New Zealander Rebecca Perrott, fourth in the Olympic 400m freestyle final in Montreal, was 20 seconds adrift in third place, a relative ocean in racing terms.

Together we had smashed my world record by five seconds. We were both elated, it was an amazing feat. We had produced the swiftest two efforts ever seen in a race that was way ahead of its time. Those times would hold us in the top 10 fastest women in the world rankings for 21 years until the season before the Sydney 2000 Olympic Games.

Coming second is always hard. It was a touch. I knew I could and should have won. My psych-up was off. I should have had more confidence to take my opportunities, but I didn't.

Looking back on it, I would come to appreciate that I had been a part of an Australian duel that was the envy of the world that day. Both of us and Australia had every reason to feel proud of the epic history that our rivalry had produced.

I had to lift myself up for the 400m and then the 200m freestyle. The 400m podium was a match of the 800m event and the 200m had the same three medallists, but with Perrott ahead of us Aussies.

I had one last shot: the 200m butterfly, a technical and treacherous race but one I loved. It had made me—it got me on the Olympic team at 13. This was my baby. It was going to be tough. The last two Commonwealth record holders were ahead of me on the clock. The favourite was my roommate Linda Hanel, who at the start of the year had taken down Canadian Olympic finalist Wendy Quirk's Commonwealth standard and then improved her own mark to 2:12.80, almost two seconds faster than I'd even swum. Wendy was the experienced local favourite.

Rooming with your main rival in a race is complicated, especially during the hours before the finals. Our nerves were on edge. I asked if she wanted to go with me to the food hall to grab something to eat but she turned round, opened her red suitcase and started rifling through it. There it was! With a huge smile she held up a can of tuna. It was her favourite pre-race meal, her ritual. So, she'd smuggled the can all the way from Australia. We both laughed and relaxed.

Back at the pool, something clicked. My stroke was solid, flowing and I felt invigorated in a way I hadn't for all my freestyle races. Preparing for the final, I closed my eyes and let my mind wander back to the Olympic trials in 1976. I could hear the voices of my coach Dick Caine and Olympic champion Kevin Berry: their enthusiasm flicked a switch. I knew just how to race this one. Confidence brimming, I stepped onto the block with a smile on my face. One last nod of determination as I stared down the lane, blinkers on, and I was set.

The first 100m was paced and controlled, before I made the third lap mine and turned for home in the lead and feeling strong. There was no stopping me. I nailed my finish and looked up at the board: the Commonwealth record had been felled in 2:11.66.

I'd missed the world record by just 0.46 of a second and now had the third fastest time in history.

Wendy was second, with Linda delivering a second bite of the cherry for Australia with bronze. I'd made the podium three times at the Games but at last I was on top. Relief washed over me.

The head coach of Canada at the time was our own Don Talbot, who paid plaudits to what he'd witnessed:

> *"Michelle Ford is Australia's most underrated swimmer, according to Canada's coach Don Talbot. Australian Talbot says he wishes he had Michelle swimming for him. [...] 'Michelle Ford has undoubtedly been one of the outstanding swimmers in these Games. She was responsible for the exceptional efforts in the 800m and 400m [...] She swam very well in the 200m freestyle and won the 200m butterfly with one of the finest efforts ever. It says a lot for her courage that she can come back after a number of defeats and still swim her best times. The dread of being second no matter how good the winner, may have driven swimmers out of the sport.'"*
>
> *(E.E. Christensen, 'I Wish I Had Michelle – Talbot', Sun Herald, August 11, 1978)*

When Just the Girls Are Grounded

It was time to celebrate. One week of competition and the team had done well. The final tally: the hosts had 14 golds in the pool under Talbot's tutelage, and Australia was next with 10 crowns.

It was time to put some normal clothes on, relax and have fun. Back at the athletes' village, we dressed and waited for the team meeting. We were told there'd be one meeting for us girls, and another for the boys. How strange, we thought, especially after such a great result.

The female team manager then told us we were grounded. The only outing we were allowed was to the dining hall and back. The rest of the evening would be spent in our rooms. I wasn't a party girl but I did cherish the chance to let my hair down and see something of the town. We all did. We all needed it.

Disappointment turned to anger the next day when we heard that the boys had been allowed out with no curfew and no controls. The story made headlines back home:

> *"Australian girl swimmers are furious today over celebration restrictions placed on them. [...] but the management gave the males ... an open ticket for a night on the town."*
>
> *(E.E Christensen, 'Girls Grounded by Buck', Sun Herald, August 11, 1978)*

Two Berlins

Some of the team flew home after Edmonton while a smaller squad travelled on to West Berlin on August 13 for the third World Championships. Three athletes per country were allowed in each event. This would be the last chance we would get to race the very best in the world before the 1980 Olympic Games.

The United States came ready for battle, their men unchallenged as the world's top team, their women determined to turn the tables on East Germany after the Montreal shocker.

The media reported from the East German press conference that two of the GDR stars had withdrawn. Reporters were told that Petra Thümer, the double Olympic champion in my best freestyle events, had a heavy cold, and Christiane Knacke, who'd set a pioneering butterfly pace, had slipped in the shower and hurt an elbow. Their absence left the GDR with a mixed team of veterans and juniors in Berlin being prepared for the Moscow Olympic Games.

A year after their Montreal Olympics game changer, a new wave of GDR girls had joined established stars to dominate at the 1977 European Swimming Championships in Sweden. Petra Thümer set world records in the 400m freestyle for the title a month after she had broken her own 800m standard at trials in Leipzig in eight minutes 35.04.

A week after the Europeans, Christine Knacke, an up-and-coming junior who finished second in the 100m butterfly to teammate Andrea Pollack in Sweden, raced at a duel meet in East Berlin and became the first woman to break the minute barrier. At the same event, Olympic champion Ulrike Tauber completed a trio of world records in the 200m medley in just six weeks.

The trouncing of continental opponents in Sweden was part of the biggest ever seen in international championship waters: between 1974 and 1989, East German women claimed a staggering 92 percent of all titles and 90 percent of all medals at the European Championships, which featured many of the leading swimming nations of the world from a continent of more than 50 countries.

The questions ran and ran.

What We Didn't Know Back Then:
Three Tales from Stasi Files and Whistleblowers
1976

At the GDR Olympic trials, Petra Thümer finished second to compatriot Barbara Krause, with both women inside world-record time. Krause wiped three seconds off the mark but then didn't show up in Montreal and Thümer took the double 400–800m gold in world-record times. At the Montreal Games, East German officials told the media that Krause was ill.

Years later, state documents would show that she had returned a positive test for an anabolic steroid because doctors had miscalculated the dose of banned substances they had given her and the East Germans could not risk anyone testing positive in competition.

1979

Renate Vogel, 1972 Olympic relay silver medallist and 1973 three-time world champion for the GDR, finished second to a West German in the 100m breaststroke at the European Championships in 1974. She was treated like a failure by coaches who she had complained to about medicine she felt had deepened her voice. She asked to come off the tablets and leave the sport but was told, "No!"

So, the swimmer made her plans. She travelled on holiday to Hungary, within the Soviet Bloc, and with the help of friends was given a West German passport, a false identity and a ticket from Budapest to Munich. Once free, she told Austrian broadcasting network ORF in Vienna and other media that she had been doping through injections, pills and substances mixed into her food at sports school from the age of 14.

Despite her statement, the GDR continued to deny and refute the claim that their athletes' performances were enhanced by doping. Renate would later confirm that she was never approached by anyone at FINA or the IOC to inquire about her revelations.

1989

A decade after Renate's revelations, Christiane Knacke echoed the story when she told Austrian media that she had been given steroids from the age of 13. They came from her coach Rolf Gläser, who would later be convicted of bodily harm to minors. He was the coach who told media asking about deep voices at the Montreal Olympics that the East German women had "come to swim, not sing". Knacke said that in the year leading up to her historic 59-second 100m butterfly in 1977, she had put on 15 kg of weight: all of it muscle. Ironically, like many other GDR coaches employed abroad in the 1990s, Gläser would work in Austrian swimming before his 1998 conviction.

Lessons Come in Waves

Berlin was divided in two by its wall: the Democratic Republic of Germany (GDR) to the East, the Federal Republic of Germany (FRG) to the West. We'd be swimming in the 1936 Olympic Games pool next to the Olympic Stadium at the 1978 World Championships. Both had survived the Second World War.

The pool had been renovated for the World Championships, with new stands big enough for a 20,000-strong crowd. It was a majestic scene.

The day before racing began, we were reminded about the importance of team presence. In Montreal, we'd been intimidated by the blue tracksuits of the GDR as well as the USA. Here, it was the USA in their red, white and blue tracksuits. They looked dominant and surreal; they exuded pride and confidence. Their demeanour stood in stark contrast to our somewhat bedraggled crew.

Their team consisted of more than 30 swimmers, coaches, a masseur, doctors and physiotherapists. They had it all and they had come to show that Montreal was a blip for their women, but they had learned lessons and now travelled with a complete entourage of medical and other staff.

We were a strong and competitive team but we felt inferior. The American war cries were a constant reminder that perspectives on might and mindset matter. They had presence; we did not. Still battling funding, Australia had just eight women and six men at the championships.

No two championships had the same program in those days: the 200m freestyle would be my first race, followed by the 400m, the 200m butterfly and then the 800m freestyle (which was my first race in Edmonton, but would be the last in Berlin).

However, all psyched and ready, I found out I'd been scratched from the 200m. Tracey had also been withdrawn with 'an arm injury'. I was told, with a wink and a nod, that this was 'strategic'. We were not favourites to win the 200m and would struggle to get on the podium at our best but the move worked for one coach-athlete partnership and not the other.

Coach Buck told the media, "This measure is taken to ensure the best performances in our primary events."

I was baffled. I loved competing and would rarely withdraw from races. The more I raced, the sharper I got and the 200m was a way of breaking the ice, soaking up the atmosphere, and getting a feel for the pool, the blocks and the pace of the starter, before my main events came round.

I watched the 200m in the stands with my father. A lot of parents had travelled to Edmonton but few had continued on to Berlin. My father had been with me since the last couple of days of the Honolulu camp. He'd coached me and his presence was reassuring at a time when I needed him. Edmonton had been challenging and left me doubting the guidance I was getting. It meant the world to me to have someone there I could trust.

His reading of my preparation in Hawaii was spot on when he wrote a postcard to my mother:

> Dear Jan,
> ... Michelle is training well + happy. 2:17 in set of 5 descending 200 'fly. Stroke is good. [...] She is not keen to swim the 800. She never has been!! But time will tell. I would not push her as her 200 'fly could be great.
>   Love Ian

We analysed other swimmers—how they prepared for a race. The lessons never stop. When it was my turn, I got off to a solid start in 4:13.36. I broke American Shirley Babashoff's championship record for a ticket to centre lane 4 in the final.

The sun was still high in the European summer sky as we lined up for the showdown. That suited me, as daylight provides better visibility than the glare of floodlights. In a race in Hobart earlier that year, the bright lights had made it impossible to judge the distance to the wall. I'd rammed my head into it in a freestyle race and that had convinced me to start wearing goggles.

I wasn't a fan: the black foam glued to the plastic frame sparked an allergic reaction and I developed a painful rash around my eyes. However, looking to match any advantage the others might have, I pulled my goggle straps over my cap and adjusted the lens.

I'd practised this many times in training.

All seemed well as the gun fired but the impact of the dive dislodged my right-eye goggle. Water flooded in and my focus switched from the swim to crisis management. When the goggle had completely filled up, I closed that eye but the squinting dismantled the other goggle and I was soon swimming blind.

The whole thing spiralled out of control from there on several levels. My mind was racing. I wasn't sure what was best. Should I throw them off and risk losing momentum and place in the race? What if I did toss them off; would I ever get them back?

A swimmer's worst nightmare followed: both sides were now full of water. I forced my eyes open and although everything was a blur, I could make out the black line at the bottom of the pool. However, on the last turn, I misjudged the distance from the wall and was too far off to get a good push for the sprint home. I shut my eyes once more, put my head down and sprinted to the finish.

I ripped my goggles off in anger at the end of the race and saw that I'd finished fifth, something of a miracle under the circumstances but that was no comfort. Tracey took gold in a world record of 4:06.28, with Americans Sippy Woodhead and Kim Linehan on the podium and the GDR's Barbara Krause fourth.

I was glad Australia had something to celebrate but to be honest, my focus was not on anyone else at that point. If the highs in sport leave you soaring, the lows can be crushing.

Chain Reaction

The ebb and flow from the best of times to the worst of times can be brutal in sport but the most enriching lessons are those learned at the low points; you just don't know it at the time.

To cap the crisis of my 400m freestyle, a miscalculation in the 200m butterfly made matters worse: I just missed the final. That same day, after watching Americans Tracy Caulkins and Nancy Hogshead defeat Olympic champion Adrian Pollack of the GDR, I wrote a postcard home to a friend with a simple conviction: *"I am going to win the 800 and show them all I can do it."*

The last day of the championships dawned with both Australians through to the 800m final, alongside Americans Woodhead (world-record holder in 200m freestyle) and Linehan. Strange as it was, the best of the GDR were missing, with the one East German challenger in the final barely able to break nine minutes.

It was going to be a fireworks finale for the four medal contenders. At times like these, those last-minute pep talks from your coach can be critical to the confidence and belief you take to the starting blocks.

In search of that last important, tactical psych-up, I went to look for my coach John Rodgers. I noticed that he was still up in the stands talking to someone and seemed ruffled. I waited. He waved me on to the marshalling area and told me that he would be down to see me.

I'd later learn that he was organising the next invitational meet in Australia and was on the hunt for potential participants at the very moment I was getting ready for a final in which Australia was contending for gold and silver. That was symptomatic of the skewed priorities of some of those steering the ship. Apparently, they'd forgotten that the swimmers were the engine.

I left my father in the stands, telling him John would be down soon, and headed for the marshalling area. I found a seat near the door to make sure my coach could see me. My competitors arrived one by one, eyes down, fully focused. No one spoke. The grand clock on the wall ticked away and I started to get agitated. Perhaps he just wouldn't make it in time to say anything. I knew what to do but the reassurance of your coach just before you walk out to race can work wonders. The lack of it can achieve the opposite.

There was no sign of him as the official ushered us towards the door for the march out to the blocks. He appeared in the doorway at the last minute. Too late.

I slipped out of line briefly, with everyone watching and listening. I asked him where he'd been. He muttered something over the top of my words and I couldn't catch what he was saying. Relieved he'd shown up, I was also really mad at him. My mind was fixed on that and not the race. My mood fuzzy, the walk out to the blocks was a blur.

I tried pulling myself together, repeating in my head, "Never mind, just get on and do the job!" What followed felt like the longest 16 laps I'd ever swum.

Tracey set the pace, with the Americans and me following close behind. By the end of the race, the energy reserves I needed had been depleted by pre-race frustrations over Coach Rodgers. The spark had gone out. His distraction had become mine and now, as we raced down the last two laps, Tracey was out front close to the pace we'd both swum in Edmonton just over two weeks earlier. The 200m champion Sippy started sprinting and became the third person ever to break 8:30 and Kim outreached me for bronze (8:32 to 8:33).

I was eight seconds slower than I had swum at Commonwealths. It hurt me and, moreover, Australia. We still had the two fastest swimmers in history by a big margin and no stone should have been left unturned to make sure we both swam to the very best of our ability and capacity at the World Championships.

Coach Rodgers bore some responsibility but on a personal level, I'd learned a hard lesson, one that would stand me in good stead on the way to the next Olympics. I'd allowed too many external factors to get in the way of the job. I walked away from Berlin disappointed but aware of the balance and total harmony that an athlete's mind needs for optimum performance. I had to be singularly focused on what I had to do, and to trust but never rely on other people: sport is like the rest of life.

Although horrible at the time, those two 1978 incidents came just when I needed them: two years out from a competition like no other, the Olympic Games. I knew I could do better and swore that I would not let them happen again!

The championships produced 13 world records in the 29 swimming events. Tracy Caulkins of the US, 15 and from Nashville, emerged as the new queen of women's swimming with four golds and as many world records at the helm of an American sorority that claimed nine gold medals—seven individual and two relay—across 14 events.

Even Caulkins didn't get it all right: like me, she miscalculated in the heats and missed qualifying for the 200m breaststroke final in which she would have been a podium shot.

There were no records for East Germany. It was almost as big a talking point as their moments of sheer dominance in other years. The same session as our 800m event also featured the women's 100m freestyle and that produced the only GDR gold in Berlin: Barbara Krause set a championship record of 55.68 seconds, just shy of the 55.41 world record she set a month earlier at the National Championships in the same city but on the other side of the wall.

However, the rumour was that all of the GDR's eggs were being put in the Olympic basket and they would be invincible in Moscow come 1980. Even so, their slowdown in Berlin was a mystery to all of us. Talk of doping was still rife but it wasn't the East Germans in the headlines on the last day in Berlin. News came through that Russian Viktor Kuznetsov had been disqualified and stripped of his bronze medal in the 100m backstroke after two tests found him guilty of cheating with anabolic steroids.

More School, Less Swim

By the time I returned from the 1978 Commonwealth Games and World Championships, I'd had 67 and a half days leave from school that year. September, October and November were the only months left when schooling could be the sole focus for an Australian swimmer.

My first task on arriving back home was to collect all those carbon-paper copies and stencils from my friends and squeeze six months of work into the next three until the end of the school year.

I simply had to set the swimming aside and get back to it on the way to Christmas.

Diary Entry
Tuesday December 5, 1978—21°C

At 5 am, I awoke and got ready for training. It was the hardest session I had done since I started back training two weeks ago. It consisted of 4x800 metre medleys on 12 minutes. I was very tired and sore after it. I had the usual rush when I got home from training but today mum took me to school so that I could do some of my depth study (assignment) which I am very nervous about because I am afraid I won't have it finished in two weeks. Mr Simpson (maths teacher) asked me if I was training again for the Boston trip. I think he sensed I was back in hard training.

When I arrived home from school, I was so tired I flopped onto my bed and had a sleep before Lisa Burns came to pick us up for training. At training I was still sore, so luckily, I got an easy session. The cameraman was there and took a film of me for the promotion of the next KB Games. I still am worried about my school project.

Diary Entry
Saturday December 9, 1978

Saturday was a nice day but unfortunately, I had a bad start of 9.5 kilometres. After this hectic session, I went home and once again flopped on my bed. I awoke just before one o'clock. Mum had arrived home and started to prepare lunch. I was just about to take my first bite, and someone knocked at the door. The next two and a half hours I spent with this 'someone', my English tutor who worked through my English course for 1979.

The assembly hall of St George Girls High school was full to the brim for the end-of-year Speech Day. I was happy and relieved as I sat in silence soaking up the babble and chirp of everyone trying to find the right seats in the right rows.

I'd made it over the line—just. I'd be joining my friends for our final year next term but a stern warning had been delivered.

My report card reflected my struggle: *"Michelle is an enthusiastic and hard-working student. Michelle's absences have influenced her results this year"*; *"Considering the amount of time Michelle has been away this year, she has performed well. Her conscientious attitude has been her main asset"*; *"Michelle is always diligent; her interest in her studies is most pleasing"*; *"Unfortunately, Michelle missed a lot of work which she found difficult to pick up. Her disappointing result does not reflect her eagerness"*.

An athlete's life is not easy! I'd tried to catch up with everything but it was overwhelming: nothing could make up for the time I'd been away nor the lethargy and yawning I'd brought to classes every day. I'd set myself an impossible task.

It was obvious. Nothing less than total devotion to my studies would do in 1979, my last year of high school.

Chapter 12
Dress Rehearsal

"Through practice, gently and gradually we can collect ourselves
and learn how to be more fully with what we do."
– Jack Kornfield, mindfulness mentor

By the end of 1978, my routine had been adapted to include appearances at functions and photo shoots to help secure funding for the Australian Olympic Foundation (AOF). The new body had the task of issuing grants from government and sponsors, to help athletes cover the costs of training.

The sea change had started to wash through sports such as swimming as a result of the pressure placed on the West by the Soviet Bloc's game-changing model of heavy subsidisation of sport and its direct challenge to the Olympic Charter's 'amateur' Rule 26.

Unable to control the way the communist world had gone about making sport a poster for their political system, Western nations sought ways to direct funding into elite programs without athletes receiving the support directly. The journey away from a ban on receiving any financial help for the 'job' of being an athlete in Olympic sports had begun, though the fledgling economy was under the lock and key of regulators. Private investors were wary when it came to whom the money was actually going to and what it was being spent on.

In swimming, Rule 26 remained in place and would still be reinforced for several more years by many national federations around the Western world. However, they could have moved with the times soon after a meeting of leaders at the International Swimming Federation (FINA) agreed to relax the 'amateur rule'.

At a gathering in Kuwait soon after the 1978 World Championships in Berlin, FINA bosses said that any financial support must be filtered through national federations but the idea was to allow local clubs and associations more flexibility to find the money needed to run their programs.

Many sports, including International Association of Athletics Federation, 'IAAF', today known as World Athletics, went further by allowing those freedoms without any threat to the 'amateur' status of athletes, so that in countries such as Britain, trust funds were already providing support to leading names such as Sebastian Coe (World and Olympic Champion, current president of World Athletics and, since 2020, a member of the IOC).

Swimming's 1978 decision was conveyed to us by Syd Grange, the Australian representative on the ruling FINA Bureau, or board, as reported in the *Sydney Morning Herald*:

> "International amateurism rules have been relaxed to allow swimmers to endorse products and accept individual sponsorship. He [Grange] stressed that under the new FINA regulations, swimmers could now accept remuneration from endorsements and sponsorships to offset the cost of travel, accommodation, equipment and training ... the FINA regulations had also provided for state associations and the ASU (Australian Swimming Union) to receive a percentage of ALL funds acquired by swimmers through the endorsement of products, advertising and sponsorship. Under the new regulation, swimmers can also receive remuneration for teaching elementary swimming but are barred from coaching."

The move was welcomed by sports organisations that would no longer have to rely solely on government handouts. In contrast, the ASU interpreted this ruling to say that swimmers, while able to accept funds to offset their training and travel expenses, could not have any direct relationship with sponsors.

All deals and funds had to go through state or national federations. Private businesses and donors lined up enthusiastically but when they realised that the ASU would take an 80% share, leaving the athlete with just 20%, many sponsors baulked and walked away, determined not to see their investment disappear in administration and perks for the sporting gentry.

Kellogg's, the cereal giant, became the first sponsor to make donations. It committed A$50,000, while the Leyland motor company provided the first grants to assist athletes in their training—purses of $2,000 issued through the AOF. In return, they could link their brand to athletic excellence.

Any dollars were welcome but they were a drop in the pond for athletes. Sports federations continued to beat on the doors of parliament with constant pleas for support, to no avail.

The lobbying had a consistent message: to be competitive on a world stage, we had to keep up on the conveyor belt of sport's evolution. Trying to hold down a full-time job and keep up the training required to take on the full-time athletes of the Soviet Bloc was not sustainable.

Even for school kids, there was no provision in the West like that in the East: the sports schools of the GDR allowed athletes to cover the academic curriculum so that neither school nor sport were compromised.

The Master Plan

It was January 1979. I was 16 and on the cusp of my last year of high school. If I was to get that ticket to university, there would be no compromise because of swimming. Opportunities for women were far fewer in those days so I'd set my goal at becoming a physical education teacher or physiotherapist. The competition for such places was high, so I needed good grades.

My mother always said that 90% of anything is in the preparation—and any plan includes sacrifice. Swimming would be my sacrifice in 1979. There could be no more two- to three-month absences.

So, a plan was hatched: I'd continue to follow my training and racing regime to the end of January 1979. The start of the school term would then mean a sports lockdown: no travel and no yawning in class. My coach was informed: I'd be picking up in the pool again after my exams in November, when I would switch hats and move to Nashville, Tennessee, to train full-time for the Moscow 1980 Olympics under the guidance of Australian coach Don Talbot, the mentor to waves of champions, including world-record-holding siblings from Australia, John and Ilsa Konrads.

The only swimming trip of the year was to be from December 28, 1978 to January 17, 1979, taking in training and racing in Los Angeles, Boston and Nashville.

The day after returning to Sydney, I raced at the NSW State Championships and by the end of the meet had another five titles to my name. I set 16-year age records in the 200m and 400m medley, won the 100m and 800m freestyle and 200m butterfly, scratched the 400m freestyle due to jet lag and was awarded the meet trophy.

It was books, books, books from there on. Even the Australian National Championships in April were forfeited, with my swimming reduced to much lighter fitness work to keep me ticking over. The rest of the plan, my diary from 1979 confirms, was this:

August '79: Midterm exam

October '79: Year 12 final exam. 'The Higher School Certificate'

November '79: Depart for Tennessee, USA to begin intensive training

March 1980: Australian Olympic Selection Trials

February – May 1980: Full-time training USA (Nashville)

June 1980: Home for training camp

July/August 1980: Moscow Olympics

A Twist of Fate

Temptations to travel were turned down. I was more alert in school and friends commented on the difference in me. I was on the right track, or so it seemed.

The curve ball arrived on June 4, 1979—a letter from the Australian Swimming Union:

Dear Michelle,

It is with pleasure I congratulate you on gaining selection to compete at the Spartakiade in Moscow next month. As usual, it is harder for our people to compete at their top when in fact, it is out of season for them. However, I feel confident you will acquit yourself with distinction and be a good ambassador for Australian swimming.

Yours Sincerely,

W Slade,

Vice President ASU

The Spartakiades of Peoples of USSR was a large multi-sport event including athletes from across the Soviet Union and, for the first time, invitations to compete had been extended to others from around the world as part of Moscow's Olympic preparations. It was a chance to get a glimpse of life in Russia, feel the atmosphere and better understand what was awaiting us in 1980.

My study plan was in place and working well but here was a great opportunity that pressed one of the biggest buttons in sport: leaving no stone unturned. The lure of Olympic gold is irresistible to the elite athlete. Rules change, technology moves on and records get broken, but the moment when the best of the best come together in one race on one given day for the ultimate test ensures that the outcome lives eternally.

As Angie Cook, Australian middle-distance track champion of the '70s, noted in an article in The Sun Herald on October 21, 1979:

"It is not always the times on the clock which signifies a great performance. The ability to produce the best on the day and to overcome the pressures from within and without are the stamps of a competitive and skilled athlete."

A year out from Moscow 1980, here was a chance many others had not been given. I wanted to seize the day. There was one big barrier in the way: my midterm exams— compulsory and counting towards finals—were due to begin on August 3, the day I was due to arrive home from Moscow.

It was time to return to the headmistress's office with a begging bowl.

Behind the Iron Curtain

Our Soviet approval to travel with departure and arrival times came just days before we were due to leave, dictating a scramble to obtain visas. An ominous deal also had to be struck with my headmistress: I'd have to sit the midterms the day I flew into Sydney, there would be no compromise.

We left for London on July 19 and would fly to Moscow after we'd acclimatised for a few days. We had to deal with 24-hour flights through 10 time zones and giving the body clock time to adjust is especially important if journeys are to end in peak performance. Racing would start on the 25th and the Spartakiade would run until August 5—a dress rehearsal for the Olympic Games a year away, schedule and all. Eight thousand Soviet athletes would compete with 2,300 from 90 visiting countries.

Everything was clean, big, empty, drab, grey and austere, from the airport to the people and the Russian capital's buildings. The traffic on vast, utilitarian boulevards was as sparse as the scenery. I'd seen nothing like it.

The Olympic village was still under construction, so we were assigned to the Hotel Moscow for our nine-day stay. We soon learned to ignore the plan. We were taken instead to the Hotel Rossiya, or «Россия», without explanation. It was massive and very odd indeed. There were no phones to call out on, so we could not contact our parents to tell them where we were; nor could they easily find out. Phoning into Moscow was a complicated exercise even if you had a number.

Built in 1967 at the order of the Soviet government to house Communist Party officials and visitors to the Kremlin, the Rossiya overlooks Red Square. The stark and square kilometre-long walls of the hotel stand in contrast to the beautiful Byzantine cupolas of Saint Basil's Cathedral and the steeples of the Kremlin. Next door, a kilometre away, the 'Gum Store' was one of the few stores in the Soviet Union that had no shortage of consumer goods.

Rossiya was the largest hotel in the world back then. Built to house members of parliament and visitors, it could house 4,000 guests and it was rumoured to have cameras and listening devices in each of its 3,200 rooms. Each room of 11 square metres (120 square feet), each corridor, each floor and each elevator were identical. To get to your room, you had to know which lift to take to the right floor before knowing which corridor to walk along to the next lift shaft that was linked to the floor your room was on.

It was easy to get lost and if you were, the 'floor attendant'—the lady in charge of each floor and there to control who came and went—only spoke Russian, so it was important to show the number on your key.

Somewhere in the colossal edifice there was a 2,500-seat concert hall, and there was a police station on one side of the building. One of the many rumours about the place was that jail cells were located behind unmarked black doors near the barber shop. It was all very intimidating.

At check-in, we were given one small white, starched towel and a cake of soap each. There were five swimmers and a coach/manager on the Australian team but boys and girls were put on separate floors and told not to mix. On the first day we took the hotel towel to use at the pool and when we returned, we were confronted by the attendant screaming something. It was explained to us that if anything went missing from the room, the attendant would have to pay. She'd be watching!

It took us a good quarter of an hour to get to the dining hall each day. It wasn't really worth the effort! On the first day, we were presented with a soup with something white floating in the middle of it. It turned out to be an egg. We pushed the bowls aside and waited for the next dish. A few salad leaves with some strips of meat on top arrived. It was tongue. We prodded and poked but didn't eat. There were no corner shops. We'd surely starve!

In Red Square the next day, there was more drama. Dressed in jeans and our Australian tracksuit tops, we were heading for Lenin's Tomb across the cobblestones when all hell broke loose. Whistles blew and a group of uniformed police officers shouting "Nyet!" flocked towards us. We'd crossed one of the red lines that mark where you can and cannot walk.

Interaction with the Russian people was strained. They were distant, perhaps because they were conscious of being watched; perhaps because they'd been warned about 'Western foreigners'. It felt like this might be an issue when the Olympics arrived. There was a genuine fear of what the Soviet Union called "ideological contamination from tourists". The CIA mentioned the theme in intelligence dispatches:

"Handling the unprecedented number of tourists represents a monumental task for authorities not attuned to Western travellers … team accreditation issues such as Chinese and Taiwan, Israel and German representation are sure to surface as they do before every Olympiad. Perhaps of greater concern to organizers will be how to handle interaction between Westerners and Soviet citizens, including possible action by dissident Soviet groups."
(CIA Report: USSR: Olympic Games Preparations

In the Gum Store, contact was more relaxed, though we were told "the walls have ears". Some of the more courageous Muscovites discreetly approached us to see if they could buy our Levi's jeans and other goods that they couldn't buy in their shops.

There were queues outside shops that seemed to have very little in them, while foreigners and high-ranking officials had access to specialty shops called Beriozka, the name of two chains of state-run retail stores that sold luxury goods, such as chocolate and caviar, for foreign currency. Most Soviet citizens had no foreign currency and were not allowed in.

Nothing was boring about Moscow. It was all an adventure into another world, another time. We were completely cut off from home and being monitored everywhere we went.

The Spartakiade

We wanted to practise in the competition pool but it wasn't available, so off we went to the Chaika Pool, one of the city's public outdoor 50-metre pools.

We could see the pool but it took us a while to work out what "access the pool via the change rooms" meant. A water tunnel led us into the complex and eventually we arrived at the main pool. A heavy mist rose off waters that were kept toasty by thermal heating. It was very Gorky Park. And far warmer than we were used to.

No matter. The whole trip was about accepting and learning. Besides, it was out of our control and it was the evening before racing when we would finally get to swim in the competition pool.

The meet was over seven days, with the precise schedule of the Games that were a year away: my 200m butterfly first, then 400m freestyle the next day, the heats of the 800m freestyle on the penultimate morning and the final on the last day.

The tight budget meant we were a handful of swimmers with a coach some of us had rarely met, Forbes Carlile. We were a close-knit group and we turned to each other for support.

Linda Hanel, the 200 'fly specialist who was a rival back home but a teammate here, was my roommate: we were the only girls on the team.

We were both capable of making the podium in the 200m. We were sitting watching the races from the stands when it hit me: "Did you see that? The swimmers don't even have time to stop!" I'd noticed that the starter wasn't following the rule that swimmers must be stationary on the blocks before the signal to go is given.

In heat after heat, half the swimmers were being left on the blocks as the others got a super-fast start. No false starts were called. Come our race, I tried my luck: when the whistle blew to get on the blocks, I stepped to the front and got set without waiting for the command. The gun went off! Not protocol—but a great start!

Awareness counts. A year ago in Edmonton and Berlin, although my times were world-class, I'd lacked conviction and self-assurance. I'd learned a lot from the experience of a season that didn't go according to plan and left me shy of where I wanted to be.

I felt different in Moscow. There might have been any number of reasons: the excitement of being in an Olympic city, the small team, and the attitude of a coach who treated us with respect and worked both with us and our home coaches.

It was also out of season for us and some of the pressure was off. My job was to rehearse my own program. For whatever reason, I felt good and realised just how lucky I was to be rehearsing the Games program and feeling settled in an environment that could easily have been unsettling.

Over the next seven days, we five Australian swimmers collected four golds, a silver and a bronze. All my races delivered gold for me and the three wins made me the most decorated foreign athlete. I was also super happy for Linda, who won the 100m 'fly on the last day, when I won the 800m free. She told the *Sydney Morning Herald* that her secret of success was the 'psyche-up' she got from me because I'd told her time and again to "just go for it".

The importance of the rehearsal was not lost on the media back home:

"Sydney's Michelle Ford, 17, last night won her third gold medal and Australia's fourth at the Spartakiade Games in Moscow, the 'rehearsal' for next year's Olympics.

The Sans Souci school girl won the women's 800 meters freestyle by a margin of nearly four seconds in the Lenin Stadium Pool. The win meant Michelle became the first foreign competitor from 90 countries to win three gold medals.

It was a thrilling climax to a week in which she has also won the women's 200 metres butterfly and 400 metres freestyle."

(The Weekend Australian, *August 4–5, 1979)*

We landed in Sydney at 7 a.m. on August 3, the day of my exams. A gauntlet of media, lights, cameras and questions later, I was being rushed to school by my parents. I'd promised my headmistress and teachers I'd be there. It was crazy to think that I could manage a two-hour maths exam coming off a 30-hour flight, but the promise had to be fulfilled.

Still, it was all worth it. The exams had to be passed but my goal, Olympic gold, was alive and kicking. It felt closer than ever. On August 17, two weeks after my midterm exams, I wrote in my diary:

"I have gone to Russia, won three golds, finished my trials, and got the confidence back that was lacking since Berlin. I am so pleased that I went to Spartakiade and passed my exams."

Sometimes it's worth deviating from the set plan. I now had another three months to complete my final exams before I could breathe swimming again.

'Glorification of the State'

While my head was back in my books, the debate about how the West could respond to the East's sport-and-school support system rumbled on.

"There is a system in the Soviet Bloc countries which unashamedly uses sport for the glorification of the State..." as the Olympic History magazine put it (17 TNA: PRO FCO 28/4223). In the aftermath of the Montreal Olympics, Australian reporter Rod Humphries, under the headline 'Mass Sport Secret of Success' noted: "The German Democratic Republic (GDR) had invested $A43 million in 1971, matched by another $A61 million in 1974 and had budgeted up to $A80 million each year for the lead-up to the Moscow Olympics, covering 72,187 swimmers."

Although the world was beginning to question that approach, Americans led the way in finding a competitive response. How to build a system that would respect the amateur code yet support athletes in the way their opponents from the East did?

There was no government funding of sport in the US, and that led them to reform their collegiate system. The NCAA (National Collegiate Athletic Association) thrived on many millions of dollars pumped in by both college alumni and private interests to support the new wave of sporting scholarships for amateur athletes.

It was the answer to all the dreams of Australia's male swimmers: a program where they could combine swimming and a university education. In turn, US colleges fed their competitiveness with recruitment drives in search of international talent.

However, women had a different experience. The AIAW (Association for Intercollegiate Athletics for Women) program was not regulated by the same NCAA ruling and was therefore forbidden to offer scholarships outside the US, but in 1979 heated discussions to align the two organisations were under way.

There was new hope of international scholarships for women in the near future as Title IX sex-based equality legislation, under which colleges were obliged to provide for women what they provided for men, started to gain momentum.

The thought of going to America on a scholarship was enticing. A US university scholarship would be ideal and I worked out a plan with my parents. It would allow me to continue my swimming while earning a degree. The timing was perfect.

Part 3
Long March To Moscow

Chapter 13
Boot Camp

"I can be changed by what happens to me. But I refuse to be reduced by it."
– Maya Angelou

Time's up," the examiner called. It was mid-November 1979, and my last exam was done after two weeks of eight tests and toil! I breathed a sigh of relief. A sense of satisfaction washed over me and my shoulders felt like they were relaxing for the first time in months.

My last day at school. My uniform packed away, it was time to get back to the pool. The clock was ticking. The Olympic Games were only eight months away. I had not been back in the water for four months but, fortunately, I never took long to find my competitive form after any setback or time out of the water. My fitness built from a very young age was ingrained.

Armed with an intensely active childhood and a healthy logbook of strength and conditioning training, I was hopeful that my absence from the pool since my return from Moscow in August would not have put me too far behind in my preparation.

Athletes make sacrifices to get the job done. The hardest things we miss are those important moments in our life that can't be honoured or enjoyed because destiny and determination draw us away.

The plan was set. There was no time to say goodbye. My formal for the leaving class of '79 was scheduled for November 22 and sadly my plane left for Nashville, Tennessee, on the 18th. I wanted to celebrate our six years spent together as friends since we were 11—but I needed to be elsewhere.

I was off to a rigorous training routine pioneered by Australian coach Don Talbot. He'd recruited a team of international stars in Nashville with the aim of bringing the house down in Moscow, regardless of the flag.

Winter, snow and a steamy, chlorinated, indoor 25-metre pool greeted me in the country music capital of the USA. I'd visited the Nashville Aquatic Club (NAC) the year before on our US tour but that hadn't prepared me for the boot camp that awaited me.

Don had us climbing ropes and paddling around the pool on our hands while our legs were tied to skateboards. Buckets were tied to our waist to make progress excessively heavy, a process that suits strength and endurance.

In the pool, the mileage was brutal. There was no mercy. The military-style regime was a shock to the system. I'd known some of the toughest coaching in the past few years, but this was next level and crazier than I'd ever known. We were asked to do some insane stuff.

Within a couple of weeks, I was asking myself why I was there. The agony was intense. I was not alone in thinking that: every team member was swimming their hearts out for that pot of gold at the end of the Olympic rainbow. Each of us had our individual goals and aspirations: we gave each other strength and encouragement to endure this arduous regime.

At 17, I'd never experienced the same level of exhaustion before. My hands were blistered from climbing ropes that I never mastered, a 'weakness' I was punished for by having to stay back to do them again after training in the pool. The fatigue was intense. I had pangs of loneliness when memories of home flooded back and Nashville felt a very long way from home, family and friends.

However, I also knew I had to forge on, buckle up, knuckle down and set aside complaining and self-pity. I was getting a slug of Australian hard 'yakka' (work), a dash of American positivity and ... competition, competition, competition—something that I would not have got had I stayed home.

I had signed up for this and if that's what it took for gold, I just had to keep going and remind myself of what I'd known and told the reporters before setting off to Nashville:

"Swimmers must pass through three thresholds on the way to greatness. The first is hurt, the second pain and the third agony—I know them all".

(Janet Hawley, 'Michelle's psyching herself for Moscow', The Age, November 17, 1979)

White Christmas and a Whisper of Trouble Ahead

My world revolved around swimming but some snippets of news filtered through, including updates on the 52 American diplomats and citizens being held hostage during the Iranian Revolution after a group of students took over the US Embassy in Tehran on November 4, 1979.

Another item far more significant in terms of our daily dedication to sport reared its head, but it felt too far-fetched to believe. The news barely drew the eye of the swimming community. At a meeting of NATO representatives on December 20, Western governments raised the possibility of boycotting the Olympics in Moscow in response to the presence of Soviet military forces in Afghanistan. The Soviet–Afghan War began after the Soviets, under the command of Leonid Brezhnev, launched an invasion of Afghanistan to support the local pro-Soviet government that had been installed during Operation Storm-333.

My interest was arbitrary—all I was focused on was the next session. If I wasn't training, I was eating or sleeping, and any spare time was spent writing letters home. On Sundays, I made a weekly call to my parents.

After a month in Nashville with Christmas approaching, homesickness set in. It had been very tough and I was longing to be home with my family enjoying the summer and the busy life we led. Instead, I was in Nashville and not really enjoying myself! Some of my training partners were heading home for the festive break. Not me. It was too expensive and too far away.

I spent an American-style Christmas Day with my adopted family, the Parish clan. They were welcoming, warm-hearted and amazingly considerate people and made me one of their own. I'd never seen a living Christmas tree nor had snow at Yuletide. We talked about Australian Christmases in summer and the family asked me how Santa could come down the chimney when most houses 'down under' didn't have one! It finally dawned on me why Father Christmas was dressed in winter robes.

Christmas came and went with no let-up in a daily training regime that started with 5 a.m. wake-up calls. I ticked off my countdown calendar to the Games. Seven months to go. It felt like an awfully long time but there was a break in the clouds: racing! Speed tests in Toronto, Cincinnati, Texas and Florida were scheduled ahead of a return home in March for Australia's Olympic trials.

I'd swum in Australian colours at the Texas International a year ago but this time the selectors back home had decided not to include me on their team. Had I done something wrong by coming to America to train? Whatever the answer, it felt strange to compete against my fellow Australians on a different team.

A Champion for Change

Australian trials were scheduled to start on March 20, 1980, four months out from the Moscow showdown, making me the first of the Nashville squad off the blocks in search of selection. My teammates from England, Canada and America would have another three months to prepare.

As is the case today, Games selection criteria differed from country to country in 1980. Although the Olympic rules imposed by global swimming regulator FINA allowed three entries per country in each event, only America, Russia and GDR (the big three at the time) were likely to battle for podium sweeps. The rest of us rarely had enough money to send a full team.

Australia would only send those who had a serious chance of making finals and medals. Back in November 1979, a circular from coach Forbes Carlile had identified 55 swimmers *"likely to be considered for selection for the Australian swimming team, however, the likely number, to be approved by the AOF (Australian Olympic Federation), the national Olympic Committee who ratifies the team, will not exceed 25 swimmers".*

The coveted places were considered by many to be the ultimate achievement. The aim for me was to place in the top three and swim under the Olympic qualifying time standard to be on the way to the bigger goal.

Many at the time thought that holding trials five months out from the Games was far too soon. It was feared that some of those selected would consider it 'job done' and lose form on the way to Moscow. Only one coach and two assistants had been named despite the insistence of Carlile and others on a ratio of five athletes to one coach, with sports science staff on top. That's what we needed to be competitive with the best, but nothing had changed since Montreal except the names.

Known throughout the swimming world for his publications and tenacious blend of scientific research along with his coaching success, Forbes Carlile was a prominent voice in Australian swimming. He had attended Scots College, one of the most exclusive private boys school in Sydney, and the University of Sydney under Professor Frank Cotton before graduating with a Master of Science. He later lectured at the university in human physiology and pioneered work on elite athlete training methods, including the use of interval workouts, pace clocks, logbooks, heart-rate tests, training under stress and electrocardiography studies of the ventricles. His approach was the first of its kind back then.

At the Munich 1972 Games, Forbes was not an official coach but had travelled there with a TV company as an expert commentator and coach to Shane Gould, whose historic tally of five solo-event medals at a single Games—three golds, all in world records, a silver and a bronze, all in solo events—has never been matched by a woman at the Olympic Games. American Michael Phelps is the only swimmer to have emulated the feat, with five of his record eight golds at Beijing 2008 claimed in individual races.

Shane and another of Forbes' world-record-breaking distance freestyle racers, Jenny Turrall, both used the two-beat kick he had pioneered as part of his 'even-paced' swimming method for distance swimmers. The two-beat also became my trademark.

Too outspoken for many of those in power, his calls for change after the failures at Montreal led to him being appointed as the head swimming coach for 1980.

A strong advocate for sports science, Forbes had long empathised with the need to make home coaches part of an athlete's final journey to the blocks on the big occasions during training camps and competitions. By 1979, the ASU had finally been persuaded that home coaches would be welcome to work with their swimmers right up to the last training camp before Moscow. They had to pay their own way, of course, and there were "no guarantees".

A master of the written word, Forbes insisted on open communication between coaches and swimmers. His 10-page 'Moscow Training' circular was addressed to swimmers on yellow paper and to their coaches on blue paper. It noted:

"Throughout the swimming world today, it is recognised that team preparation should have a firm scientific base, with constant monitoring of swimmers. All leading countries are making strong efforts and spending a lot of money to make ground in this respect. ... The team needs constant services, preferably of a trained physiotherapist, provided all the time. There is no major swimming team in the world, East German, Russian, American, British, etc. which is not provided with this service. At the Games, it is completely unsatisfactory to rely on a masseur who is dividing himself between two or three sports. The British and other teams are doing much more. If there is 'not enough money' to thoroughly prepare the Australian swimmers for Moscow, we must despair of our situation."

In an Olympic cycle, money flows from the purse of the Olympic federation and, in most cases, government, but the decisions on who and how many make teams are made at the national-federation level.

We felt that Forbes was standing up for our interests at a time when the money needed to keep up with elite sport around the world was still missing. There was nothing for coaching staff, nothing for medical and no help with appropriate training-camp sites. We were a few months out from Moscow, and the plan was still in draft.

Even so, my preparation was all systems go. And I kept reminding myself of the different pathway I'd chosen and that my parents had helped plan for me, summed up by a *Woman's Day* article on the eve of me heading to Nashville the previous November:

"Bright and awesomely determined, Michelle will spend the next 8 months in America with expatriate coach Don Talbot. ... 'In America, they use all sorts of advantages we don't – like filming swimmers underwater and sports scientists to advise how to pull through the water. They use sports psychologists. I have had times when the body has been fit, but my mind has let me down. Everyone today has their own trick to psych themselves up and psych out the competition. I've had swimmers come up to me at the start of a race and say, 'What's the matter, Michelle, you look sick!' People do anything to rattle your concentration!'"

Boycott Threat Gets Real

On December 24, 1979, Russian troops entered Afghan territory to reinforce the country's communist regime against Islamic rebel forces. In early January 1980, Soviet nuclear scientist and dissident Andrei Sakharov called for a boycott of the Olympic Games.

It had hardly registered with athletes when US President Jimmy Carter gave an ultimatum on January 14, 1980: the Soviet Union had a month to pull out of Afghanistan or it would face trade embargoes and a boycott of the Olympic Games.

Twelve days later, Canadian Prime Minister Joe Clark joined the fray, setting a February 20 deadline for the Russians to leave Afghanistan or his country's athletes would follow the US lead and not be in Moscow come July. Athletes began to understand that their world was to become a pawn on the chessboard of global politics.

President Carter urged the IOC and its 89 members to move the Olympics to Greece on a permanent basis to rid the Games of politicisation once and for all but the idea was rejected, in part on the basis that contracts had already been signed with hosts.

When the US deadline was ignored by the Soviets, President Carter pressed America's allies to join a boycott.

Athletes across the world were bewildered. We were being drawn into matters we had barely heard about and, for the most part, didn't understand. Many of us were not even voting age in our respective countries. We had devoted years towards this moment. We had to believe this was only a threat by the US administration. All would be well. Heads down, we got on with the job.

That was very much the mood in Nashville. Either we did not want to listen or thought that none of it would amount to much. To think that a boycott would happen with only six months to go before the Games was preposterous, unimaginable. Surely it was a smokescreen, a move to offset other political issues challenging the Carter presidency, perhaps? Maybe the situation in Afghanistan would peter out?

The timing did not bode well. We were in a Cold War and 1980 would mark the first time a Soviet Bloc country had hosted an Olympic Games. Many outside of sport were concerned. The British parliament, keen to draw attention to the treatment of dissidents in Russia, had aired the possibility of boycotting the Moscow Games as early as October 1978 but then Prime Minister James Callaghan had said that "any action on the Moscow Olympics should be left to the British Olympic Association and sports federations".

That was not how the US administration of 1980 saw things. On January 23, President Carter included this devastating line in his address:

"... that with Soviet invading forces in Afghanistan, neither the American people nor I will support sending an Olympic team to Moscow".

Athletes held their breath. The IOC was thrown into disarray and politicians stood firm.

Margaret Thatcher and Malcolm Fraser, the respective prime ministers of Great Britain and Australia, agreed that a boycott of the 1980 Games would hurt the Soviets most. Fraser took the US line and began knocking hard on the doors of sports federations and the IOC, demanding that the Summer Games be cancelled, postponed or moved to another site.

On February 12, eight days before the US ultimatum ran out and the day before the opening of the 1980 Lake Placid Winter Games in New York, IOC President Lord Killanin confirmed that the IOC would stick to its contract with Moscow.

The Winter Games slipped through unscathed but there'd be no escape for the Summer Games. Predictably, on February 20, with no withdrawal of Soviet troops from Afghanistan, the US president slapped grain and technology trade embargoes on the Russians and confirmed that the United States would be boycotting the 1980 Olympic Games in Moscow. Other Western governments, including Australia, followed.

Had they given any thought to the impact of their stance on athletes? Did they understand just how long it took to prepare for an Olympic Games?

The fallout from the high costs of hosting the 1976 Games in Montreal coupled with the 1972 Munich massacre (in which two members of the Israeli Olympic team were killed and nine others taken hostage) meant that just two candidates bid for the 1980 Olympics: Moscow and Los Angeles.

Moscow won hosting rights for 1980, and down the line Los Angeles for 1984. By January 1980, the sports venues had been built in the Soviet capital, plans were locked in and ticket sales launched. The official invitation from the IOC to the 90 affiliated and recognised National Olympic Committee (NOC) members was sent. The deadline to accept was May 24.

Teams were yet to be finalised but parents and those interested in travelling to the Games were bidding for tickets, making travel plans and provisional hotel bookings. Athletes and coaches looked at their plans and knew that they had no control over what might happen. All they could do was keep on working.

How sport fits into a complex world in which organisers have close relationships with politicians but politics is supposed to play no part in sport has been debated since the early days of the Olympics and it continues to be a big theme to this day.

Athletes had been caught in the crosswinds of political storms on many occasions.

In 1980, athletes felt they were simply being used in a game of political football. As I prepared to leave Nashville for the selection trials back in Australia, the situation had escalated.

Opinion polls showed that the majority of the Australian public were not in favour of a boycott. Of the 23 national sporting codes in Australia that were to be represented at the Olympics, several took an early executive decision in favour of boycotting, while others like swimming sought direction from the membership.

Boycott or no boycott, it was time to race for my ticket back to Moscow.

My first national age championships in Adelaide competing as a 10-year-old in the Under 12s in 1972, in lane 4 in the blue swimming costume. I was first in record time in the 100m Freestyle.

In 1974, I was the fastest 12-year-old in the world in 100m Freestyle, establishing records in 14 strokes and distances, except Breaststroke.

With Kevin Berry ahead of the 1976 Olympic trials. Kevin was the 1968 Olympic champion in the 200m Butterfly.

My grandfather Oliver Alldis.

With my parents and younger brother William after I had just broken the 100m Freestyle world record for a 12-year-old in 1974.

A close-up of my Freestyle technique.

Psyching up before my 200m Butterfly race at the 1976 Olympic trials at the North Sydney pool.

The 1976 Australian Olympic swimming team. I am in the front row, second from the left.

Australia's Michelle Ford walks to the blocks, dwarfed by champion East German Kornelia Ender, before her 200 metres freestyle heat.

A newspaper clipping from the 1976 Olympic Games which shows 14-year-old me behind Kornelia Ender from East Germany.

With my letter of congratulations letter from East German Petra Thumer after breaking her world mark.

With training partners (L-R) Trevor Cracknell, Max Metzker, and Ron McKeon.

My dad Ian and me in the stands watching and analysing a swim meet.

Our secret departure at Sydney Airport in 1980, with my younger brother William.

The Australian Women's swim team on arrival at Moscow Airport. I am holding the koala my brother gave me. From L-R: Rosemary Brown, Lisa Curry, me, Lisa Forrest, Georgina Parks, Michelle Pearson, Karen Van de Graaf.

Celebrating my 18th birthday in the Olympic Village with Mischa Bear.

Me with the Gold Medal for the 800m Freestyle.

My Gold Medal for the 800m Freestyle.

Media Interview with Channel 7's John Devitt after the 800m victory ceremony.

The victory ceremony for the women's 800m Freestyle at the 1980 Moscow Olympics.

The score board after the 800m Freestyle event with an Olympic record.

Me with GDR Innes Diers (2nd) and Heike Dahne (3rd).

The Australian flag that accompanied the national anthem for my victory ceremony.

Receiving the Gold Medal.

Showing my Gold and Bronze medals to my grandparents Beatrice and Frank Ford.

Signing autographs with young fans.

Australian Sports Star of the Year, 1980

Preparing for a race.

Public petition to Australian Swimming to be put on the 1984 Olympic swim team.

Giving an interview after receiving the MBE in 1984.

On graduation with my Masters degree in 1984 from the University of Southern California with Robin Fiene (L) and Cindy Bodenstedt (Centre) from the USC swim team.

With Thomas Bach (L) and Sebastian Coe (R) on strengthening the athletes' voice.

Chapter 14
Trials and Tribulations

"It is obvious that we can no more explain a passion to a person
who has never experienced it than we can explain light to the blind"
– T. S. Eliot

It was March 16 and I was on my way home for the Australian Olympic trials after four months in Nashville.

As the plane descended over Botany Bay, I knew that the mad dash from final exams to Don Talbot's uncompromising school of toughness had transformed me back into a solid, fit and happy competitor. His program and the American way had paid dividends.

Trading the summer months for winter and swimming in an indoor, 25-yard pool had its advantages: my turns, which had cost me fractions of valuable time on every lap raced in past years, were sharper. Just saving 0.1 of a second at every turn of an 800m adds up to 1.5 seconds, which is often the difference between gold and silver, or in some races, gold or no medal at all.

The team spirit in Nashville was strong, positive and dynamic, reflecting a trademark of the USA swim team in general. It was uplifting and had reignited my self-belief and esteem after the hard knocks of Berlin in 1978 and the 'talk-it-down' mentality of some in the swim community back home.

By choosing to go to America, even when working with an Australian coach, I seemed to have fed the parochial minds of some in Australian swimming who fed the media doubts about my capacity. Reports suggested that I was not a medal chance for Moscow. It was toxic but my time in the USA had taught me how to rise above it.

Confident that I would make the team, Don had calculated that I didn't need to rest up for trials. "You can't afford to ease back and lose form through a taper, Michelle; there's no time," he'd said. "We're still months out from the Games—stick to your goal."

The job in Melbourne at trials was to just make the team inside qualifying time for my main events. The coach's parting words were a no-distraction mantra: "Do not lose sight of the end of the rainbow—the Olympic Games."

I was entered in six events: the 200, 400, 800 and 1500m freestyle, the 200m butterfly and the 400m medley. It was a lot to get through in just four days of trials and I'd be up against rivals who had tapered to race in peak form to secure their spot.

The challenge was simply "a good training program", Don had insisted.

In the midst of it was a familiar double header: the 800 free before the 200 'fly. I knew I was fit enough but the Australian girls were world-class in those events and sailing through with a 'good' time was not an option.

I'd been through all of that in my head a dozen times by the time I landed in Sydney after the 30-hour journey from Nashville.

After a happy reunion with my family at the airport, I was finally on my way home. My room was exactly as I'd left it: medals and trophies displayed neatly in the cabinet by the door, school books piled up where I had left them before my quick exit, my record player in the corner and my noticeboard above my desk with a poster of the 1976 Australian Olympic team taken during the flag-raising ceremony in Montreal.

Pinned below it was a newspaper clipping with a photo of me as a tiny 14-year-old walking behind the imposing figures of East German swimming star Kornelia Ender on the way to the 200m freestyle heats. My mother had placed a new pinboard above my bed, with the pins of every national Olympic team that I'd collected in Montreal.

The spirit of my grandfather was here in my room where he'd set out my quest, listened to me giggling at it, but had understood that the seed had been sewn.

The harvest drew closer.

1980 Olympic Trials

There we were in the ageing icon of a pool where Australia had mopped up at a home Olympics in Melbourne in 1956. The home team claimed eight of the 13 solo and relay titles in the pool between them.

To this day, it remains the last time that Australia topped the mighty USA on the medals table in Olympic waters, though our women dominated with eight out of 17 golds in a larger event program at the COVID-delayed Tokyo 2020 Olympics held in 2021.

Some of the legends of '56 had returned to this now bleak and austere building to cheer on the new wave of Australian Olympians at the Moscow trials.

Despite much talk of boycott, we were optimistic. On the first day of the trials, the Australian Swimming Union announced that its delegates would be voting in favour of sending the team to the Moscow Games when the matter came up at the Australian Olympic Federation's annual meeting on April 17. That sent a strong message to the Fraser administration in Canberra and lifted our spirits in the pool.

Over the four-day trials, I did what I set out to do. I won the 800m and 1500m distance events very comfortably over my rival Tracey. I took second place in the 200 'fly and 400 medley and was third in the 400m, qualifying in all four of my Olympic events.

It had been precisely what Don Talbot had predicted: a "good training program", with no break in the work geared to Moscow in July. We'd planned it perfectly.

As we awaited the team announcement, I sat contemplating the tall ceiling of this majestic building with its floor-to-roof windows and years of golden history and grime. The iconic swim centre would close its doors for the last time that evening and the greats of 1956 were sitting there alongside us. How were they feeling? It must have been a wrench to say goodbye to the hallowed waters in which you'd made your name an eternal part of Australian sporting and Olympic history.

A new wave of names were about to be added to the book of green and gold teams. The loudspeakers crackled. Here it was. Boys first, girls second.

A shiver ran up my spine when they read out my name among the 11 men and nine women selected. Each of us was applauded by the crowd as we walked out and assembled on the deck. Only six of us had made it from Montreal to Moscow for the Games of the XXII Olympiad: Mark Kerry, Mark Tonelli, Max Metzker, Linda Hanel, Tracey Wickham and me.

As I shook hands with Dawn Fraser and the other legends, words Kevin Berry had said to me years ago came to mind: "Your first Olympics, you learn. The second, you win!"

We stayed in Melbourne for two days of team-building and instruction on logistics: training camps, uniform fittings and travel arrangements. It was all systems go. I was now one step closer to the Olympic goal than my friends in Nashville who were still months shy of their trials. The waiting was all the more stressful because of the US government's declaration that it would not support a team going to Moscow. "But what would a boycott achieve?" my American teammates were asking.

Back to Nashville

With a lump in my throat, I waved goodbye to family and friends once more. It was time to get back to Nashville and the training and race preparation aimed at making waves in July.

It felt less daunting now. I'd made the team and Don Talbot's regime was about to shift from winter slog to spring honing, with more frequent racing making it more fun. And more of what I was used to—quality reigns. Give me quality any day.

The US Nationals in Austin, Texas, were due on April 9, after which there'd be several other competitions up to June and my return to Sydney to join the Olympic squad.

In Nashville, all talk centred on President Carter digging his heels in. At a special meeting of American athletes, he pre-empted a vote due at the United States Olympic Committee on April 12 by declaring that no US athlete would be going to the Games.

However, the Olympic Charter specifies that only a country's Olympic Committee, and not its government, can decide who participates at the Games. The American Olympic Committee's vote during the week of the US Nationals would be critical.

Australians feared that the American decision would steer our own government, causing a serious dilemma for many families, including my parents, who had already bought their tickets, prepared and, in some cases, paid for their flights and hotel accommodation in Moscow. My father felt that even if a team did travel, parents and fans should reconsider their own plans to show empathy and understanding with the decision-makers facing up to the Soviet Union and its invasion of sovereign territory. His view made headlines:

> *"Father of Olympic swim hope, Michelle Ford, strongly opposes the Australian government's boycott of the Olympic Games. Mr Ford said last week that the boycott, if imposed, would 'settle nothing and could boomerang on Australia.' Michelle, 17, is training seven hours each day. She told her father by phone that the Australian government's opposition to the Games was 'dampening' her enthusiasm for training[...] 'Is Mr Fraser going to get any positive results from not sending athletes? I can't see how not sending athletes to Moscow can hurt the Russians,' said Mr Ford. 'But I think the government should stop Games' spectators going to Moscow and spending Australian money there.'"*
>
> *('Olympics Ban Upsets Stars', Sydney Morning Herald, March 15, 1980)*

Letter to Olympians (April 21, 1980)

Before my departure, I signed a petition launched by a group of Australian athletes rallying against a boycott:

> *"We all no doubt have differing views on the boycott question and ultimately the decision to participate is an individual one. However, we feel most, if not all of us would accept the following as adequate reason for our participation:*
>
> 1) *The ideals of the Olympic movement are indivisible. If they are not adhered to in full, they will be destroyed.*
> 2) *Those ideals, participation by the youth of the world, pursuit of excellence, and internationalism, belong to no particular political group, and we, as aspirants to those ideals, must resist political intrusion.*
> 3) *To suggest that those who wish to participate are somehow traitors is shown to be nonsense by the weight of the Australian public opinion. We should see the Olympic movement as an important event which reduces international tensions."*

We were caught between two stools—our allegiance to our government tested by our dedication and devotion to Olympic sport and the futility of a boycott when it came to any expectation that the sacrifice of athletes would change the course of a conflict far removed from our lives.

On the pool deck in Nashville, we were no longer asking how we were swimming. It was all about whether we'd even make it to the Games, but I recalled Don's calm determination when he'd said, "stick to my plan".

Hope and Despair

The snowflakes and crisp morning air had given way to a warmer 14°C and we were finally able to move to the outdoor 50m heated pool that was part of the local country club. I also moved house to the Gilbert's family residence, which was closer to the pool. It was a huge relief to leave behind the winter freeze of those 5 a.m. starts wrapped in my parka waiting for someone to open the door at the back entrance of the stifling indoor pool only to be engulfed by a swirl of humid, chlorinated fumes escaping the hatch.

Outdoors! I could finally breathe again.

A mix of British humour, Southern American slang, Canadian and Australian colloquialisms made up for the lack of cultural activities and things to do in between the slog in Nashville—and they were an antidote to and salvation from mounting tension over the boycott. We were sitting ducks awaiting our fate.

Words from the ancient history of the Olympics spoke to all of us at the mercy of the political crisis in 1980:

"Through the 12 centuries of the Olympic Games, many wonderful athletes competed in the stadium and the hippodrome of ancient Olympia's sacred area, moving the crowds with their great achievements. Although mortal, their Olympic victories immortalised them."

We were officially 'amateurs' in our era and our job was seen as representing our nations and performing for the glory of sport in a spectacle of precision, tactics and true grit. Sport mirrors life in many ways: wins, losses, good times and bad, battles, courage, camaraderie and respect. And resilience.

The threat of having the Olympic Games torn away was crushing our spirits and testing our will to keep working. However, the Nashville Aquatic Club (NAC) swim team held strong. We had no choice and that bonded us, regardless of nationality.

As the clouds grew darker, contingency plans were already being made to make sure the US Olympic trials would be held. The American Swimming Association was planning to reschedule their event for after the Olympic Games in August, as their summer highlight was no longer trials for anything. The Canadian trials would still go ahead before the Games. It was chaos and the burden fell on athletes, coaches, clubs and parents as governments rallied their respective National Olympic Committees to tell Moscow they would not be there.

Then, out of the blue on March 25, the British Olympic Association, in the face of the resistance from the UK government, voted 22 to 4 in favour of sending a team to Moscow! The decision was underlined by the stipulation *that "naturally, if circumstances change, the BOA would re-examine the situation".*

We celebrated with our British teammates at Nashville, Jimmy Carter (the British swimmer, not the US president) and Phil Hubble. Everyone had been sure it was a no-go after British Prime Minister Margaret Thatcher had backed a boycott in line with the US government.

President Carter headed in one direction at every step of the development of the crisis. He stuck to his line throughout all meetings with the IOC and heads of state, imposing trade embargoes, placing restrictions on Olympic broadcaster NBC to stop payments to Russia, and making offers of reimbursements for the 6,000 American supporters with tickets to the Games.

The suggestion that athletes get to the Games under their own steam and compete as individuals was an audacious attempt to bypass the boycott, but it never took wings. It was said that US athletes would have their passports withheld if they tried, but that was never confirmed.

We arrived at the US Indoor Nationals in Austin ready for racing between April 9 and 13 amid talk of the impending big vote. Saturday the 12th was D-Day. It dawned and we awaited word from the US Olympic Committee (USOC) meeting in Colorado Springs. I was lining up to race when everything suddenly stood still. It was as if everyone had been struck dumb. Everyone looked frozen to the spot. Then the gun fired and the race started. That's American pride. Come what may, we go on!

During the break before the relays as the last events of the meet, the news ricocheted around the venue: USOC had voted that morning not to send a team to Moscow in July.

"The USOC has decided not to send a team to the Summer Games in Moscow. The United States Olympic team shall be selected in the usual manner in order to recognize the athletes who have been training as Olympians, and be it further resolved that if the President of the United States advises on or before May 20, 1980, that international events have [changed] ... the USOC will enter its athletes in the 1980 Summer Games."

(Excerpt of the USOC telex to IOC Headquarters, April 13, 1980)

In effect, it was over. The USA would not be in Moscow.

What Now, Australia?

What did it mean for Australia? The rules of the International Olympic Committee stated that the National Olympic Committees *"must be autonomous and must resist all pressures of any kind whatsoever whether political, religious, or economic in nature".*

The USOC did not receive government funding but Australia's Committee did and the situation was more convoluted.

Like me, many Australian athletes had helped with efforts to raise the estimated A$2.5 million that the fledgling Australian Olympic Federation (AOF) said it required to pay for a team to be in Moscow after the poorly funded fiasco of Montreal. It was a ripple compared to the much bigger budgets flowing into sport in the Soviet Union and the GDR at the time.

While the AOF was independent of government in its statutes and constitution, state support was desperately needed to cover the shortfall of sending a team to the 1980 Games. There would be no money from a government sticking to its line of *"Russian troops out or no Games".* The US decision had hardened hearts further as *The Australian* newspaper noted under the headline '*US Vote Spurs Fraser*' on April 14:

"It's hard to predict what effect the USOC announcement will have on the Australian Olympic Federation. Anti-Russian feeling in the United States is running very high at the moment and the Afghanistan question has been compounded by the tense situation in the Iran hostage crisis."

Four days out from the vote of the Australian Olympic Federation, the government was piling on the pressure, but AOF secretary-general Julius Patching held firm:

"We still abide by the principles of the Olympic Charter. Olympic committees must not be guided by or dictated to by governments. Whatever we do, it will be done with care – and with the intent of protecting the Olympic movement and the interests of our Olympic athletes."

On the other side of the world in Nashville, the alarm clock woke me with a jolt. I was due on the early flight to Edmonton, Canada, via Chicago, to compete later that evening in the Homecoming Classic on April 18 and 19.

It was D-Day on the boycott question in Australia and my mind was all over the place. Would we go? And if we didn't, should I pack up and go home? Or stay and enjoy the summer and work out which university to study at, having had my eye on UCLA? I had no answers and my host family was waiting to get me to the airport.

I grabbed my bag and we were off to meet my travelling teammates. With my competition suit, goggles and cap packed into my hand luggage to be ready for a quick change for my warm-up at the other end of the trip, I slumped into my seat and watched Nashville disappear from view.

In Chicago, we had to rush to make our connection. Then at security, a truth struck like lightning: I had no passport with me. Sweat started to drip down my face. With my mind in a fog of questions over the big vote back home, I'd thought it was a local flight to Canada, not 'overseas'. I'd overlooked the Canadian border and now I was stuck! In Australia we can fly for five and more hours and still be in the same country.

Watching my teammates disappear on to the flight, I felt stranded and slightly alarmed in a city known for its high crime rate. At the help counter, I explained my dilemma and they suggested I get my host family to fly the passport up with the crew on the next flight out of Nashville. That might allow me to catch a later flight to Edmonton "or the first one tomorrow morning".

The attendant was switched on enough to realise that at 17, my safety was paramount, so she arranged a room in the airport hotel for me to wait in. Lying on the bed, I felt tears rolling down my cheeks. The boycott, the passport and the pressure of feeling very alone in a big world far from home had got to me.

In just a few hours, I'd hear whether I'd be going to the Olympics.

The phone rang. It was the airline informing me that my passport had arrived and that I'd be able to leave on the next flight to Edmonton. I grabbed my things and rushed back to check-in. Running through a flock of yellow robes of chanting Hare Krishna followers, passport and ticket in hand, I arrived at the gate breathless but bound for Edmonton.

My Last 800m Freestyle?

The mad dash from the airport was a welcome distraction and I made it just in time for the 800m freestyle. I raced as the general assembly of the Australian Olympic Federation got under way in Melbourne half a planet away.

I imagined this might be the last 800m of my career if I didn't make it to Moscow. I accepted the moment for what it was and in winning I reconnected with what swimming meant to me: there was harmony and satisfaction in racing. It was exhilarating and all the more so when I managed to cut out all the noise.

I'd learned to shun distractions in that 1978 season of soaring followed by hard knocks, while Don Talbot had reminded me constantly of his mantra—"Stick to the plan … do not lose sight of the end of the rainbow—the Olympic Games."

I had no intention of doing that but the decision was not in my control and it was the same for my NAC teammates.

"Ford wasn't about to bask in the victory long. She's got more important things on her mind. She's looking for a victory back home. 'They're [the Olympic Committee] voting tonight to see whether we boycott the Olympics or not,' said Ford.

*The Canadian swimmers are on pins and needles too, waiting for a decision.
But the kids could do nothing but push the problem to the background."
(Jim Matheson, 'A Passport to Success', Edmonton Journal, April 18, 1980)*

Deciding Not to Decide

I put the phone down and my Nashville teammates wanted to know what my parents had told me. Was I going?

I had no idea! The wait would go on. The 26 national Olympic sports federations in Australia met on April 19 to ratify the Olympic team and cast their own votes on our participation at the Games. They endorsed 273 athletes, coaches, administrators and medical staff as members of the Australian Olympic team—204 competitors and 69 officials.

After the team was given the thumbs up, Australia's Deputy Prime Minister Doug Anthony addressed the assembly. Harry Gordon recalled the moment in his 1994 book *Australia and the Olympic Games (The Big Split)*:

"He told delegates that the Soviet Union wanted control of Middle East oil, that it had destabilised the Indian Ocean, that world peace was at risk; he also suggested that any division between the United States and its Allies (on the issue of the boycott) would amount to a devastating victory for the USSR. He asked the conference to make a decision not to send a team to Moscow."

A marathon debate then ensued and it was decided not to decide: they would do so on May 23, the day before the IOC deadline for acceptance to the Games. The Australian Swimming Union delegates spoke in favour of sending a team to the Games but other sports begged to differ and it was agreed to grant the AOF executive, a group of 11 men, the power to take the decision on May 23, the day before the IOC deadline for acceptance to the Games. Five more weeks of uncertainty! But at least they hadn't backed the boycott.

The rest of the Homecoming Classic unfolded and my exploits and frustrations once again made the local media:

*"Ford ... took six races; 200, 400 and 800 free, 100 and 200 'fly and 400 IM ...
However, she wasn't doing handstands when the meet was over. 'I've phoned my
mom back home in Sydney, and she told me they've delayed the Olympic boycott
vote for another five weeks,' said Ford, a possible medal winner in Moscow. "I just
wish they [the Australian Olympic Committee] would make up their minds one
way or the other. It's really depressing. You don't know if you're coming or going.
Should I train hard or shouldn't I?"'*

(Jim Matheson, Edmonton Journal, April 21, 1980)

Feeling Lost

I'd felt so buoyed in Edmonton but back at the Nashville Aquatic Center, the spark had gone with the fight in me ebbing as fast as it had flowed. Not knowing was almost worse. Despite their own depression over the US decision, the team around me rallied to support me, encourage me, pace and push me in training. Like their laughter, their strength was infectious.

I watched how the Americans rebuilt; their enthusiasm was inspiring. Talking about my dilemma when they'd been left with no hope was embarrassing. I wanted to go home. I'd had enough. However, my parents insisted I stay.

It was getting ugly in Australia with the tide of media and public polls turning in favour of a boycott. Households were split and the country was divided. It seemed everyone had an opinion and some were belligerent and frightening.

Seeing the way that the wind was blowing, the government called sporting associations and even individual athletes offering 'under-the-table' payments to support the boycott. A 1984 report from the House of Representatives on payments to athletes and teams who did not participate in the 1980 Moscow Olympics would reveal that seven sporting codes/teams took government payments totalling $488,000 and $36,000 went to six individual athletes.

The next blow came on April 25 when the Canadian Olympic Committee announced they would follow the USA and boycott the Moscow Games. My NAC teammates from Canada must have been devastated. They never returned to Nashville.

France was next to declare on May 13 and it came down on the other side of the coin: its athletes would be going to the Games. But two days later, the Federal Republic of Germany joined President Carter's boycott. All the while, the lanes at Nashville were emptying. I desperately wanted to go home but my parents pointed out that it was now winter in Australia and there were no decent pools to train in. I was to stay in Nashville.

Australia's crucial vote loomed large. Both at home and abroad, the world was watching to see which way a nation that had been to every Olympics since 1896 would jump. Under the headline *'Boycott Suspense'*, *The Sun* reported on the morning of the vote:

"With two days remaining for final decisions from several countries, the Carter administration said it was confident its list of supporters would grow. A department spokesman said the support of Australia, whose Olympic Committee votes on the issue today, was 'critical to the U.S.'

America's allies generally endorsed President Carter's call for a boycott. However, with the exception of West Germany, most of the autonomous Olympic Committees in Western Europe have voted to go. Most of Carter's support has come from Third World countries in Africa, Asia, Latin America and the Middle East. Apart from Australia, decisions remain to be made by Brazil, Japan, Spain, Tunisia and Venezuela."

Games On!

Restless in Nashville, I counted the seconds on the digital clock on the bedside cabinet: 1 a.m., 1:30, 1:45! What was taking so long? Then the house phone rang and I tore off my bed covers and ran to the kitchen. It was 2 a.m. and my host family had left the lights on so I could see my way. I'd barely lifted the receiver when I heard my parents say, "We're off to Moscow!"

"What?! Really?!" The questions flowed but I was no longer listening to the answers. My parents could tell and said they'd call back later. Their news was confirmed with the morning headlines on May 24 screaming: *'Photo Finish Vote on Olympic Games'* (The Sun) and *'6–5 decision rebuff to Federal Govt'* (Sydney Morning Herald).

The president of the Australian Olympic Federation (Syd Grange) said when announcing the decision:

"There's always been conflict in our loyalties to the government and our loyalties to amateur sport. The great problem the executive faced was to try and reconcile these loyalties, and it wasn't an easy task."

Mr Grange said the executive reached its decision *"after a long and very critical discussion – we looked at the attitude of the government, we looked at our responsibility and we tried to reconcile the two and we decided we should send a team".*

He also said that *"any group or individuals who felt so strongly about the boycott issue that they did not want to go to Moscow could withdraw from the team"*, and that *"the Australian team would go as normal, march, carry the flag and observe all the usual formalities".*

In shock, I called my coach, but being Australian, he already knew! Then my thoughts turned to my teammates at the NAC in Canada. How was I going to tell them? I felt a rush of emotion. A smile became a chuckle and laughter, followed by guilt, first towards my American friends and then about the training I hadn't done because I'd been so low. Ted Power caught the mood swing in *The Tennessean* on May 25 under a headline *'NAC Swimmer Headed to Moscow'*:

"In a year so full of disappointment for most of the senior swimmers at the Nashville Aquatic Club, some good news was due: and, Thursday, at two o'clock in the morning, the good news finally arrived as Australian Olympian Michelle Ford got the word she would be competing in this summer's Moscow Games.

Ford, 17, who has been training at NAC for the Games since November, didn't mind being jostled from bed to answer the phone call from her parents, who dialed their daughter from Sydney with the news that the Australian Olympic Committee had voted 6–5 to send a team to the boycott-torn Olympiad.

'I knew they were going to call, but I didn't know what the outcome of the vote might be,' said a relieved Ford. 'I had been thinking we weren't going to go, but when France voted to participate last week, I think that might have set a new trend.'

The Australian decision was no doubt a hard pill to swallow for the other members of the Nashville Aquatic team, many of whom had their Olympic dreams dashed by the U.S. boycott. Ford said the members of the team congratulated her just the same, though.

'The team was really pleased for me. But it's hard to explain how I feel about them not being able to go. I'd like to prove to myself that I could beat everyone in the world, but although I won't have that chance, I'm still really happy about going,' explained the distance freestyler, who will swim three individual events at the Games which begin July 19."

The Aftermath

We had been given a green light but there was still a feeling that it was amber and could switch to red at any moment.

The AOF decision was a slap in the face for our prime minister Malcolm Fraser, whose anger led to the charge that he'd taken it all too personally. Meanwhile, behind the masquerade, his government continued multimillion-dollar trade of Australian wheat and minerals with the Russian state.

Syd Grange's appeasement to the government that anyone could withdraw from the team "if they felt strongly about the boycott" was an invitation for the government to try to prove its point and show that it has sportsmen and women on its side. Financial incentives were offered to athletes and sports codes if they opted out.

The media took the same tack, applauding each individual athlete withdrawal, and in the frenzied atmosphere, a key public poll days after the AOF's decision showed 50% of respondents in favour of boycott, 40% opposed and 10% undecided.

The cloud had not lifted and the AOF's 6–5 vote in favour of sending a team just wasn't accepted by those who intended to keep fighting for a boycott. Time was running out to accept an invitation to the Games and the feverish campaigning had serious consequences. Beyond the crisis of conscience among athletes, those of us who decided to go to Moscow became targets.

Prime Minister Malcolm Fraser said that it represented "... a failure of executive leadership [of the AOF] and a denial of national responsibility" to send a team to Moscow.

However, in a television interview on 24 May, and reported in The Canberra Times, he gave the team his qualified blessing, saying, "I cannot give them my blessing to go, but I can say that I hope any athlete who does compete in Moscow makes damn sure that he or she beats everyone else in whatever the event may be.

"Because, whatever views Australians might have about whether or not they should be in Moscow, now that they are going it is all the more important that they win and win as well as possible. So in that sense, they certainly have my good wishes. In that sense, they have my blessing."

Mr Fraser said he wanted all Australians to get behind those who compete in Moscow.

PR spin for TV, maybe, as his comments did not match the reality of what was going on behind the scenes with the government's financial incentive being offered to athletes to pull out. Neither the prime minister nor the government made any effort to call out the vitriol that some media and public were directing to the athletes, with death threats and calls of "traitor" an everyday event.

Chapter 15
Secret Send-Off

"A hero is an ordinary individual who finds the strength
to persevere and endure in spite of overwhelming obstacles"
– Christopher Reeve

The government support for a boycott that had the backing of five out of the 11 Australian Olympic Federation executives contributed to a toxic environment for athletes. The country had never seen anything like it before.

By late May, more opinion polls were swaying towards a boycott on the grounds that it was unsafe for the athletes to go to Moscow.

The death threats and calls of "traitor" directed at athletes were coming from our own citizens. The situation was so precarious that my mother sought permission for me to bypass the Olympic training camp in Sydney and go straight from Nashville to the pre-Moscow holding camp in France. She wrote to the ASU:

May 1980

Letter to the Executive Committee, The Australian Swimming Union

Due to the present situation in Australia regarding Olympic athletes and the problems confronting Michelle personally if she were to return to Australia before the Olympics, and after much consideration, I feel it would be in Michelle's best interest to remain in the USA for the present time and to travel with the other swimmers in the US to meet the team in Vittel France on the 1st July.

It is unbelievable to me when I as an Australian born parent must tell a 17-year-old girl whose grandfather fought for Australia for 3 years in the Middle East in World War II and who herself has never voted for any particular government and who I have taught to always be proud of the Australian flag that right now it is unsafe for her to return 'home'.

Indeed, it is hard for me to take out a personal insurance cover for her but not for my other 3 children.

Jan Ford (mother)

Still in Nashville, I had been told to report to the Warringah Swimming Centre north of Sydney for the three-week Olympic training camp before leaving for Europe, but the week before my scheduled flight home, my mother's fears were more than justified by the headline splashed across the front page of The Clarion, a weekly publication for journalists: 'DEATH THREATS – Athletes become targets as nation divides over Olympics'.

The story revealed how swimmers aged 16 to 22 years old had received multiple threats to their lives and those of family members. One said "… your body will be found floating in the Harbour", another "… I hope you die".

We had no idea who had sent the threatening notes and the people screaming "traitor" at us in the street were complete strangers. It was unsettling, menacing and the mood stood in stark contrast to the attitudes I'd become accustomed to in the United States.

Despite the threats, I had made my mind up. It was time to go home. Don Talbot handed me my last workout on a warm, sunny afternoon. Don never showed emotions, but he confided in me that he was pleased Australia was going and we would get to honour the work we had done. The whole team had turned up to say goodbye and it proved impossible to focus and get through the session.

Tracy Caulkins, one of the most versatile swimmers in history, the most decorated and admired of all my NAC teammates, and a best pal who had helped me so much during my time in Nashville, walked towards me with two envelopes in her hand. They were addressed to the British swimmers who had been training with us and who would also be in Moscow.

Recently having had both her world medley records broken by the GDR's Petra Schneider but no longer able to challenge her in Moscow, Tracy said, "Could you please give these letters to Jimmy (Carter) and Phil (Hubble) when you get to Moscow … a good luck message from the team."

We chatted a bit, then she looked me in the eye and said, "Michelle, we want you to go to Moscow …" She stopped for a moment, emotions running deep, paused, and after a big sigh, added, "… and represent all of us here. You will be swimming for us. You are one of us and we're so proud of you."

Tears welled. We hugged each other. Tracy, a winner of four golds at the 1978 World Championships, would have gone to Moscow as a multi-gold prospect. A world-record holder in both butterfly and medley during her career, she pressed on to a home 1984 Olympics in Los Angeles and claimed gold in both medley finals and with teammates in the medley relay. She met Australian sprinter Mark Stockwell at the Games. They married and have lived most of their lives 'down under' where Tracy became president of Swimming Australia.

Back in 1980, the friendship of those in Nashville meant the world to me but left me feeling torn. Unlike them, I'd been dealt a great hand. I not only had a shot at proving myself and a chance to live the Olympic dream, but they'd given me the gift of standing up for all those who could not be there. Their grace was my gratitude.

I had mixed feelings about going home, too. The Australian Government's boycott campaign was unrelenting. It put Australians on a collision course with each other, pulled society apart and the pressure on athletes to step down was intense. I asked myself whether it was worth it. Should I just give in to the government and accept their offer of $6,000 to withdraw? Or stay true to myself and get my act together for the greatest challenge of my life?

Glass Half Full

The US decision in April to boycott had quashed my appetite for training and I had begun to question why I was doing it. It was too demoralising to slog up and down empty lanes on my own and most of the time I swam well below my best speed, except when members of the Nashville Aquatics team turned up to keep me going by training alongside me.

I'd now been told that I could go to the Olympics and my thoughts turned to going into battle knowing that my preparation had been compromised. It was a time of utter confusion for athletes outside the Eastern Bloc.

For orientation, I kept returning to my grandfather's words, the quest he'd set me and the confidence he'd given me. Politics had distorted everything. That the Games were in Moscow didn't matter for me; it was about competing at the Olympics, wherever they were being held.

The politicians just don't get it, I thought. They don't understand why we get up in the morning and swim for hours on end; why we give up so much and put so much time and energy into it without receiving a dollar. We were striving to achieve something that the whole nation could be proud of. Instead, we were now the villains. I felt it was unfair, unsporting and un-Australian.

Cracking Under Pressure

I had never given up before and wouldn't do so now. Excuses don't make champions, I was told. But now it was our own government offering incentives to reach for an excuse to not follow through on all the work, commitment and calling.

The Australian Olympic Federation had stood by its decision to send a team to go but Prime Minister Fraser and his government refused to accept it and insisted on a re-vote. They were unforgiving.

IOC member Kevan Gosper, chairman and chief executive of Shell Australia and dual Olympian himself, sided with the boycott, joining Sydney Grange (president of the AOF, FINA board member and president of the Australia Swimming Union), Julius 'Judy' Patching (AOF Secretary General), Jack Howson (general manager of the 1976 Australian Olympic Team) and Eric McRea. Gosper broke ranks after the IOC rejected his idea of delaying the Games, which, like President Carter's idea of shifting the Games permanently to Greece, would have broken the contract with the Moscow organisers.

> *"A member of the Australian Olympic federation executive, Mr Gosper issued a statement explaining why he believed an Australian team should not go to Moscow. Mr Gosper, former Olympic runner, made a 40,000 km round trip from his London base to vote in favour of the boycott. [...] Mr Gosper said he regretted that the International Olympic Committee of which he is also a member, had not agreed with his suggestion that the Games be postponed for a year."*
>
> *('Gosper Appeals to Athletes', Sunday Telegraph, May 25, 1980)*

Australia's other IOC member, David McKenzie, voted against the government's push for a boycott as did Phil Coles, John Rodda, Tom Blue, Bill Hoffman and Lewis Luxton.

By May 29, soon after the vote, athletes and teams who had qualified for an Olympic berth began to pull out. Some withdrew for personal reasons, some for political reasons; others, particularly the national sporting federations, many that hadn't qualified, opted for the financial incentive the government was offering to withdraw.

Our head swimming coach Forbes Carlile and teammate Tracey Wickham withdrew for different reasons. While Forbes was in favour of the government's stance, Tracey explains her reasons in Lisa Forrest's 2008 book Boycott, 'I remember ... secretly I was hoping that Malcolm Fraser would say we're not going ... so I could get out of this. Because I knew I could not go, I wasn't ready.'

All the lobbying hit home harder in some sports than others and no sport was left untouched. Of the 273 Australian athletes and officials originally selected to represent Australia, only 123 made it to the Games.

In the end, 65 countries boycotted and 2,300 athletes bypassed the Moscow Games. Of the 612 medals awarded at the 1976 Montreal Olympics, 180 (29%) were won by athletes whose countries did not attend the 1980 Games. However, in women's swimming, we would still face the dominant force in the world-record books: the GDR.

A Call For Harmony

Not all media commentators backed the boycott and the papers were full of reader letters in support of the team going to Moscow. Coverage also focused on the injustice of asking young Australians who had trained for years to sacrifice it all even though trade with Russia continued.

"When it disagreed with the decision, the government had embarked on a course which threatened to wreck the Olympic organisation in Australia and in doing so divided Australian society. Meanwhile, … the Fraser government continues to foster and expand profitable trade in a wide range of goods of strategic value to the Soviet Union with some of those profits flowing to members of the government, including the Prime Minister."

('ALP Attach Govt "Damage" to Olympics', Sydney Morning Herald, May 30, 1980)

"The saddest part about the wrangling over the Games is the divisive effect it is having on the Australian community. And young athletes who have trained for years for the 1980 Games suddenly find themselves in a crisis of conscience. The athletes are young people whom we can be proud of, they deserve the sympathy of us all. Above all, they do not deserve condemnation."

('Don't Blame the Athletes', Sunday Telegraph, June 1)

However, government campaigning had tipped the scales, and athletes and officials were left to feel the heat. In a plea for tolerance and understanding, our team doctor spoke to the Sydney Morning Herald for an article headlined *'Appeal to Lift Threats'* on June 5:

"Olympic officials yesterday appealed for the end to a campaign of threats and insults against members of the Olympic team. Team doctor Brian Corrigan said it was intolerable and un-Australian for young sportsmen and women to be called traitors for wanting to compete at Moscow – even by their own Prime Minister. He did not understand how Prime Minister Malcolm Fraser could put so much pressure on young athletes. 'It is grossly unfair,' he said. 'Athletes have never started a war, only politicians.' Both competitors and officials have been abused in the street and on the telephone since the federal government's call for them to reconsider going to Moscow."

The Australian Swimming Union continued to publicly back our mission to Moscow as we gathered for our training camp in Sydney from June 15. Training camps had not been a positive experience for me in the past, but this time I was looking forward to being in a closed environment among teammates away from the noise and controversy.

We were teenagers. Aussie kids with our hearts set on racing at the Olympic Games. I felt committed and psyched on the day our 22-strong Australian Olympic swim team assembled at the Dee Why Surfrider Motel on the Northern Beaches of Sydney.

One Rule for the Boys ...

Compassion, team-building and a feeling of belonging should have been the order of the day, but management had a few surprises waiting for us.

The female and male swimmers and coaches were separated for the pre-Olympic training camps with the males getting to stay at the far more luxurious hotel by the beach, while we stayed at a far less salubrious motel down the road.

Evening dining would be together at the men's hotel, and breakfast would be at the respective hotels. Really? The 'womenfolk' on their own in the current climate? We were such a small team, the boys aged 17 to 22, the girls 15 to 18; was there any real need to separate us, I wondered?

We arrived at the three-storey motel, home for the next two weeks. After bumping our bulging suitcases along bleak corridors, we found our door and pushed it open: it was 3x3m, with two beds aligned on either wall, a table by the window and a small stand-up cupboard in the corner by the door. Washing facilities were down the hall. We each placed our bags on our assigned beds. I collapsed on the bed, head in my hands. This is what 'the girls' were worth. The boys had the beach. Déjà-vu memories of Montreal and Edmonton came flooding back.

It wasn't just the accommodation. We were back to daily weigh-ins for the women's team, each morning the same routine: lined up, weighed and scrutinised. At least now the weigh-ins were at our motel away from the boys but an ounce gained was the subject of whispers around pool deck.

I watched as laxatives were taken in time for weigh-ins to make sure the dial was on the ounce. The anxiety and denigration wore heavily on all the girls. We heard no talk of any weigh-ins for the male swimmers.

The exercise was neither meaningful nor based on sound scientific research and, sadly, the reaction of our coaches and managers overshadowed our good work in the pool. It felt like Montreal '76 all over again for some of us: four years on, at 17, we were now among the oldest girls on the squad. No lessons had been learned.

A New Plan

Separating the men and women's teams in the pool proved complicated, especially because coaching becomes more specific and requires a closer relationship between the guide and the athlete at the elite level. We were far shy of the ratio of one coach to five swimmers prescribed by our former head coach, Forbes Carlile.

Bill Sweetenham would be my Olympic team coach at the newly built, indoor Warringah Swimming Centre. He was an experienced hand. Tough and unrelenting, Bill had similar qualities to my first coach. He was inspiring and told it straight.

We clicked immediately. The doubts were put to rest as a squad of the 18 who had made it through the political maelstrom bonded as a unit.

Even in that bubble, we were not deaf to the noise outside as the government kept up its campaign to stop the plane taking off to Moscow. We were constantly on the pay phone at the pool to family checking that all was well at home. The threats were still being made and everyone was worried about what might happen.

Then news came through that the AOF had caved into government pressure and would hold another vote on its decision to send a team to Moscow. The date was set for June 19.

In typically brash style, head coach Bill Sweetenham told us to get back to work. "All will be well," he told the team. We doubted him and it seemed the other coaches, Joe King and some of the home coaches who came to the training camp, did too. We were on tenterhooks for the next three days and some of that translated to poolside banter that could either be interpreted as a psychological strategy or a damaging distraction, depending on how the athlete chose to respond.

My teammate Rosy Brown was talented, diligent and trained amazingly hard. I admired her. We had been on teams before and often roomed together. Like me, she had recently returned from the US and a couple of our races coincided. We were both training under Bill's guidance and had just completed a tough series in the pool when he said how thrilled he was with our times and demeanour in the water. He shared the good news with the other coaches.

I was about to push off the wall for a swim-down after the hard set when one of the other coaches asked him, "So, who do you think will win in Moscow?" I sank lower in the water in an effort to stay out of view and strained to hear the reply. "I bet Rosy …" Bill replied. There was no mention of me. I'll show 'em, I thought. Calm washed over me down the next lap. Perhaps I had overheard wrong; or perhaps it was his way of shaking me up.

We were all on edge. The AOF decision on whether we would go to the Games was looming.

Flag or No Flag

The manager summoned us to a meeting. His words were blunt and sad: "Linda [Hanel] will not be travelling to Moscow with us. We have put her on the flight back to Melbourne today."

My roommate from the Moscow Spartakiade the year before and fellow 200m butterfly ace was gone. I felt dumbfounded and crestfallen.

I knew that she had been struggling and now realised just how much. She had left without us being able to say goodbye, another victim in a game of political football.

The viciousness of the boycott debate had taken its toll yet again.

The manager went on to explain that since the vote, and because of the mounting pressures and unrest of the Australian public, all Olympic departures were to be made in secret. Only close family and friends would be allowed to farewell us. He said that all teams had been told to leave Australia for Moscow as soon as possible and our departure was being brought forward to the next day, with our training camp continuing in Vittel, France, before heading to Moscow a week later.

Silence marked the training session that followed, our arms turning over only through habit. We had just been told that we were to sneak out of the country like thieves and vagabonds. We understood. The latest vote had reignited the hostility towards the team.

The AOF compromise to the government was that the team would march behind the Olympic flag in the opening ceremony, not the Australian flag, which would have been dipped in honour of a communist regime at loggerheads with the world.

However, unlike many of the other participating Western nations, the AOF maintained that for any Australian athlete who made the victory dais, the national flag and the national anthem would be played, as reported by the *Sydney Morning Herald* on June 20, 1980.

Polls now showed 52% against us going to Moscow. The opposition leader asked the prime minister to "stop bullying athletes" and give them the full support of the government. Fraser dug his heels in again and kept up his 'don't go' missive to sporting codes.

We would be the first and still to this day the last Australian Olympic team to leave the country in secret without an official send-off.

Chapter 16
It's a Man's World

"All animals are equal, but some animals are more equal than others."
– George Orwell

There had been four years of waiting, training and building up. The last six months of indecision, worry and concern had sapped our attention and energy.

Boarding the flight to Europe finally meant we were actually going to the Games. No turning back! Taking off to compete for your country overseas is special. There's that moment when the plane rises above the clouds and the light streams in. It was really happening. The Games were two weeks away. No more hiding. The athletes' truth is race day!

While we faced constant turbulence, it was all plain sailing for our competitors in the East. They must have been rubbing their hands at our plight.

It was July 2, 1980, two days earlier than our scheduled departure to avoid a security storm at Sydney Kingsford Smith Airport.

We'd been told to be discreet but leaving 'in secret' wasn't quite what we'd imagined. Dressed in our green skirts/trousers and cream shirts, with mandatory green-and-yellow striped tie and blazers tucked away in our bags for fear of attracting attention, we filed into the departure hall with our families and friends there to greet us alongside those members of the media who had been tipped off.

"The familiar green blazer may have been missing but there was no mistaking Australia's Olympic swimmers at Sydney Airport yesterday when they left for Moscow via France. The squad – like all other Australian representatives taking part in the Olympics – had been asked by the Australian Olympic Federation not to wear their uniforms for two reasons – to keep them in good condition for the official opening ceremony and for security."

('Swimmers Go, but No Blazer of Glory', Sydney Morning Herald, *Wednesday July 2)*

Now reduced to 17 swimmers, two coaches and two managers, we were all thrilled to be on our way at last. My parents had purchased tickets to Moscow but like other swimming parents had cancelled their trip, maintaining that the lack of tourists would make an impact on the political situation without preventing athletes from competing. At the last moment, they asked if I wanted them to go. I did, but with too much uncertainty swirling around, I told them that I needed total concentration and would worry about them if they made the journey. They understood but I knew they were disappointed.

Having crowd support had always given me a boost but while saddened, I had agreed that it was for the best. My parents had been to every major global and regional championship I had ever swum in, but they would be back home watching on TV this time.

On our way through the terminal, we were pulled aside by reporters. Our answers were straight to the point: we were proud to be Australian and to represent our country. My seven-year-old brother, William, clung round my neck and refused to let go. It was always hard to say goodbye but there was excitement in the air this time. Families and swimmers had lived through a terrible time and it was a great relief for all of us to know that the plane was about to take off. My parents were never overly indulgent when it came to expressing their feelings, a trait I inherited, so it took me by surprise when they presented me with a stuffed koala. Ever since Dawn Fraser gave Shane Gould a cuddly kangaroo toy on her way to the podium in Munich, a stuffed kangaroo had been our mascot. A koala was different.

Qantas flight 15 to Frankfurt, Germany, took off at 2:30 p.m. Seated in the non-smoking section, we managed to organise sleeping space on the floor between the rows and across the seats with the arm-rests up. I laid out the woollen blankets provided by the airline, made a bed between the rows of four and wedged myself in, ready for a long sleep.

At the other end, there would be a 400 km bus trip from Frankfurt in Germany to our training camp in Vittel. In my mind, the journey was sorted, settled and nothing to fret about—until mealtime. When the trays came round, there were no bread rolls and the obvious carbohydrates, like potatoes and dessert, had been removed. Protein was served. The girls looked from side to side and noticed that the boys and staff had the lot.

We asked the crew if we could have something more and were told that they had been given strict orders not to serve us. We didn't understand at first, and then realised that they only meant us, the girls. Denied the liberty of a night out on previous trips, we were now denied a decent, rounded meal.

The obsession with diet had gone too far, we thought. As the hours ticked by, my stomach was growling but the flight attendants carried out their orders to the letter. By the time we arrived in Frankfurt, the girls were famished but the boot camp was not over for us yet. The 'nil by mouth' instruction lasted another six hours on the bus to Vittel. We arrived fatigued, hungry and angry.

Forty hours from Sydney, we scrambled off the bus to explore the luxurious Club Med and Spa Resort in Vittel. The venue had been changed at the last minute due to security risks, and this was a real treat.

Letter to My Family: July 8, 1980, Vittel, France

Dear Mum, Dad & all,

Well we finally made it to Vittel after 40 hours flying and a 5h30 min bus ride. Vittel is a small town of 2,000 people and Club Med occupies most of it. There are three hotels here that belong to Club Med: 'The Grand', 'L'Hermitage', and the 'Nouvelle'. The Grand is the central hotel where most late-night activities are held. Luckily, we got the best deal. Our rooms are old but spacious and the view is overlooking the golf course. Everyone is very nice to us, although not many speak English.

I am still training hard and my times are coming down and I am feeling better in the water (we are still doing the same mileage). I think I start cutting back (tapering) next week. I swam my first 800m for a time trial. I felt ok. It was the 4th day since our arrival and I was suffering from jet lag. Last night Bill gave us 50x100 metres on 1 min 20 (depart). He said he would take off two 100's for every one under 1 min 5 sec. I held mine around 1 min 4.8 seconds (1:04.8).

The weather was very cold last week but hopefully it will get better. The food is really nice here but everything is either too spicy or cooked in garlic – too much, and it gives me indigestion when I am swimming. It would be a great place for a holiday though!

We are going out to eat lunch at some castle today, so it should be good. As usual we are not doing much except swimming, sleeping and eating, but not too much! I only have one complaint about this place and that is there are no washing facilities, but I suppose the bath is big enough.

I am sharing a room with Lisa [Forrest] again (same as in Sydney training camp) and I am sure we will be together again in Moscow, which is good because now we get a few privileges, as all the other girls were out of the room at 1.30pm with the boys watching the steeplechase when they were supposed to be in the room. The girls were then ALL LOCKED IN OUR ROOMS FOR 6 HOURS. The boys, however, were allowed to stay and watch the steeplechase. Ridiculous but that is the stupid management.

We are leaving here next Sunday (13th July), one day early to go to Darmstadt (Germany) where the US team trained for the World Championships in 1978. It is 30 minutes from Frankfurt Airport.

I was going to ring you yesterday, but you can only ring from the post office and only at a certain time. Unfortunately, I missed out but will try and ring tomorrow.

Love Michelle

P.S. HAPPY 8th BIRTHDAY WILLIAM

The Village Gates

Flying through Soviet air space to Moscow one week later, we peered out of the small, grimy plane windows to see if we could see the lights of the city, but it was all trees, trees and more trees.

The unchanging, monotonous yet entrancing landscape sent my mind on a fast flight through the past eight months since my final exams at school: the move to Nashville, the intensity of the work, the longing for home, the constant calls and the letters sent. The boycott drama had been the last of the temptations to throw in the towel. However, the courage, blessing and humility of my new friends at NAC had helped to keep me strong.

We were coming into land and it was time to switch off distractions and plug into the Nashville positivity I had tapped into during my time with the team there. Even though I had left behind a hostile and unfortunate situation, I still had some even bigger hurdles to conquer.

Olympic laurels were not going to fall in our laps. The Eastern Bloc countries had an uninterrupted training program, and an army of East German girls awaited. It was three per nation per event. Boycott or not, nothing would make a difference on that score in any women's event.

My memories of muscular girls in Montreal four years earlier had not faded. But by 1980 the tide had turned, not in the 200m, but in the event I had only taken up after Montreal, the 800m freestyle, with two world records under my belt. At 17, I was wiser and was the Western world's number one threat to GDR dominance in the pool in Moscow.

The plane rattled and swayed on its descent to the newly built Sheremetyevo International Airport. We had changed into our dress uniforms with green-and-gold-striped Olympic blazer, the Australian coat of arms on the left pocket, and the words 'Australian Olympic Team 1980' embossed in gold letters below it. The dream would now be an Olympic reality.

Russia, then the core of the Union of Soviet Socialist Republics (USSR), is a land of great contrasts. Its capital, Moscow, famous for its Bolshoi Ballet, the Moscow Circus, St. Basil's, Red Square and other iconic institutions, buildings and places, is also grey, bedecked in cold monolithic buildings and divided by wide, charmless boulevards.

Sport was one of the realms that had flourished behind the Iron Curtain. Under the umbrella of 'physical education', naturally talented athletes were spotted from an early age, plucked out and prepared for the ultimate stage, the Olympic Games, the vehicle for showing the world that their system was better and infallible. East Germany and other countries in the Soviet Bloc followed the same model.

At the airport, I noticed a stark contrast with Montreal. While there were some army tanks when we landed, the heavy machine guns that guarded and surrounded us in Montreal four years earlier after the Munich massacre were nowhere to be seen. The presence of stern-faced soldiers, many carrying less-imposing guns, was enough to suggest that the safety fears raised in the boycott debate were heavily overdone. Who was going to attempt anything here in the most militarised state in the world?

Security was unlikely to be an issue though it would keep us busy for a while after arrival. The airport had been opened in May but everything felt and smelt so new that it seemed as though the construction had finished yesterday, the white-tiled walls dotted with the colour of Olympic signage. The airport was also reserved for Olympic traffic only, with VIP lanes to the right and the rest of us, the athletes, to the left.

We had started the day with a 6 a.m. workout before taking the five-hour flight to Moscow and then after a lengthy security process at the airport, there was a 90-minute bus ride to the accreditation centre next to the Olympic village. We wouldn't be official until our Games ID cards were attached to a lanyard and placed around our necks.

Fatigue was creeping in and we were all in need of wholesome sustenance. We were shown refreshments in the self-serve fridges: water, Fanta or Pepsi, the newest sponsor after Coca-Cola pulled out because of the boycott. Carbonated sugar drinks for us were enough to blow the caps off the coaching staff, but they were just what I needed. However, one gulp and I knew the contents were not what we expected. It was a drink and it was fizzy, but it tasted nothing like a Fanta. We all opted for water after that.

At the gates of the Olympic village, we reached the last of the security checks for the day. A guard checked my accreditation and started rummaging through my handbag. He pulled out a white envelope, stared at the writing on it and hoisted it high in the air. Raising his voice, he treated me to a piercing stare and repeated "dis, dis, dis". It was a question. "What is dis?" More guards rushed in. I couldn't think for a moment but the problem dawned on me when he pointed at the name written on the envelope.

I laughed but they didn't seem to find it funny. The envelope was addressed to Jimmy Carter.

"English swimmer," I said.

"Nyet, nyet, dis, who dis?" he insisted, pointing at the name. In a clipped Russian accent, he read, "Carter. Jimmy Carter!"

More guards rushed in to take a look at the tricky object. I didn't dare look away. My teammates were watching, a slither away from falling about on the floor. I imagined what it might be like for Jimmy when he arrived with the British team. Keeping a straight face, I waited. They talked among themselves and eventually, the guard said "Okay" and handed back the envelope and the bag. I was free to go.

The Olympic village was big, bold and imposing. Eighteen buildings, each 16 storeys high. All identical. The enormity startled me. Divided into three clusters of six buildings, this was to be Moscow's new housing estate after the Games. The prefabricated blocks of two- to three-bedroom apartments were all the same; kitchen areas that were not functional except for a kettle, the bathroom and toilet so small you could hardly fit in. Only two elevators serviced the building, when they worked. The two beds, side tables and a cupboard were a very snug fit in each bedroom.

It was tight but nothing like the one apartment that 14 of us had squeezed into in Montreal. Compared to that, this was spacious!

Designed to host 14,000 athletes and administrators, the village was 20 km southwest of the city centre in an oasis of its own. During the Games, it would be home to a melting pot of people and cultures. Running down the middle of the buildings was a vast open promenade that also served as the central thoroughfare for the village transport—a two-carriage 'auto train' to everywhere, including the international zone with its shops and the dining halls.

There was a 24-hour medical centre, a cultural centre with a cinema and two TV rooms, a reading room, a 'phonotheque' (a place to listen to records), a dance hall, a games room and a discotheque, all free of charge. There was to be no popping into town. A small shopping centre adjacent to the dining halls would have to do. There was a telephone exchange centre to make and receive calls, as well as telefaxes. However the main attraction was an ice-cream parlour: morozhenoye (Мороженое), the Russian word for ice cream, was the first local one we learned.

The hosts, always the largest delegation, had a record 560 athletes, 100 more than the Soviet Union had in Montreal. The mighty GDR (East Germany) was the second largest delegation with 364 competitors.

Despite never boasting big team numbers, Australia had 176 team members, including 123 athletes—96 of them male and just 27 females, with the long road to equality stretching far into the future. (Paris 2024 is set to be the first 50:50 gender participation in Olympic history.) We only had three doctors, two physios and a masseur for the entire team.

The addition of women's rowing, basketball and handball to the Montreal Games, and more recently women's hockey into the Moscow Games, had increased female participation, but it was still limited to only nine of the 21 sports. This ratio of just over one in four was magnified in the village where only two blocks (N1 and N3) were assigned as the 'Women's Quarters'.

The protocol that prohibited men from accessing the women's quarters included this quaint phrase about the female houses: "... though not isolated from the rest, they will be off limits to men."

Meanwhile, 16 blocks of 80 apartments were allocated to team administration, medical officers and male competitors. The Australian women's team had been assigned two floors in building N1, and on the other side of the central promenade in N2 were the men's quarters and the Australian headquarters.

We were lucky to be in the closest buildings to the entrance, the international zone and dining halls, which made our coaches happy as they were concerned about us walking too much, fearful we would have sore legs.

The window of our two-bedroom apartment opened to the 'Square of Nations'. It was customary for each nation to fly their flag in the village throughout the Games, and a flag-raising ceremony was conducted as each team arrived. Even though certain governments had asked that their national flag not be flown in ceremonies, the village became a spectacle of colour and life, with a blend of official and unofficial flags brought to the Games in the suitcases of athletes proud to display their national colours and symbols.

The Olympic Games is the only forum in the world where participants from every nation (130 countries back in 1980 and today, 205) can come to participate and live together irrespective of nationality, race, colour or creed.

For optimal performance, conditions should be as stress-free and streamlined as possible. We had learned at the Spartakiade the year before that conditions in Moscow were far from our Western 'norms' and that these Games were not going to be a walk in the park. Our beds, our food, the transport, the venues and even our schedules would not be in our control. This is a feature of all Games but it was exacerbated in Moscow by language and cultural barriers that required us to be flexible and understanding, and sometimes questioning.

However, arriving five days before the start of racing had helped us to familiarise ourselves with the geography and timetables of the place. Our first supper said it all. It was well-intentioned, but everyday essential ingredients such as meat and vegetables were simply missing.

Part 4
Against the Odds

Chapter 17
Mind Games

"Victorious warriors win first and then go to war, while defeated warriors go to war first and then seek to win."
– Sun Tzu, Chinese philosopher and military strategist

With a hit-and-miss supper and a straw pillow to sleep on, my first night confirmed I was back in Moscow but nonetheless the first full day in the Olympic city couldn't be anything but special: July 15, my 18th birthday.

At 6:30 a.m., just before dawn, four days out from the Games' opening ceremony, we were off for our first swim in the Olimpiyskiy Pool with its floor-to-high-ceiling glass frontage. Our destiny would play out in its lanes over seven days from July 20.

We were here for racing, not partying. A birthday, whatever the number, was no free pass to an easy day in the pool. Down corridors, through locker rooms and out onto the deck, the smell of wet cement was pervasive. The sharp bits of unfinished mortar between the tiles in the pool were further evidence that the builders had just left.

Despite that, it was clean, pristine and felt familiar. I stood for a moment visualising a full crowd in the stands, imagining the silence that falls just before the gun goes off. It was a dream no longer, we were living what we had worked for.

Bill Sweetenham, the head coach and the man guiding me and the other distance freestyle girls, was browsing through the schedule when he called me over. It was six days to the 200m butterfly; seven to the 400m freestyle; then, after the rest day and the penultimate session of finals, the 800m in the closing session of the Games in the pool was 11 days from now.

Time to taper! Or so I thought. In my head, the 200m butterfly was my first shot at gold. It was also my favourite event. That would mean starting to ease back on the workload, some sharpening, fast 50m sprints and feeling good.

"No. Not yet," Bill insisted. "We've got the 800 on the last day." Translation: the

4 km sessions would continue until the last days of competition, and through my first two swims.

He knew the 200 'fly was my pet event and that it was my birthday, so maybe he would think again and go easy on me, just today, I was hoping. Who was I kidding?! Twenty minutes after the rest of the team had boarded the bus for the village after their workout, I was still swimming up and down. The athlete-coach game of attrition began: the athlete tests the coach's resolve, and the coach refuses to budge: "... keep going!" The athlete backs down, does the work knowing full well that the coach has thought it through.

I mumbled at being last out; he stood firm. I thought I knew best; Bill, just as nervous as me about the days ahead, put on a show of assurance and control. I was so mad—but trained to obey.

"Happy birthday, Michelle," said Bill after the session. "I'm very pleased with you. I really think you can win." There were smiles back and forth. The code of silence kicked in. A good but normal start to a day at the office.

Back at the village dorm room, birthday wishes and a gift from the head of the Olympic village had been placed on my bed. I'd been given a raccoon tail for my 14th birthday at the Montreal Games and it was still hanging on my pinboard at home. On arrival in Moscow, we'd received a 'goody bag' with a face towel and some make-up; not that I wore make-up, but it was fun to try it on. The new box was wrapped and lined in red velvet, inside a diamond-shaped object made of coloured glass: a big bottle of perfume, Russian style.

Phil Coles, the head of the Australian delegation, had asked a few of us to go to the international zone for a photo shoot after lunch, before heading to the bus for our afternoon workout.

To my surprise, they presented me with a Misha bear, the official mascot for the Games, for my birthday. The media back home ran pictures of me and the Soviet bear and me and my koala, with headlines along the lines of 'Rival Bear Hugs for Birthday Girl Ford'.

All the challenges of the past few years had been solid preparation for taking everything in my stride—the straw pillows, a toilet cubicle so small the door crunched your knees, dough balls for bread that were the highlight of most meals, and a daily change of travel times to the pool because "the bus got lost".

Others were thrown by those things. I'd learned to accept the roadblocks—climb over them or walk around them—my eyes were fixed squarely on the mission. Block out the noise, I kept saying to myself. After another hefty set done in the pool, I boarded the bus and noticed my coach smiling at me.

His relaxed demeanour and confidence in me were reassuring. I believed he had my back and had worked out the best winning strategy. My opposition was a team looking for podium sweeps—a trifecta—in every race. Bill and I had to believe and be smarter.

After three weeks on the road, we were excited to receive letters from home, even though they'd been written at least a week before we'd got to read them. In the village post office, for a high price, we could also place an operator-assisted call home or send a telex to a nominated post office number in Australia for forwarding or 'calling through'.

Our manageress would collect all incoming letters and telexes for us and place them on our beds. Envelopes addressed to 'Michelle Ford, Olympic Village, Moscow' delivered mostly good luck messages from friends and family, while telexes were simple notes like "Good luck Michelle STOP"; "We are all cheering for you love STOP". They were heart-warming.

In the midst of piles of encouragement, a few different types of letters slipped through: I was "un-Australian" and "a traitor". Didn't they get it?! We'd come to an Olympic Games, not a political rally. I was proud to be Australian and proud to represent my country. I understood why some had opted not to come to Moscow but I didn't understand why we were being subject to this hatred. I ripped those letters in two and threw them in the bin.

My teammates were feeling hurt by the onslaught, too. It was so unfair but for the most part we bottled it up and blocked out the noise in an effort to focus on performing well. We'd come so far and weren't about to give up.

At the Pool

Back at the pool for one last session on July 19 before the opening ceremony, our time slot coincided with the team in blue tracksuits and swimsuits with the white DDR written large on them. Bill fixed a peripheral, eagle eye on them, his hand in his pocket holding a stopwatch. They'd been watching and monitoring us too, while the discreet filming of our workouts by the Russians didn't escape our notice.

We strolled casually around the pool, made our camp and started stretching. I purposely turned my back on the pool to show the East Germans I had no interest in them. I wasn't going to let them know I cared. I had my game face on.

They acted in a similar fashion. One by one they exited the pool, picked up their gear and headed for the changing rooms, but their coaches remained on deck. Bill noticed and switched the whole squad around, placing the male sprinters in the lanes nearest the East German observers and the distance squad furthest away. His instructions were the quietest I had ever heard. The watchers departed.

When my next 4 km session was over and the rest of the squad was gone, Bill pulled me to one side and spoke to me as if he didn't want to be overheard, even though there was nobody around! He told me that having watched the East German girls, he had total confidence in me.

He said, "The 200 'fly will be your toughest race, I believe, but I am confident with your 400 and 800m freestyle." His timing and message were impeccable: just what I needed. It was confirmation and reassurance that I could do it. My self-belief soared. Shoulders back, I got changed with a big smile on my face. Days before the start of racing, it was all coming together just in time. I was swimming well and felt strong in the water.

Bill and I were on the same page. We understood each other and that it would only work if we were one. We both knew the East Germans would try to own every race. The coach was clearly nervous at this late stage in the game and wanted reassurance that we were on track for me to deliver what he believed I was capable of. He set me an 8x100m test set off a short rest and asked me to hold 1.03 splits every 100m for an eight-minute, 24 second set. With the set done, no words were needed. He just smiled.

The sun shone that morning in the pool even though the sky outside the giant windows of the Olimpiyskiy Pool was grey. With rain threatening and the odd squall blowing through, I wondered about the opening ceremony that evening.

Bill's instruction rang loudly in everyone's ears: those who were swimming the first day were not to march. My first event was not until the second day, so the decision was down to me, as were any consequences of spending hours on your feet late into the night.

The Opening Ceremony —Central Lenin Stadium

Olympic fever had Moscow in its grip. The government had spent the equivalent of US$2 billion, a Games record, to prepare the stadiums, village and infrastructure. The Olympic Games were to be their showcase to the world, and with this, the first broadcasts of the Soviet Union to the Western world. The Games were also estimated to have incurred a deficit of just over US$1 million.

In protest of the Afghanistan invasion, the Australian team would not march behind our national flag. Instead, our joint flag-bearers, Denise Boyd from athletics and my swimming teammate Max Metzker, carried the Olympic flag. It was the first time we had two flag-bearers, male and female. However, agreement had been reached between the Australian Government and the Australian Olympic Federation for the national flag to be flown for any team member who made the podium.

To this day, you can read many references which say our flag was not flown and a neutral flag replaced it at medal ceremonies, but that was not the case. As all Australians who made the podium in the pool or cheered us on will testify, we were honoured by the sight of the Australian Blue Ensign rising up the flagpole in Moscow. Sadly, athletes from Britain and other nations had to compete under the symbol of neutrality.

Since Montreal 1976, I had wanted to relive the excitement of the opening ceremony—the thrill of walking into the stadium, the adrenaline rush, and the sights, sounds and colours of all the teams. It was unforgettable.

On the other hand, I knew that the final approach to racing was a critical time: make or break for some. Five hours of standing around would be long, too long, perhaps. Would it jeopardise my performance or lift me up? I had lived through a lot to get to Moscow but the thought of throwing it all away for the thrill of marching scared me.

The ceremony was also going to be longer than usual. Until 1980, Olympic opening ceremonies only consisted of the parade of nations and rituals associated with the official opening of the Games. However, the Soviet Union wanted to put on a spectacle to impress the rest of the world and an artistic performance was included after the ceremonial parts.

The boycott frenzy had piled on the pressure from Australia: only medals would send a strong message to the government and prove to the public that coming to the Games was the right decision. The fact was that we had to perform to save face, and the swim team would be first off the blocks.

In the canteen with teammates, I explained that I was going to watch the ceremony from our delegation headquarters on our only TV. Although athletes could move into the stands to watch the 'show'—the theatrical part of the ceremony—there would be a lot of standing about and I didn't want to risk that draining me ahead of the heavy lifting to come in the pool.

I had just finished speaking when a voice came flying across the table, loud and clear. Peter Evans, a breaststroke specialist from Perth and making his Olympic debut, said, "It is a once-in-a-lifetime experience, Michelle." It would be twice in a lifetime for me, but Peter was insistent: "You cannot miss this for the world." He wouldn't let up and his enthusiasm began to unravel my logic as my emotions took over.

I changed my mind. My gold satin marching uniform, what we called our Wonder Woman outfit, lay dormant in my suitcase ready for the occasion but thankfully word had come through from headquarters that it was too cold to wear a short-sleeved dress, so we girls were told to march in our travel uniform.

We were just about to leave when my roommate, Lisa Forrest, ran back to grab some small Australian flags that she had brought with her from home. We'd been told we weren't allowed to take cameras or flags, but that didn't stop us. We all agreed that if we couldn't march behind the giant Australian flag, we would wave the little ones!

The Australian team was in line to walk out immediately after Greece, which always leads the parade of athletes in recognition of having been the birthplace of the modern Olympics in 1896.

Following Australia was the team from Afghanistan—the country at the epicentre of the boycott. It was a conundrum. They were there but all my international teammates from Nashville—Americans and Canadians—were not. It was a cruel reminder that the athletes were pawns used by all sides in the political game of chess.

Diary Entry – July 19, 1980

We awoke at 6.30 am which we will continue throughout the competition. The weather is not looking too prosperous for the first day of the Games, so I found it difficult to decide whether to march. I was about to say I would not march but while I was waiting for the bus the wind was blowing quite strong and I found out that our teammate Max would be the flag carrier. I forgot about the decision while we did our workout of 4000 meters. I felt good in the water and Bill was in a great mood because he saw the East German girls and became completely confident in me. He also said that my 200 'fly would be the toughest race which I suppose is true. Anyway, we will see.

Lunch was the same as usual – horrible – the same food is served up for every meal, but I think breakfast is the worst.

The opening ceremony was fantastic. That same feeling once again raced through me, and I was on cloud nine. The effects were spectacular. Everyone knew they would put on a good show. We were only away for 5 hours and did not stand much at all. I am so glad I marched, and I am so glad we came to the Games.

We all jumped on a bus and came back to the village. Georgina and I had dinner and went back to the rooms (headquarters) to see the end on TV.

Must go now 21:10 – Hope everyone does well. M

Chapter 18
The Blue Suits

"It's hard to beat a person who never gives up."
– Babe Ruth

There's no feeling in a swimmer's life quite like the first time you walk on to the deck of an Olympic pool on the opening day of competition.

Result sheets are a blank canvas but there's a buzz of anticipation in the air. Nerves and excitement are tangible as coaches clutch stopwatches and swimmers find their place in the melting pot of warm-up with every stroke, distance, plan and pace seeking its place in the melee.

Years of effort, physical and emotional energy, and the dedication of athletes, coaches, parents, family and close friends will be poured into a sparkling pool.

I stood on the Moscow pool deck looking across towards the East German team.

There was more to the difference between us and them than doping. The Eastern Bloc had its own interpretation of the Olympic Charter's Rule 26 on amateurism. They were a highly tuned professional outfit—a machine—not a team of individual 'amateurs' scrambling to do the best with the backing of parents and often the goodwill and commitment of underpaid coaches and unpaid helpers like we were. They looked invincible. The money, the science, the technology and even their swimsuits were more advanced. They had an adequate number of coaches per athlete, their own physios, psychologist, dieticians, massage therapist and doctors—anyone and everyone to service the athlete. We had none of that. The disparity was blatant.

Just as we had been in Montreal four years earlier, it was obvious that Australia was behind the curve and at a disadvantage. Our poverty of progress in developing a professional system to match that of the GDR and, in other ways, the USA, was something Forbes Carlile had pointed out before he quit as head coach prior to the second of our three training camps on the way to Moscow.

Some of the GDR girls were known to us, some were new. Of the six teenagers who accounted for 11 victories at the 1976 Games in Montreal, only two made it to Moscow. Years later, we would come to understand that there was a huge price to pay for many of the GDR girls, both those who made the podium and others who never competed internationally and were unknown to us. It all came at a cost to generations of opponents as well.

The Olympics is not just about the fittest athletes and best-laid plans, but also those who have the strongest minds and the ability to accept and adapt in spirit and attitude at speed. I didn't think of it in the same language back then, but the way Bill Sweetenham would later describe what he had subtly been bringing out of me sums it up perfectly: it was time to switch from defence mode into attack mode.

Notes that I had kept from coaches and others down the years had a common theme: "Michelle, you underestimate what you are capable of" and "You don't know your own strength!" The qualities my grandad had seen in me at 10 were alive, kicking and about to be put to the test.

The smug look on the faces of the East German coaches riled Bill but his poker face reminded me to wear mine. With my metaphoric blinkers in place, I shut out anything that was not in front of me or that might spook me. I focused on the one thing in my control: me.

Diary Entry
Swimming Day 1 – July 20, 1980

Well, today began with an overcast sky which is not unusual.

Because I did not have to compete today, I could sleep in and go to the pool at 9am for the start of the heats (10am to 11.45). I ate breakfast in our room this morning. Before leaving for the pool, I decided to go and collect my first-day issue stamps.

Everyone did quite well but there is only one individual final tonight, the men's 200m butterfly. After the heats, I got in and did a 3000-metre workout which felt better than yesterday. We left the pool at 12.30pm and headed back to the village, a 40-minute bus ride. We went straight to lunch which did improve slightly with more variety, and then back to the room. The other girls had come back earlier so they were asleep when we came in. I slept from 2 to 3.20pm.

We left again for the pool at 4.45pm and boy was it raining. By the time I got to the bus, my wet gear was even leaking. I am sure it was the heaviest rain since we have been here.

I did about 600 metres tonight and felt fantastic. Unfortunately, Mark Kerry and Glenn Patching did not make finals in the 100 Backstroke. Phil Hubble (my English friend and training mate from Nashville) came 2nd in the 200 fly which was great, and I'm sure he was pleased. It was sad when he had the Olympic flag in the ceremony instead of the Union Jack (British flag) for the victory ceremony. I did not stay to watch the 4x100 women's medley relay because I wanted to have a good rest for my 200 metres butterfly tomorrow. I got back at 8.20pm, had dinner and went to bed.

The others are still not back, but I better go as it is 9.30 and I must wake at 6.30am ready for tomorrow!'

Nite. M

Swimming Day 2 – July 21, 1980

Three world records, with their first gold in the only female final … I awoke to the news that the East German women had dominated the opening day.

Today, it was my turn.

200m Butterfly Heats

The first of my six heats and finals in Moscow was a flashback to Montreal: I was in the last heat alongside Andrea Pollack, the reigning Olympic champion, the 'mega-armed' girl I had met on the bus as a 13-year-old in 1976.

My nerves were firing but I was composed, calm and confident. I loved the 200 'fly and after only a few strokes, I realised I was back in my best shape. By the halfway turn, I was neck and neck with Pollack. I'd been trained from a young age to 'explode' down the third lap and found myself passing my opponent with some ease. "Slow down, slow down" was running through my mind: this was not the moment, there was no need to build up lactic acid in heats.

'Easy speed' was what I needed: just enough to guarantee a place in the final. First at the last turn, I breezed home as the fastest qualifier for the final in two minutes 12.72, the gauntlet thrown. I leaned over and shook Pollack's hand. I could tell she wasn't pleased. I had the ticket to lane 4. I'd be flanked by three East Germans in 3, 5 and 6.

200m Butterfly Final

Pollack, who had led a podium sweep in Montreal, was back to see if the DDR could deliver all three medals again. The 'call room', where swimmers check in and assemble before a race, was small, with a glass wall and a floor-to-ceiling curtain that separated the preparation area from the main swimming hall on the other side.

With my towel draped over my shoulders and my eyes fixed on the ground, I took a vacant seat. No one talked. No one dared look at the other. This was already the start of the race. Each of us was locked in thought—our game plan was our universe.

A loud cheer from the spectator stands shattered the uneasy silence. Barbara Krause had taken gold in the 100m freestyle, lowering the world record twice in 24 hours.

We were next. Lined up in lane order, Krause's teammates beside me, I glanced out the glass door to see her time. There was a slight nod from the East German girls to each other and then it was back to race-face. My canary-yellow tracksuit in stark contrast to the steely DDR blue, we walked the length of the pool to the starting blocks. I looked up at my teammates over the other side of the pool and felt in control. I knew Australia needed a medal and this was our first chance.

My trainers and tracksuit discarded, I heard my name being called, first in French then English, and struggled out of my t-shirt with the tightness of the neck almost pulling my cap off. After a sharp tug and readjustment, I was set as lane 8 was being announced to the crowd.

There was still time to follow my ritual: my cupped hands splashed cool water over my arms and face. With some of the tension gone, I stood to take my place behind the blocks. I took two deep breaths, did a rub and shake of my arms, a shrug of my shoulders and then waited for the whistle.

"Take your marks …" Bang! Then another whistle.

Agneta Mårtensson of Sweden had false started in lane 8. We were all called back. A second false start would mean disqualification. I recomposed myself and took a few more deep breaths.

In lane 4 as the fastest qualifier, I was caged between Ines Geissler in 5 and Sybille Schönrock in 3, with defending champion Pollack in 6. I'd never heard of the two girls either side of me and had no idea how they would swim the race. Geissler was 17 and Schönrock a week shy of her 16th birthday. Until their Olympic trials, they had never been selected for the GDR. Moscow was their first international competition. They were part of the first generation of GDR swimmers to have flown under the radar until the Olympic year.

There were no mistakes on the second start and we were off. I stuck to the plan, turning within a stroke of them at the 50m mark. Had I gone out too fast? Had they watched my heat and decided to draw me out faster than I had wanted? They would have studied my race tactics and known I was capable of negative-splitting (swimming the second half of a race faster than the first). Taking me out fast would risk my back-end speed.

Geissler led at halfway by half a second under one minute 03, with Schönrock, me and Pollack next through in that order and all within 0.07 of a second of each other. It was fast.

Everyone assumed it would be a GDR sweep. To have a chance of ripping the form guide up, I had to be no further back than my opponent's hips at the 100m mark. Things were looking good but the East Germans seemed to be working as a team:

one would surge, then fall back as another surged and on it went. It felt like being trapped in an accordion.

I stuck to my plan and exploded down the third lap, only to find them doing precisely the same. I held my position, and it was neck and neck into the last turn. The East Germans were powerful off the walls and I found myself behind the girls either side of me upon breaking into stroke. It felt like I was in a test set with the boys back home.

I wasn't wearing goggles but the blurry blue outlines either side of me were clear enough. I had no idea where Pollack was. She was surely close! My body was starting to hurt, something I had rarely felt in a 200 'fly. It hit me like a ton of bricks, a feeling commonly referred to in swimming as like 'a piano falling on your back'.

Twenty metres from home, I screamed inside my head, "Keep going! ... you can do it!"; anything to block out the pain of cramping arms. My stroke shortened. It was the worst I had ever felt in a race but I was within a stroke of the East Germans as we battled for the wall.

I mis-timed my finish and glided in, but at least I'd made it! Looking up at the scoreboard, I wasn't expecting a great result. Yet there it was: bronze, half a second ahead of the defending champion.

Australia's first medal of the Games! The first Olympic medal of my career!

Thrill kills pain at such moments. A weight had been lifted. The Australian team cheered me off the deck on my way to get ready for the ceremony. There was relief on the faces of the coaches and managers, too: for them, medals were the only currency.

Being third means that you walk to the podium at the front of the line-up, so the GDR girls had to look at my yellow tracksuit, a reminder that the blue sweep had been halted. We exchanged no words and they shook my hand with something resembling a half-smile.

I'll never know what they truly thought. Geissler had a best time of 2:15.81 at 16, a touch faster than I was at 13 to earn a place on my first Olympic team. I later learned she had finished in sixth place at the 1979 GDR Nationals, but a year later here she was with gold in an Olympic record of 2:10.44, Schönrock 0.01 of a second away and me a second further back.

Nothing could wipe the smile off my face though. Any medal was an amazing feat. After gold and silver were presented, it was my turn. I stepped on the podium. When the medal was around my neck, my mind was racing, coming to terms with what I'd achieved. No one, not even our media, had given me a chance in this race.

When the GDR anthem started, a tear rolled down my face. There it was, to the left of the two GDR flags—the Australian flag. It was a wonderful sight and a wave of emotion washed through me: I felt sad that my parents could not be there to see it and that my grandfather was no longer with us, but also felt a strong bond to Australia and my fellow citizens despite everything that had happened.

I hoped they would be proud of me.

For me, in this moment, it was more than just an Olympic medal.

The Doping Room

On the victory lap round the pool deck, I was pulled aside. "Michelle, how do you feel seeing the Australian flag up there for the first time?" asked a reporter. I looked down the pool to where he was pointing, with the flag already being taken down and my teammates waving at me. I mumbled something like, "I can't believe it, I can't believe it's really true".

Tears welled and the reporter put his arm around me for a second before our team manager, Peter Bowen-Pain, took hold of my elbow and led me off in the direction of the doping control room. On our way along the deck, I was called up to the media box in the stands for interviews with Channel 7 and ABC Radio.

I was able to articulate my feelings better on air after the first rush of excitement had left me. At some stage, the manager tapped his watch and said firmly, "We only have one hour to sign in for testing, or you will be disqualified!"

On the way there, we passed the team and Bill was waiting. "We need you in the water to warm down," he said with a wave of his hand towards the swim-down pool. I managed a few laps and felt the tension easing in my arms and shoulders but the manager intervened once more. I knew I needed more easing down to swim out the lactic acid but also understood that the doping protocol was critical.

The control room was small and had a toilet cubicle at one end. A few other swimmers were sitting there and a fridge full of drinks was available for those who needed liquid before they could produce a urine sample. Interesting choice, I thought: alongside the fizzy drinks and water was beer. No wonder the guys got back to the village at 2 a.m. after a lengthy stay in doping control!

I had been instructed to avoid the water, and the beer was not for me with the 400m freestyle awaiting me the next morning, so lukewarm Fanta it was, with the fridge more of a cabinet than a cooling device. If it took too long to produce a sample, there was an option of returning to the village's medical centre and sitting it out there.

The first four in every event plus one at random were to be tested. I waited for the East Germans to arrive and when they did, they went straight in, produced a urine sample, presumably, and left. The rest of us were left thinking, "How?!"

Eventually, I was ready. I chose a sample bottle from a row of them with yellow lids and took it to the toilet cubicle, only to realise that I was being followed. A complete stranger had to watch me. Somewhat embarrassed, I asked, "Is this enough?" and was told, "A little more." Task completed, I offered up the container. "No, you must take it back to the desk and put your name on it," the stranger said.

The medical personnel then placed a piece of tape with my name on the bottle. I felt slightly uneasy with the whole thing. I had no idea what would happen to my sample after that. Having been in there almost an hour, I was keen to get back for a proper swim-down but saw that everyone had already left. That was fine by me. I just wanted to get back to the village, eat dinner and get to bed ready for my 400m heats in the morning.

Swimming Day 3 – Tuesday July 23, 1980

The alarm woke me at 6:30 a.m. Rolling over, I felt the pain of muscles that could have done with a proper swim-down and a good massage the night before. I got neither.

My fastest first 100m ever in the 200 'fly had shocked my system into lactic overload on the way home. I had never felt such burning pain in that event before and was mad at myself for allowing the GDR girls to draw me out at their pace, not mine. They'd won a tactical game and I'd broken my golden rule of never allowing others to overwrite my race plan. The 400m would be different, I told myself.

400m Freestyle Heats

After a drink of chocolate milk and two bread rolls for breakfast, I was off to the pool for the heats on my second day of racing. I had a spring in my step from the night before.

However, in warm-up, my arms and shoulders were stiff and sore. I felt lethargic. I would have to swim it out of my system over long, steady laps ahead of the trickiest part of my program. Few swam the 200 'fly/400 free double. In fact, there had only ever been one swimmer in history who made the Olympic 200 'fly podium and won medals in international championship racing over 400m free: Ada Kok, the Dutch star of the 1968 Olympic team who was the first 200m champion to be dubbed 'Madam Butterfly' after winning gold in Mexico City.

My dilemma in Moscow was clear: none of the East Germans were doing my double and so I would be facing a new crop of three fresh girls ready to fire in their DDR suits. My coach knew it and told me to take it easy in the heats by holding back in the first half of the race. I was in the last of three heats with the third East German, the other two having been split by Holland's Annelies Maas, all in four minutes 13-plus seconds.

Off the blocks, I was startled by the fast start of Petra Schneider, the world-record holder in the 400m medley. I knew I'd have to catch her but was determined not to make the same mistake again. At the halfway 200m mark, I was a good body and a half behind the East German but feeling fine, relaxed and holding a solid stroke pattern and count.

Two laps later, heading into the last 100m, I was easily able to catch Schneider and passed her on the way to the wall. I finished on 4:13 as the third fastest through to the final, with Schneider on 4:14 but masking the might she would bring to the final. All three East Germans would be to the left of me, the canary suit sandwiched between the blue suits. The scene was set for 6:30 p.m. finals.

400m Freestyle Final

The warm-up had begun but we were still on a bus weaving through the streets of Moscow. The way looked unfamiliar. The driver seemed lost but there was no way of telling: asking him would have been lost in translation. The transport took us on a different route each time but here we were weaving in and out of the Moscow streets. We were starting to get worried. The finals would start precisely on time and sweat was starting to break out on my forehead. We were 'lost' for over one hour. It seemed to be on purpose.

By the time we got to the pool, warm-up was almost over. I got changed as fast as I could but the competition pool would be emptied in a few minutes before finals began. My opportunity for timed 100s, start practice and pace swims appeared lost, but for Bill. He called me over to the second pool behind the curtain and pointed out that my event was fourth on the program, with the men's 1500m, the longest Olympic race, being before the women's 400m.

The warm-down pool and the diving pool were far from ideal for warming up because of the lack of lane organisation. The warm-down pool was also only one metre deep which made long, easy and uninterrupted swimming difficult, but it was better to use it than have no warm-up at all.

Pulled from pillar to post, our two coaches were trying to stay on top of a difficult situation. Those who were not competing that day had taken an earlier bus to workout before the warm-up period began. They had no idea what had happened to the rest of us.

In the midst of the chaos, the coaches had managed to pull off a small coup: they had borrowed a massage table from another team so they could give massages to those racing in finals that evening. The media ran the story back home highlighting the gap between us and the East Germans:

> *"Australian swim coaches are in a more difficult situation than anyone. Because of the lack of staff (two coaches, a manager and manageress) compared with an East German staff of at least 20, the Aussie coaches have to do all the rubdowns and general preparation work to get swimmers ready for their races. There are four masseurs with the East German team."*
>
> *('Swim Team Fires in a Complaint', Daily Mirror, July 22, 1980)*

I abandoned the idea of having a massage because time was so short. It was more important for me to be able to sit and talk to my coach.

Bill told me, "You need to hold back on the first 100, then begin building from the third lap." Wearing goggles would help me see better across the lanes. With a nod to Carmela Schmidt, the East German nearest to me in lane 4, he concluded: "Let's see you level with her at the 300 metres, this is where the race will be decided." I nodded and went off to the call room, goggles dangling in my hand, towel lapped over my shoulder. The same as the night before: in silence with my eyes down.

Beyond the glass wall, the rafters were being tested as the partisan crowd of 10,000 roared Vladimir Salnikov home in the 1500m freestyle. That final remains one of the most famous in history because Salnikov claimed gold in a world-record time of 14 minutes 58.27, the first sub-15-minute swim in history, with the hosts also taking silver. Our own Max Metzker will always know the answer to the question, "Where were you when Salnikov…?" Max was right there, sprinting from fourth at the last turn to bronze, just 0.19 of a second shy of Andrey Krylov's silver.

I was up next. Behind the blocks, I spat in my goggles to stop them from fogging. As they called my lane, I could hear the Aussie team screaming a chorus of "Go Michelle!" It was energy for the fight.

My start was fast but breaking out of my streamline into my stroke, it was clear that the powerful East Germans had stolen a march on me again. I told myself, "Don't panic, stick to the plan, get into rhythm, stay smooth, strong, long; hold back."

Schneider, in lane 7, had gone out well inside world-record pace, drawing Maas, in lane 5, with her. It wasn't long before her early courage proved to be the end of Dutch hope, with the fast-start tactic the same one that the GDR girls had used on me the night before.

I turned in third place at the 200m mark. Schmidt then made her move and while my 'engine' felt fine, my arms (my 'wheels') started spinning as Ines Diers and Schneider piled on the pressure and opened up clear blue water.

It was a battle for the bronze with Schmidt. Just ahead of her at the last turn, I drove off the wall only to find she'd rocketed off hers and was now up with me in just one push of her powerful legs. It was stroke for stroke all the way home, but I just didn't have the same power left in me.

Diers took gold in an Olympic record of 4:08.76. Schneider was a close second, with Schmidt and me home within a couple of strokes. I didn't look up at the board. I didn't want to know. This was the Olympics, it was about placings, not times, and coming fourth by the swing of an arm was the worst place to be—out of the medals. I turned to congratulate Schmidt but she was already over in lane 6 hugging her teammates. It was the first time I had seen real emotion in the East Germans.

I was glad to be walking away but was then told to show up for doping control. There was no ceremony and no interview this time, but I did have another long stretch in doping control after my swim-down.

My head was down and I was disappointed. The best thing that can happen in those circumstances is to take the focus off yourself for a moment and cheer your teammates on, so before I went to doping control, I stood with the squad cheering our two boys on in the 100m breaststroke final. We leapt up and down when Peter Evans, who had persuaded me to go to the opening ceremony, took bronze, a fingertip from silver and only a hand from the gold medal won by Britain's Duncan Goodhew. Just over a second away, Lindsay Spencer finished sixth. So near, yet so far. That's what the Olympics is all about.

In the village that night, I wrote in my diary:

I was disappointed tonight with my swim, but what made it worse was hearing the Olympic anthem instead of the British anthem when Duncan received his gold medal. That would be worse.

Max and Peter had claimed another two bronze medals for Australia, but gold remained elusive. The fourth day of racing also drew a blank.

Swimming Day 5 – July 24, 1980

The men's 4x100m medley relay final was a belter. The USSR were joint favourites but when Sweden was disqualified for being too hasty on one of the changeovers, Australia was among a wave of the next-closest contenders for top honours, alongside Britain, East Germany, France and Hungary.

The Soviet Union had saved their best quartet for the final but our small team didn't have four reserves to step down after heats. There was just one switch: Glenn Patching was replaced by Mark Kerry on backstroke, with team veteran and 1975 World-Championship backstroke medallist Mark Tonelli called in to step up for butterfly.

Viktor Kuznetsov was back in the Soviet fold after returning from a doping ban at the 1978 World Championships. He set the pace on backstroke and was a second ahead of Mark Kerry before Peter Evans made up half a second on Arsens Miskarov. Yevgeny Seredin gained a touch on 'fly but Mark Tonelli had done enough to keep our hopes alive.

The team was screaming as Sergei Kopliakov left the blocks with 0.81 of a second advantage over Neil Brooks. Born in England, like me, Brooksy, 'the big bloke', as the media called him, rocketed off the blocks and was level with the Russian after only 20 metres.

Brooksy was a few days shy of his 18th birthday, but he was about to give himself the best present. Into the turn, our man had the edge but the Russian dug deep to get the bigger drive off the wall and draw level again.

It was neck and neck for 40m but then about 10m from home, Brooksy bounced ahead. Sheer guts and passion drove him for one long, last, decisive reach for the wall, 0.22 of a second ahead of the hosts. Gold for Australia in 3:45.70! Britain took bronze.

The Aussies were going wild—athletes, a handful of Australians in the crowd, and even the journalists and commentators were leaping up and down in the media box with veteran Australian swimming commentator, Norman May, famously calling the race in a live broadcast with "Gold, gold to Australia, gold ..."

There were not many Australians in the crowd that day, given the boycott, but as *The New York Times* noted: "A small but vocal band of supporters, furiously waving Australian flags from the stands, cheered them on, and they responded together in the pool after it was over, with victory signs up to the few who had made it to Moscow."

Intermission

I now had three days before the 800m freestyle showdown—but not three days of peace and calm.

The noise in the village was becoming unbearable. The manicured and mosquito-infested garden squares between the accommodation blocks had become meeting places for night-time discos, with athletes' music blaring out from boom boxes (a trendy new toy back then) and radios.

'Moskau' by the group Dschinghis Khan (we called them Ghenghis Khan in Australia) was a hit song in Russia at the time and was played incessantly. Athletes from different nations would form a big circle, arm in arm like Russian dancers, and then end the chorus with a thunderous cry of "HA!"

We had no idea what the lyrics meant but the English version came out back home while we were at the Games. Australia's Channel 7 used it as the theme for their coverage of the Games and the single came out in a die-cut Channel 7 paper sleeve. A massive hit, it topped the charts for six weeks.

The village was abuzz. It made for a very busy 'rest day' in the pool on July 25 after five days of racing, with two to go. All the while, new athletes were arriving for events that would take place during the second week of competition. The place was never still. It had become a beehive where everyone had their own task and timetable to follow.

Complaints to management resulted in the official disco being opened for longer. The idea was that the athletes would go there instead of partying at the village but that didn't quite work. The disco was small and athletes don't like walking if they can avoid it.

It's an impossible and meaningless exercise to compare results with parallel competitions. The Olympic Games are special for that reason. No other competition has so many distractions: unfamiliar food, packed living quarters, straw pillows, bus timetables and technology that you can't rely on, and just the scale of everything. Basically, you get the kitchen sink thrown at you.

I felt for those who were kept away by their governments and the political situation. It was tragic. Nothing compares to that one moment in time.

Bread Fight

Steadily through the Games, the food got better and a rumour spread that our demands had caused shortages of food for the citizens of Moscow.

The dough balls were finally overtaken as the best thing on the plate, so athletes found another use for them in the diner on rest day as the monotony of village routine set in. We were sitting chatting when a two-day-old, hardened bread roll flew across the room and landed on our table. Someone on the British team had lobbed it our way.

We threw it back and laughter broke out but before we knew it, the whole dining hall was thick with flying dough balls being bombarded back and forth. Russian guards rushed in to rescue the situation and we left trying to suppress our giggling over the newest sport at the Games: the big bun fight.

The next day the rules changed: one dough ball each. They can't really have thought that would stop us, but it was never the same again: a bread war had been averted.

Chapter 19
The Tidal Wave

"Champions aren't made in Gyms. Champions are made from something
they have deep inside them – a desire, a dream, a vision.
They have to have the skill, and the will. But the will must be stronger than the skill."
– Muhammad Ali

With two days of racing left at the Olimpiyskiy Pool, the East Germans were thumping the rest of the world's women, their five podium sweeps in the first five days a measure of dominance never seen before in Olympic waters. They had surpassed Montreal. Meanwhile, the Russians were dominating the men's competition.

There were only two events in Moscow where the GDR girls had national records slower than the best time of a foreign opponent entering the Games. The first was the 200m breaststroke, in which the Soviet Union's Lina Kačiušytė, the Lithuanian world-record holder, led a podium sweep for the hosts on day 4. The East German contenders were the last three swimmers home. A nod to the political master, perhaps? We'll never know.

The other threat was the 800m freestyle—me. I was the only Western opponent left standing with a chance to halt the GDR wagon. With two world records in the vault and a best time of eight minutes 25, I had swum 10 seconds inside the European and GDR national record of Petra Thümer, the 1976 Olympic champion.

The Spartakiade in the Moscow Olympic pool the year before had been useful but I had raced at a time when my focus was almost exclusively on my final school exams.

No other GDR swimmer had swum inside eight minutes 42 over the past four years. Now, two weeks before the Games at the GDR Olympic trials, two swimmers had gone inside 8:40, with a third close behind. Three swimmers we had never seen in international waters before were suddenly medal contenders in Moscow.

I had returned home from Nashville to a fitness and pace test set by Bill Sweetenham and had done eight minutes 42. It was clear that I was "nowhere close to where I needed to be". Since April when President Carter had drawn the final red line and the United States Olympic Committee went ahead and backed the decision declaring that the USA would not be in Moscow, I hadn't known what to do. I wanted to give up. Weeks of disruption and demotivation had followed. I missed sessions and valuable preparation time, so it was no wonder when I turned up at training camp that Bill had some concerns. I did too!

Yes, there was the hard work and punishing sets that had me in tears in the water but face to face, we clicked: he understood what I wanted. He wanted it too. It was only a matter of weeks before the Games and, as with all new partnerships, we had to go through the growing pains. There were moments of great doubt along the way. They are just part of the process—until the media gets a whiff of 'division' and either thinks it knows the story or has spoken to someone else who does.

The headline in *The Sun* declared: *'Coach has Michelle near tears'*. The second line read "*... and she loves him for it!*". It had appeared two days before the start of the Games and centred on the timing of my taper.

Distortions and media sensationalism had been a part of my swimming life. I had learned to put the blinkers on. However, for family and friends on the other side of the world, it wasn't quite so easy. Their reaction to overblown headlines disturbed me when they shared their concerns with me on one of our rare phone calls.

I had moved on from my disagreement with Bill over the timing of my taper, which I thought would affect my ability to be at my best in my pet event, the 200m butterfly. He had his eye on the 800m freestyle because he believed that was going to be my golden shot.

It was all done and dusted in no time at all, but it took days to filter home and then blow up in the media, causing unnecessary concern, particularly against a backdrop of rumbling debate about the boycott and our security and welfare.

Coach-athlete relationships can be trying at the best of times but tensions run no higher than on the cusp of the biggest race in the life of an elite swimmer: the Olympic final. Emotions ebb and flow, blunt words are spoken but all of it happens alongside a show of admiration, faith and confidence-building. Having miles between us was tough on my family, friends and me.

My letters were taking 10 days to get home, and to make phone calls home was incredibly complicated and very expensive. Given all of that, I thought it best to keep certain things to myself. I had other things on my mind. I had taken bronze in the 200m butterfly behind two East Germans and finished fourth in the 400m free behind three blue suits.

Had I let them get the better of me through a tactical mistake? Had I fallen for their game? I knew I had and my coach noticed my mind racing. He knew we both needed reassurance and ordered a set of 100s with just five seconds rest in between each.

I looked at him quizzically. Really? Wasn't it too close to competition to be doing such a set? Then again, nothing here was 'normal'. I got to it and put in a whole series of metronomic 1.03 splits, the time he had set for me. When I was done, I looked up to find him beaming back at me, as if to say, "See, told ya!" He was spot on.

I felt strong and light in the water. When I smiled back, Bill lifted an eyebrow, his demeanour back to stern. I understood. Poker face. Give nothing away. Let them think the third and fourth places were all I had. We would hide our game. We had needed the time to ourselves to rebuild and remain steadfast in our program with no interference and no questions. The bond between athlete and coach was strong.

A sense of calm set in. We knew what we had to do.

Swimming Day 6 – Saturday July 26, 1980 – 800m Freestyle Heats

My last event of the Games. I intended to be the hunter, not the hunted. That reflected what Bill would later describe as the key task he had when I had returned from Nashville: "Michelle was in defence mode. I needed her to be in attack mode. That's a physical and mental process."

I would not be showing my hand in heats, not even trying to be the fastest qualifier. The aim was not to be the 'hare' (the fastest qualifier in the middle). I intended to be the 'fox' on the outside, working in my own space at my own pace. Draw them into my game. For a gold medal the following evening, I would have to take control and that had nothing to do with achieving a specific time. It was all about winning.

I watched Heike Dahne clock eight minutes 36.09, her fastest time ever, in heat 1. I was up next with two East Germans and my training partner and teammate Rosey Brown alongside me. Ines Diers, their hot tip to take me down, had won the 400m, taken silver in the 200m and bronze in the 100m. She also had relay gold from the 4x100m freestyle. She would be their Shane Gould if she toppled me.

So I thought it best to let her think she could. Diers, 8:40.29, Ford, 8:42.36 in our heat. I cruised home to qualify third fastest. There would be no East German either side of me in the final this time. Ines Geissler, who'd snatched bronze from me in the 400m, was next home in our heat, in 8:46.96 in seventh overall for an outside lane. Rosey, on 8:49, just missed the final and put her energy into supporting me from then on.

Happy, I set off to collect my clothes when a tap on the shoulder startled me. My heart sank. Had I been disqualified? I turned to look up at Bill and the team as the awkward official tried to get his words out. He was hesitant and uneasy. I had been chosen for random doping control, he explained. I chuckled in disbelief. Random? Right! "I've done two doping tests this week and I've got the final tomorrow.

You can test me then?" He shuffled his feet and looked at the ground.

I welcomed any testing if it made sure we were in a clean fight but this felt like a ploy to distract me. I recalled the speed at which the East Germans had managed to produce their samples and leave the testing room when everyone else was waiting for nature to take its course, but then told myself to grin and bear it. There was plenty of time until the final the next evening.

Swimming, Day 7 – Sunday July 27, 1980

A sleep-in and late breakfast were what the coach ordered. The sun, up at 4:15 a.m., had threatened that but I drifted in and out of sleep and it was nearing 7 a.m. My teammates had all left for the morning heats and silence reigned in Block N1.

Alone in my room, I sat opening fan mail and letters from friends. Most were heartwarming and motivating. However, one was different. *"Michelle, You must withdraw from your race … If you decide not to and dare to stand up on the blocks you will be a traitor to this country …"*, and on it went in the same vein. I tore the letter up. Why, I asked? My bronze, the first medal for Australia at the Games, had helped bring people together, but one week later, such letters were still coming in. How could someone have written it? And how rotten that it arrived on the day of my 800m final!

As athletes, we didn't deserve this. We had already paid dearly for the way we'd been treated in a political row that was well beyond our control: our preparation had suffered and our focus had been diminished. Then this menacing note in my final hours before the biggest race of my career. It was poisonous.

I threw it in the bin, grabbed my accreditation and headed over to the international zone to call my parents. I didn't tell them about the letter; I knew they would be upset and I was too far away for that. I just needed to hear their voices. Walking back to my room, I took in the flags and the serenity of village life, with other athletes on the move and heading to their own dates with destiny. Mine was today.

The team returned from the pool with good news: we would have six swimmers in finals on the last night. Lisa Forrest, my roommate, was third fastest through to the 200m backstroke showdown and faced three East Germans of her own; Mark Tonelli had made the 100m freestyle final; and the women's 4x100m freestyle quartet of Lisa Curry, Karen Van de Graaf, Rosey and Michelle Pearson was fifth through into what would be the last showdown of the seven days of swimming in Moscow.

When You Know Your Coach Has Your Back

I awoke from my afternoon nap to find a placard at the end of my bed. Three flags were glued to the cardboard—the two East German ones either side of and below the

Australian flag. I chuckled. It was one more assurance that Bill believed the race was mine. This was his way of saying the gold was mine. That's what I had to believe.

There was only three hours to go but there were a few more mood messages to come. One arrived from headquarters: I was not to catch the regular shuttle bus to the pool. All our finalists would ride in Australian delegation cars to the venue that evening. Bill didn't just speak the words "no stone unturned"; he practised them. We would be at the pool on time, calm and ready, with nothing left to chance this time. He had been planning it since the fiasco with the bus on the day of the 400m.

I had been going through my warm-up routine but wasn't quite finished when Bill called out, "Okay, Michelle, time to get out and get changed!" in the middle of a set. Odd! I leapt out and picked up my green Lycra (then revolutionary) race suit with the gold and white lightning flashes on it. We only had two competition suits to use over the eight days. I had already used one suit in the first five swims and it had now lost its elasticity. Tonight, I would battle in a brand-new bather that I had put aside for my last race. Tracksuit on, I approached Bill, who pointed and said: "Joe [King, coach] is waiting for you at the massage tables over there."

Just outside the marshalling area, the massage tables were lined up like a row of beds in a hospital ward. The smell of lotions was uplifting. Though we had rarely experienced anything like this on national teams because it was outside our budget, I knew how helpful this could be: my mother, a physiotherapist, used to massage me when I had sore muscles from heavy training. The one masseur Australia had for all sports in Moscow was with the track and field team, so our coaches took on the role as and when they could.

Joe coached the sprinters. He had been manager in 1976. It was his first national team as coach and I didn't know him that well, so there was a bit of awkwardness, but Joe spoke in assuring tones with his modest and calm demeanour, and I let go. It was just what I needed.

800m Freestyle – Final

We were the first race up. The call to go to the marshalling area made me jump but Bill had found a quiet corner for our last talk through the race. "Hold back over the first 100," he said calmly. "Don't let them take you with them. Stay behind them. Then start building at the 150 mark, they won't be ready for it and at the 200 metres, you can take the brakes off, then …" He concluded: "Michelle, you're looking good in the water. Keep to your program. You can do this."

In the marshalling area for the last time at the Games, the silence was deafening, the tension in the room almost crackling off the walls. The three East German girls sat apart and made their presence felt even though they sat completely still and made no eye contact. With my head up, shoulders back and a smile on my face, I took my seat.

The race had already started.

Looking straight in everyone's faces, I stood up, shook my arms and stretched when I didn't need to. The response was perfect. Other girls copied me and the East Germans were drawn out of their zone, looking around and wondering what was going on. Those 10 minutes in that room felt much longer but eventually we were called to line up in lane sequence.

The slowest of the East Germans was ahead of me, with the fastest two behind me in the queue. I didn't turn around. My eyes were fixed on the door and the stands beyond. I fed on the energy of the crowd and the buzz coursing around a pool deck lined with athletes in a jubilant mood on this last night at the swimming 'opera'.

Lane 3. Tracksuit off, shoes off. "Michelle Ford – Australie". I took a step forward, waved to the crowd and took time to appreciate the applause. Then the t-shirt with the neckline too tight: off. Cap adjusted, goggles spat in and rinsed to prevent fogging. And, ready. The massage had worked wonders.

Two deep breaths filled my lungs, the whistle blew and I repeated Bill's game plan in my head. Set. Bang! I had a perfect start but as before, blue suits had power in their legs that the rest of us simply could not match. All three exploded down the first lap. "Steady, Michelle, not yet, not yet," I told myself.

The first couple of laps are dangerous. They feel easy, too easy; good, too good. The body just wants to go, the mind has to remind it: pace yourself, do what you are trained to do. At the same time, take it too easy and there's a risk of being left too far behind. I had been taught to negative-split the race, with the back half of the race swum faster than the first and I knew I could do it, so I placed my bet and settled into my own race as the rest got drawn into a fast start by two of the East Germans.

Diers in lane 5 played a different game and tucked in slightly behind me. The East Germans worked as a unit, one to draw everyone out, another to bolt when least expected, and the third keeping her powder dry to roar home to victory.

I turned seventh at the 100m mark and imagined Bill biting his nails. I knew I was behind but hadn't realised just how far back I was until I saw Dahne's feet in lane 4. A body length! "Steady, Michelle, not yet, not yet."

It's fairly usual for the first 100m of an 800m to be swift before swimmers settle down into their rhythm on the third lap. Geissler out on the wing in lane 1 had played the stalking horse: first at the 100, she turned sixth at 150m.

One foot poised over the accelerator, the other on the brake, I swam the third lap as though I was on the steep climb of a roller coaster getting ready for the drop. Gaining ground, I pulled up to the hips of the leaders halfway to the turn, flipped and hunted them down: by the 200m mark, I had moved from seventh to second. Momentum with me, I came off the wall and into the fifth lap of 16 telling myself, "Okay, Michelle, let's go. Let's show 'em. Time to move!"

Strength and power surged through me. Body high in the water, my mind was in the zone. Dick Caine's early instruction came floating back. "Keep your stroke long, push back hard, down past your hips." There was more acceleration. Peripheral vision at the next turn told me I had a half-body lead. I could sense they were fighting to go with me. One lap later at the 300m mark, I was showing them my feet.

Too easy, I thought. But the game was far from over. They were here to win. They would surely have an answer. I feared that they would come back at me. I had seen their blistering finishes, executed with a long, slow, powerful, boy-like stroke. They had speed, stamina and phenomenal turns. They already had five podium sweeps, including all three other freestyle races over 100, 200 and 400m, and Diers had been on the podium in all three.

I felt as though I needed to make sure I had something left in the tank at the end. I had no fatigue but thought it best to let the metronome in me take over, maintaining even splits lap after lap. But looking back over my shoulder from time to time, it was clear I was pulling away, gaining almost a second on each passing 100m. By 500m, I had a lead of two body lengths. Will it be now? Will they start firing back? Should I put my foot down this early or hold back in case I need that extra kick?

The answer came at the 600m turn, with Diers in lane 5 powering off the wall and passing Dahne in 4. I noted the shift underwater at the next turn. I was a good three seconds in front and ready for her. My race had been perfect, and my burners still had plenty of fuel left to tap. I was in control and determined that they were not going to take this race from me.

I put my head down, no longer looking back. I gained another second with 100m to go. Two more laps. Time to fire on full throttle knowing that I had the East Germans beaten. What a feeling!

I felt like I was hurtling up the pool, heart beating not just from the effort but through the rush of it all. I felt like I could have kept swimming for many more laps but there was just one to go. "Let's do this, Michelle," said the voices in my head—my voice, my coach's voice, the American voices of Tracey and the Nashville team, my grandfather's voice, the voices of my parents, and all those who'd supported me through thick and thin.

Bring. It. Home.

So focused, I hadn't tuned in to the crowd much but now I heard them urging me down my victory lap. The work; the dream; the living and breathing of a life less ordinary from a very young age. This was what it was all for!

I thumped into the touch pad. Eight minutes 28.90, the first time the Olympic title had been won inside eight minutes 30. An Olympic record. Relieved, excited and amazed, a flood of emotions swept through me. Leaning back, I pulled my cap off and dunked underwater, the cool water refreshing, my hair let down; the doubts, fears, distractions, ifs and buts were washed away. I shook my head in disbelief and took a few strokes away from the wall to take in the moment from every angle. My fist punched the water in sheer elation. I was joyful, triumphant and serene. Relief washed over me.

As the GDR girls touched the wall for silver and bronze, they dropped their heads towards the wall. It might have been disappointment or trepidation at returning to coaches who had been looking for gold. Up in the stands, my teammates and the Australian media were screaming down at me. I saluted back, thinking of all those who had believed in me, my family, my friends—and all the critics and the edge they had helped sharpen in me.

We had done it! The first individual gold for Australia was in the bag.

The Victory Ceremony

Channel 7 reporters jumped down onto pool deck, pushing the Russian film crew to the side. Barely able to contain himself, a reporter stuck a microphone out and said, "Last week you were standing there in tears. No tears tonight?"

"Only tears of happiness!" I replied.

I had no formal interview training and in the thrill of the moment I couldn't muster much more than "yes, no, you know ..." But I didn't care. I had achieved the impossible, the unthinkable, the quest my grandfather had challenged me to take on. That's all there was to know.

As the interview ended, a little sign appeared at the bottom of the TV screen— a personal note that was handwritten in red pen on a torn-off piece of cardboard: "Congratulations, Michelle – The Russian TV Crew."

I was then pulled and pushed from one microphone to the next in a gauntlet of media with a medal ceremony official harnessed to my side. The team manager appeared with my koala, having taken it from my room "just in case". Congratulations were coming from left and right, including many from the Eastern Bloc, and then an Australian reporter approached me. Judy Joy Davies, an Olympian turned journalist, who won a bronze medal in the 100m backstroke at the London 1948 Olympics, grabbed my elbow and pulled me aside. "Do you know what you have just done, Michelle?" I didn't quite understand. "You've just saved the Australian Olympic Federation. Your win is exactly what we needed ... thank you!"

I walked in a daze to the back of the pool, looking for Bill who was in the preparation area with the other swimmers. Not one to show emotions, it came as a surprise when he hugged me. "Michelle, that was terrific, I knew you could do it," he said. With a big smile on his face, he turned to speak to our next swimmer up.

He knew that we had achieved the impossible: against the odds, we had turned the tide. We had shown that a little girl from Oz could take on the might of the East German machine. We had shown our government and critics the nature and value of true Olympic spirit.

Canary tracksuit wet from my dripping hair and wetsuit beneath, I stood behind the podium clutching the koala my brother had given me six weeks earlier, with the two East Germans either side of me awaiting the ceremony. At the far end, the three flags were ready to be raised with each stretched horizontally on the flagpole in a mirror image of the placard Bill had placed on my bed.

The announcer was saying something in Russian, then in French: "Michelle Ford, Australie."

It was time. Stepping to the top podium, I raised the koala above my head and waved it to the crowd. Then, after readjusting my tracksuit top, I shook hands with the officials. As I bent over, a colourful yellow, blue, green and red ribbon with the shining gold medal clipped onto the end was placed around my neck. I stood up clasping the medal. My medal.

The East German girls were next. They smiled at last. I stopped and took another deep breath. There it was: the Australian flag high above the others—and then our national anthem, *Advance Australia Fair*. Every word meant the world to me:

Australians all let us rejoice,
For we are one and free;
We've golden soil and wealth for toil;
Our home is girt by sea;
Our land abounds in nature's gifts
Of beauty rich and rare;
In history's page, let every stage
Advance Australia Fair.
In joyful strains then let us sing,
Advance Australia Fair.

Time stood still.

Part 5
The Quest

Chapter 20
Plaudits and Perspective

"You can break world records any day, but it is something else
to win Olympic gold. You get this chance only once
every four years and it might be the only chance in your lifetime."
– Michelle Ford to Australian media, July 28, 1980

Michelle Ford:
- *Australia's only individual Gold medallist, Moscow 1980*
- *the first Australian woman to win individual Olympic medals in two distinct specialised strokes*
- *the only non-Soviet Bloc swimmer to win an individual gold medal at the 1980 Games*
- *only one of two swimmers—the other from the host nation—to prevent a clean sweep by the East German women*
- *Australia's only female medallist winning gold and bronze*
- *"A special girl, a special swimmer"—Bill Sweetenham, coach*

My feet were not quite touching the ground. I was numb to what I had done. I was living the dream, floating on air. I didn't read the reviews. There was no need. After all the judgements, the critics and the pressure, I had written my own ending. The fairy tale complete.

An invitation that evening to the Australian Embassy, that had previously been out of bounds since our arrival in Moscow, resulted in a haze of jubilation as I celebrated with the rest of the team. Bottles of champagne were given to me, and tucked under my arms, I carried them back to the village.

Halfway through the Olympics, the swimming competition was over. The Australian team had won seven medals in the pool and we were elated.

The last night in the pool had been a story of victory and disappointment.

My roommate Lisa Forrest had sadly missed out. She slipped on the wall at the start of her race and was devastated. We talked long into the night and into the early hours of the morning about what our adventures, gains and losses meant to us.

Letters and telegrams of congratulations poured in from home, America and other parts of the world. Our achievements were recognised and helped to turn the tide of public opinion at home.

It was time to leave Moscow. Budgets and fears around security, even though we had all felt safe, meant that the Australian swim team and any others who had finished competition had to leave as soon as possible after their last events. My chance of being the flag-bearer at the closing ceremony was gone.

My birthday perfume, Misha bear and medals were all safely packed in my bags. Unfortunately, my koala would stay behind, as there was no room. We were bussed to the airport and left the Games as we had arrived: with no fanfare, no lights, no cameras and no official goodbye.

The plane rattled and bumped down the runway, with the force of acceleration pressing me back into my seat. It had been a wild ride for years! My mind drifted back to that moment on the sofa when I watched the 1972 Olympic Games as a 10-year-old with my father. He'd told me, "One day, if you train hard … this could be you, Michelle!"

Now it was but I knew it had taken much more than hard work. The bumps along the road, the highs and lows, the many times my resilience was tested to its limits by officials, administrators, who'd continuously put roadblocks in my way, and continued to as the next chapter started.

What had made me do it? What had me push through the barriers? Was it part of my DNA? Are champions born? Everything was flooding back. I recalled that first time I jumped into the water at three, the first blur, the first time I'd made it to the other side of a pool and stunned my parents and friends. Now, I had stunned a great many more people and helped to give Australia back some of the pride in a sporting tradition lost four years ago in Montreal.

Moscow faded from view. The job was done.

Back on the Ground

On the way home, I met my parents in the US, where I also caught up with the Nashville team to say thank you before we headed back.

A few days ago, I had been in Moscow with my teammates. Now I was on the other side of the planet watching the closing ceremony with a sense of melancholy. It was weird to think the Games had still been going after I left. My medals were unpacked from the grey airline socks I had tucked them in. They looked surreal sitting on the table. They'd been lifted, turned over, inspected and worn by the many admirers.

The closing ceremony was another spectacle of precision, beauty and synchronicity. Only eight members of our team got to march in the ceremony, with silver medallist John Sumegi, the first Australian to claim an individual canoe/kayak medal, the flag-bearer. The Misha Bear, a teardrop rolling down his cheek, floated up into the atmosphere and waved farewell. The Games of the XXI Olympiad were over. The famous last words: "See you in LA."

AMBASSADOR   AUSTRALIAN EMBASSY
                                                    MOSCOW

                                              20 July 1980

        Dear Miss Ford,

                The Prime Minister has asked me to pass
        to you the following message from himself:

                Many congratulations. I salute a
                great sporting victory.

                        Malcolm Fraser

                May I add my own personal congratulations.

                        Yours sincerely,

                        (M.G.M. Bourchier)

        Miss M. Ford,
        C/- Manager,
        Australian Olympic Team,
        Olympic Village,
        MOSCOW.

The letter of congratulations from Prime Minister Malcolm Fraser

From my perspective, the Games seemed to have performed their magic in Australia. The country was reunited and the boycott debate dispatched. People seemed genuinely proud of us.

Australia won nine medals to place 15th overall, with seven of them in the pool. We had not returned to the glory days but there was a renewed hope and impetus to find a robust response to the Eastern Bloc's investment in sport.

Our against-the-odds result in the pool had left the prime minister and his government in a predicament. How would they manage to applaud the efforts of their athletes yet save face with a nation that knew they had done all they could to stop us going to the Games? Plaudits came in from the opposition leader and the public at large, making it impossible for Prime Minister Malcolm Fraser to ignore. He did send me a congratulatory message.

However, there was no apology for the toxic environment he and his government had placed athletes in. Nor was there any mention of how the boycott controversy had been fortuitous for Australian trade with Russia.

The government's last stand came with the New Year honours list for 1981. It had long been a tradition to honour Olympians. But not in 1981, when all the honours were bestowed on those who'd towed the government line. Australian Hockey Federation president Pat Ryan and the president of the Equestrian Federation, Jack Walsh, both received OBEs (Orders of the British Empire). They were the heads of two sports that had backed the boycott without consulting athletes.

It seemed so unfair. As one teammate said to me, "The vile anger around the boycott was aimed at us teenagers on the swim team." The boys had an average age of 19 at the time and the girls were younger. It should have been that the whole Moscow team (staff and athletes) were honoured for upholding the Olympic ideal in a storm of politics that was far removed from sport.

To this day there has been no acknowledgement of that somewhat lost generation of Olympians, and many still carry the scars and mental baggage of a traumatic time. Just to hear the AOC say "Well done, guys, you were right to go and represent Australia—we're proud of you" would mean a great deal to the Olympic class of 1980.

1980 Australian Olympic swimming team

Women: Rosemary Brown, Lisa Curry, Michelle Ford, Lisa Forrest, Georgina Parkes, Michelle Pearson, Karen Van de Graaf

Men: Graeme Brewer, Neil Brooks, Peter Evans, Mark Kerry, Ron McKeon, Max Metzker, Paul Moorfoot, Glenn Patching

It was the same in Britain, where the honours list also snubbed the athletes who had excelled in Moscow. In Australia, it wasn't only the athletes who were subject to the cold shoulder by the government. Newspaper heads who had sufficiently pleased the prime minister received knighthoods while the heads of the Seven Network that broadcast the Moscow Olympics missed out.

However, the public, media and local industry saw things differently by voting me the '1980 Sportsperson of the Year'. The runner-up was Evonne Goolagong, who had won Wimbledon for the second time in 1980, as a young mother. I was also honoured with the Helms Award (now known as the World Trophy for Australasia) as Australasia's foremost amateur athlete.

Sponsors came knocking at my door but soon turned around and left when it was clear the Australian Swimming Union would be taking 80% of the pie.

Belated Birthday

A surprise, belated 18th birthday party marked the first time in five years I had been able to celebrate with my family and friends. Five years. That really brought it home to me. My parents had invited my learn-to-swim coach, friends, family, clubmates and everyone else who had supported and been there for me. My Moscow koala was even there too! It was brought home by our team manager, who noticed I'd had no room for him when I packed up to leave the Olympic village.

My mother had arranged blown-up photos from my childhood and swimming years to be posted around the room. My two Olympic medals and certificates were on display and Channel 7 was there to film my father giving me a gold pendant of the official logo of the Games and its five roads leading to Moscow, with the Soviet star at the top, and a diamond encrusted in the inner circle of the five rings. I was overwhelmed.

An Athlete's Life Is Not Easy, but It Is Beautiful!

With the target met, the world tunes in and celebrations, plaudits and honours follow. It took a while to come back down to earth after the fireworks and fanfare.

You can never tell where the next bend in the road may take you. All I knew was that I wasn't done with swimming but my education and preparing for the rest of my life had to be a priority, especially at a time when opportunities for women were so much more limited than they were for men.

When the Olympic gold dust had settled, I faced the question every athlete must answer at some stage: "What next?"

Underpinning the puzzle was my 'amateur' status. These days, sport is a profession for athletes. The best swimmers have lucrative sponsorship and partnership deals.

They can earn several times the average national household income in Australia which was a little over $120,000 in 2023.

Back in 1980, accepting $3 for the bus ride home from teaching kids to swim would have landed me a lifetime ban from Olympic sport. For me, education was the key but where was the lock that opened the door to elite athletes being able to study and train? In Australia and most other parts of the world, we had no choice. It was one or the other.

In the immediate aftermath of Moscow, the next Olympic city, Los Angeles, seemed to be the place where I would be able to combine athletic and academic pursuits.

The timing was perfect. Earlier in the year, the Title IX regulation that had been passed into US law in 1973 was forcing change at American colleges and the National Collegiate Athletic Association (NCAA). From now on, women were entitled to the same opportunities that men had benefited from for decades: full scholarships for sportswomen who also wanted to study was a legal obligation for colleges.

It was the American version of what the GDR had had for a decade: sports schools where talented children developed their skills while learning maths, German and the other subjects at a slower pace than their peers in the standard education system.

No such structures existed in Australia at the time, with my school years having been marked by a procession of begging bowls and permissions for time off only being granted with warnings attached.

The First Australian Institute of Sport Scholarship

My sights were set on US colleges but only a month after I had accepted a provisional offer, I got a call from a government official asking if I would join the group helping them to understand the needs of the athlete for the new, state-supported Australian Institute of Sport (AIS).

What had the boycott achieved? Soviet troops were still in Afghanistan, a nation that participated at the Moscow Games when others were locked out. And Australia had continued to trade with the USSR all the time that athletes were not allowed to trade with their talents.

However, the new Institute was a big step in the right direction. It would help make Australia competitive on the world stage once more.

So, on Monday September 22, 1980, I found myself standing, with the Sydney Harbour Bridge behind us, alongside government and media as the announcement was made: I would be the first scholarship holder at the new Institute when it opened in January, 1981.

The mood was summed up by a headline that had appeared in the *Daily Mirror* that morning: *'Golden Girl Quits ... Job – Dramatic Offer to Keep Michelle'.*

It was an honour to have been chosen but there was a twist in the tale. The new Australian Institute of Sport was to be opened by Prime Minister Malcolm Fraser on January 26 (Australia Day), with my Nashville coach Don Talbot back home to be the inaugural AIS Director and Kevan Gosper, who had voted in favour of the Moscow boycott with Fraser, the new chairman of the AIS Board.

Under pressure to deliver results, Don and his AIS team had to prioritise sport and I was told that my education would come second. I had given up a scholarship opportunity in the US and was now stuck.

The Institute and Australia's new plan for sport seemed to be starting off on the wrong foot at a time when athletes still could not earn a living from sport. I kept reminding myself that my future depended on my education.

In a letter to the government, I expressed my disappointment and informed them I could not accept their offer. Instead, in January 1981, I began my tertiary education at Wollongong University, studying physical education.

Swimming and the US adventure would have to wait.

Plaudits From Well-Wishers

In the days and weeks after Moscow, I was inundated with messages from well-wishers. After all the hostility the team had faced, it was a joy to see an outpouring of support for the athletes that had gone to the Games and represented our country. Here are a few notes that meant much to me and sum up so many of the other messages sent to me:

Frank and Beatrice Ford (paternal grandparents)

Dear Michelle,

We are so very proud of you, Olympic champion! So thrilled for you, we knew you could do it.

It's been a joy to follow your progress and dedication since you were a little girl. All the hard work has paid off.

We're delighted for you and can't wait to see you.

Lots of love, ...

Kay Stevenson (cousin)

Do not follow where the path may lead. Go, instead, where there is no path and leave a trail.

I think the verse on this card says it all. You did leave a trail in the 800 metres, and everyone followed. It was hard finding a card to send you. The 'Congratulations' ones were boring but this one couldn't have said it better.

I was so happy and proud that you won. Also, you weren't the only one who cried after the 200m butterfly. Everyone I know who watched you on TV cried when you did. One news reporter summed the whole thing up. World records can't be kept for ever—somebody will take them, but Michelle will always have her Olympic medals and nobody can take those away from her. He was exactly right. Anyway, you've broken world records too.

… You've won everyone's hearts, Shell. It turned out that 1978 wasn't your year and this year was yours!!

H Fosher

Dear Michelle,

Heartiest Congratulations on your Bronze medal at the Moscow Olympics I admire you not only as a champion swimmer but as a very courageous person. It must have taken tremendous inner resources to overcome the pressure of the boycott group. To win a medal against the sophisticated training techniques of overseas shows tremendous fighting spirit. I am holding you up as a heroine to my children. … It is a triple victory; a sporting victory, a personal victory and a victory for all the little people who hold lamington drives to raise money and try to do the right thing by their children for the future. Your attendance and victory at Moscow will never be forgotten but be forever an inspiration to us all.

Congratulations and all my very best wishes for the future.

Ray Watson (18th August 1980)

Great Effort in Moscow!

You shouldn't have had to cope with a pack of whingeing politicians as well as the world's best swimmers, but you beat them all. You have made many million Australians very happy. Congratulations.

Ray Watson

Carss Park Club. (July 25th, 1980)

Dear Michelle,

Congratulations on your great swim performances in Moscow.

Television sets around Australia radiated the excitement and tension of your races in the USSR. We are sure these occasions were just that little bit more stirring (if that's at all possible) for those of us associated with the Carss Park Swimming Club.

Very Best wishes for your continued success.

Sincerely,

Chapter 21
The Athletes' Voice

*Speaking truth to power is actually a form of loyalty. It is the best
and at times only way to make sure that any organisation lives up to its potential"
– Richard N. Haass, Newsweek Writer*

It was my 19th birthday, 15 July, 1981, and an A5 envelope arrived in the mailbox. The Olympic rings bottom left and embossed in capital letters the words 'COMITÉ INTERNATIONAL OLYMPIQUE, SWITZERLAND'. With a hastened sense of excitement and curiosity, I carefully opened the fine paper envelope. The official IOC letterhead shone in the top right-hand corner.

Dear Miss Ford,

May I first congratulate you on your selection as a participant in the forthcoming XIth Olympic Congress, which is an event of extreme importance to the world of international sport ...

Signed by IOC Secretary General, Monique Berlioux, it was an invitation to the Olympic Congress in Baden-Baden, a spa town in West Germany. I was to be one of the first 35 athletes from around the world ever to be called on to address the annual gathering of decision-makers.

Acceptance would lead to a flood of communication in the days ahead, including an economy class ticket and my accreditation: FORD Michelle; Special Gold Medallist guest of the IOC; Athlete.

Beyond what to wear, my head was racing with questions. What would we say now we had a chance to speak truth to power; what was there to know about the IOC? Who was who, who voted for them to be there and what kind of work did they do? I had been to two Olympics but that whole side of the coin was a mystery to me.

I was about to embark on a steep learning curve at a time of great upheaval in the Olympic movement and world affairs.

These were different times. As athletes, we felt we were treated as pawns by the political machinery. There were the horrors of the Munich Massacre in 1972, where terrorists infiltrated the Olympic village resulting in the slaughter of 11 Israeli athletes; we had the African nations boycott of Montreal in 1976, the US-led boycott of Moscow in 1980, and there was now a very real threat of a retaliatory Soviet-led boycott of Los Angeles in 1984.

Athletes were considered insignificant to the administration of sport, and in part, to our own destiny. We were told to stay in our place, that our job was to perform on the field of play only, without consideration, and we were prohibited from making any financial gain from our sport activities, let alone be able to make a living from it.

We understood that any questioning of the authorities, or the way Olympic sport was governed or operated, how decisions were made and who made them, would result in adverse consequences.

There was also great gender disparity in sport with only 22% female participation at the Moscow Olympics. The IOC was a male-only club, with not one female IOC member and few women holding executive positions in sport worldwide.

Internationally, sport was operated and controlled by the International sporting federations (Ifs). National Olympic Committees (NOCs) were static, passive bodies with no function except for the six months prior to the Olympic Games. The IOC's legal responsibility was limited to the Games period. Every four years there existed the Olympic Games (summer and winter), but between the Games there was no activity within the Olympic movement.

I was now an invited guest with several of my Olympian peers and to be active participants at the highest table in world sport was exciting, but terrifying at the same time.

United by and for Sports, declared the logo. Of the 35 invited, 25 athletes attended the Olympic Congress. It was to be a watershed moment for the Olympic Games and world sport. It was the beginning of the athletes' voice.

Breaking the Mould In Baden-Baden

On September 21, 1981, two days before the official opening of the Olympic Congress, with a sense of trepidation, we were escorted to the International Hall of the Baden-Baden's conference centre, the Kongresshaus.

A welcome speech introduced us to the team of IOC staffers and interpreters who would organise our work and stay, which included a heavy, unexpected social calendar.

The Finnish sailor Peter Tallberg, an IOC Member serving as liaison between the bureaucrats and athletes, introduced Donna de Varona, the American dual gold medallist swimmer from Tokyo 1964 and a prominent broadcaster for ABC.

Only six female athletes had been invited: myself, Australia, swimming gold medallist in 1980; my roommate Yuko Arakida, Japan, volleyball gold medallist in 1976; Svetla Otsetova, Bulgaria, rowing gold medallist in 1976; Elizabeth Theurer, Austria, equestrian gold medallist in 1980; and the two winter athletes, Vera Sosulia, Soviet Union, gold medallist in luge 1980; and Irene Epple, West Germany, alpine silver medallist 1980

We were told "There will be four five-minute presentations to be delivered by the athletes scheduled for day three of the Congress." No topics were suggested. The formalities ended with Tallberg telling us all, "It's now up to you!"

The athletes present were a convivial group, but mostly strangers as we each represented different sports. Each athlete from the East had an 'interpreter' in tow, although we later came to understand that these were their political watchers, there to make sure they towed the party line.

Many of the athletes in the room had been directly or indirectly impacted by political plays by their governments or sports. Seeing the African representative, I was reminded of the Olympic boycott by African nations in 1976, which followed the refusal of the IOC to ban New Zealand after their rugby union team toured apartheid South Africa earlier that year. I had a vivid memory of the African nations arriving at the Games Village in Montreal, and waiting for them at the opening ceremony, only to learn literally minutes before the parade of athletes that they had to withdraw.

At 14 years old, this had been my first encounter with a boycott. At the time, I had felt extremely sad for these athletes, among them medal prospects, who had their Olympic moment taken from them. The impact of the 1980 Moscow boycott only the year prior, of whether we would go or not, had been heavy on all of us. It was startling to think how many athletes around the world had been denied the opportunity to compete in both the 1976 and 1980 Games.

The conversations and banter filled the room—some serious, some casual—about home, family, their athletic exploits. The official language of the congress was recorded in our circular as being French and English, but language didn't seem to be a problem among us athletes. It was obvious that many delegates at the Congress regarded us as a mere masquerade. This feeling was accentuated when we were joined by some of the members, national delegates, whose primary aim was to be seen with their star athletes.

School visits, excursions, wining and dining. It was all a far cry from my rigorous training routine. At 3 p.m. after a copious lunch, some of us reconvened to discuss what our four five-minute speeches should focus on. It struck me that, regardless of sport, nationality or personal background, we soon found a united, common voice.

The clock was ticking. We had just one day to discuss and prepare the speeches.

The issues were multiple and complex. It was going to be tough to fit everything we wanted to say into four five-minute speeches. As Congress opened on September 22, we wrote a note to IOC president Juan Antonio Samaranch asking for more time for each presentation. He sent back word that we could have one additional five-minute presentation and a longer speech of 15 minutes to wrap up on the last day of the Congress.

Word also came through that one of the speeches must be presented by an Eastern bloc athlete, the Soviet Union's ice hockey legend Vladislav Tretiak, later to be president of the Ice Hockey Federation of Russia.

The Hot Topics

When our deliberations were done, we settled on five topics to raise with the IOC.

- Doping
- Rule 26—the eligibility to compete in the Games, called the 'amateur rule'
- The inclusion of athletes at the decision-making table and the participation of women in the Olympic movement
- Political involvement and boycotts
- Olympic ceremonies

We had agreed that there had to be unanimity between all athletes for what would finally be presented. This in itself was quite extraordinary. We were between a Moscow boycott and a possible retaliation boycott at Los Angeles 1984, in the middle of a Cold War, yet we were a small group of athletes, none of whom had met two days prior, representing East and West, North and South, working together in a spirit of esprit de corps for the benefit of all. It was truly refreshing. It was the Olympic spirit in action.

With limited time, we decided to divide into groups to write the speeches.

Svetlana Otsetova, the 1976 gold medallist in rowing from Bulgaria, would deliver the speech on women's participation, Thomas Bach, a 1976 gold medallist in fencing from West Germany, who had a legal background, would deliver the speech on Rule 26, the 'amateur rule'. Vladislav Tretyak, the Soviet ice-hockey goalkeeper, was to deliver the speech on Olympic ceremonies. And Ivar Formo, the Norwegian cross country skier and gold medallist in 1976, would be our lead-off speaker, presenting our position on doping in sport.

I had taken notes and written a speech on boycotts and injustices: the indecision and, in my case, the Australian Government offering financial rewards directly to athletes to withdraw from the 1980 team, and death threats directed at me were all still weighing on me. However, after writing the speech, I felt it would be more powerful to have someone who had been a victim to a boycott present the speech. I turned to Kipchoge (Kip) Keino, unaware that he had not participated at the Montreal Games, telling him that he should deliver this speech as he represented the African voice: those who had been subject to the boycott in 1976 after 28 African countries, including Kenya, boycotted over the presence of New Zealand, which had welcomed a South African All Blacks touring rugby team at a time of apartheid.

Kip, a two-times Olympic-champion distance runner who would go on to head the Kenyan Olympic Committee, was the only African delegate. At 41 years old, he was the oldest athlete amongst us and after some coaching, he agreed to present the speech I had prepared, of which I was very proud.

We all agreed that Sebastian Coe, the track gold medallist at Moscow and a native English speaker from Great Britain, would present the final 15-minute speech on the last day of the Congress—Seb's 25th birthday.

Looking back to 1981, every speech was a collective effort, the united voice of athletes present.

Complaining was not the way to be heard, we believed. We tried to be clear and concise in expressing our concerns and calling for action. And we said things that athletes weren't allowed to say back then.

On doping, for example, we debated what if an athlete is found guilty, should they get a life ban or not? Too harsh? Should the ban extend to the coach and athlete's entourage? Doctors? Administrators? Why just the athlete? We understood that 'life ban' may not be possible on legal grounds, but it was also clear, too, that if we went in softly, nothing would change. We had to be tough and felt that athletes would understand, too much having been tolerated, too many having turned a blind eye. It had to be: a life ban on athletes, coaches and doctors would be our demand.

On the amateur rule we discussed East versus West. How could athletes, those from the East, receive cars, houses, full medical care, food and a monthly stipend and yet not fall foul of amateur rules, while other athletes from other countries were sanctioned? Athletes who had been given nothing and even had to pay for the privilege to compete. The sting of the Cold War in sport was real; we'd all felt it. There was consensus: the athlete from the West was falling behind and struggling, tied to a more stringent interpretation of the amateur rule than in the East. Was it time to relax this most stringent, barbaric law that controlled the athlete prohibiting them any financial gain? We believed so.

While we discussed and debated, I scribbled down notes on the experiences of the group when putting together the presentation Kip would deliver: grief, injustice, lack of equality, suppression of fair play. The subject of the boycotts was raw but because of that I felt able to express my strongest feelings. Under 'Politics', I drew a star, underlined it, then wrote:

After preparing several years to participate in an Olympic Games an athlete may be faced with nothing.

- Propaganda through sport and athletes to promote political ideas.
- Athletes should not be punished by political decisions, and the IOC should be more proactive in setting up a body which governs the athlete.
- We appeal to the press of the world not to make political issues out of sporting events.
- We are proud to represent our country but make sure that it should not be abused.
- Protected from geographical boycotts, athletes need to be chosen solely on their athletic ability.

I wrote those notes at 19 years of age with far less experience and knowledge of world affairs, politics and the IOC than I have today.

If I knew then what I am aware of today, a deeper understanding of point five, for example, would have been required to ask the IOC to be genuinely neutral to achieve our wish for an Olympic realm untouched by global politics and conflicts. Just as states have used athletes as political pawns, so too have the same leaders played the IOC in their propaganda wars, making their relationships with 'neutrality' all too cosy for comfort down the decades.

Such complexities are a part of a debate that rumbles on to this day.

As numerous examples in world sport show us—not just the Olympics—simply having athletes in key governance positions is no guarantee that athletes will have a genuine say in what happens in times of crisis when global politics intervenes.

Even so, it is worth repeating as often as required what I believed back in 1981 and still do: boycotts hurt athletes. Full stop. And they have never achieved the political ends they promote.

The five five-minutes speeches presented by Otsetova, Keino, Bach, Tretyak and Formo completed, it was hard to read the audience. It was now time for the final speech by Seb Coe.

The Final Speech

Seb's birthday arrived and it was time for his first 15 minutes of fame at Congress. He, Thomas Bach, Ivor Formo and I had sat up late into the night in our hotel bistro with piles of scribbled notes in front of us as we honed the presentation to make sure our requests came through loud and clear.

We got little sleep but three hours after we agreed we had nailed it, tired but satisfied, we took our seats among the Olympic top brass and dignitaries as Seb took to the stage. This is what he said:

When I arrived here I had to admit to a certain amount of fear and trepidation at not only being included in the Congress, but also having the task of standing before you and articulating the feelings of the athletes. Well, my immediate fear was allayed. You could almost say that I felt quite in my own element when on Thursday I saw a queue forming outside the main hall for free tracksuits and inside the hall I stand here with the electric clock flashing away to my left.

We wish to record our immediate thanks to President Samaranch for his invitation to the Congress, to Willi Daume for his support and confidence in the youth of the movement, and to the whole of the Organising Committee which provided us with the support, the staff and the facilities needed to accomplish our difficult and challenging task.

I feel it is necessary at this point to outline the working conditions and problems we had to overcome in order to address the Congress.

It may have been noted by the Congress that the athletes have been looking a little bit tired—we are! We have all been working long hours in the preparation of the papers—often working into the early hours of the morning.

No discos—just discussion.

Late nights have often been followed by early mornings. Frequent visits have been made in the mornings by the athletes to schools and throughout the day to com¬munity activities.

We are the first athletes invited to participate vocally at an Olympic Congress. It is for this reason that we realise the responsibility we have in securing the future inclusion of athletes. Since the athletes will be participating in future Congresses we ask you for your assistance in providing us with comprehensive in¬formation before we arrive.

This does not mean however that athletes will arrive here with speeches formulated and written, possibly by NOCs, Ifs or even Government authorities. Only independence ensures valid contribution. This is consistent with IOC philosophy.

As a group we have rejected every attempt at political pressure in both the choice of speakers and subjects.

We came here not knowing what our role would be and we had little time to define it. Fortunately, this diverse but well-balanced group was able to address a broad spectrum of challenges.

A dynamic group was formed, we worked with cohesion and efficiency, the subject always remained more important than the individual.

Five major topics emerged. They were—in order of presentation to the Congress: firstly, drug abuse; secondly, Rule 26—the eligibility to compete in the

Games; thirdly, inclusion of athletes in the Olympic movement; fourthly, political involvement in the Olympic debate; and finally, Olympic ceremonies.

While these were not the only subjects discussed we did consider them to be of immediate importance for the future of the Games.

Time prevents us from a full analysis of these subjects, but we athletes sincerely hope that you leave this hall fully aware of our feelings.

On 'doping' we consider this to be the most shameful abuse of the Olympic idea. We call for the LIFE BAN of offending athletes.

We call for the LIFE BAN of coaches and the so-called doctors who administer this evil.

On Rule 26: it is illogical to expect one rule to be capable of attending to the individual needs of all the sports in the Olympic movement. We therefore echo the call in Congress for greater independence for International federations in determining exactly what the needs of their sports are.

The demand for a modern Olympian is considerable. Such sacrifice to the cause of the movement should never be disregarded. It is therefore the moral obligation of the IOC to ensure that within the framework of Rule 26, provision is made for the social consideration of the athlete.

With regard to the participation of women in the Olympic movement, it is considered that this institution is out of step with modern thinking in its support and inclusion of women. We simply call for female equality of opportunity.

On the subject of politicisation of sport, the athlete has the right to self-determination and on those grounds alone we reject all political pressure.

The final major topic concerned the ceremonies at the Games. The athletes wish to maintain the traditions of the Olympic ceremony and totally support the concept of one Olympic village.

Also discussed but not included in the five-minute presentation were other issues. For four weeks every four years the IOC does a remarkable job in its preparation of the Olympic sports. What happens during the Olympiad? We suggest that this time could be used to develop new sporting opportunities. Athletes and sports experts could take part in an exchange program on a world-wide basis. We would like to explore ways in which to promote the history and proud traditions of the Olympic movement, for example this was achieved here during the participation of athletes in community activities.

On the basis of the proposals of the Ifs, the support of Mr Tallberg and the commitment of President Samaranch, we strongly suggest that this group of athletes be regarded as the consulting body to help us attain the way in which athletes can participate in the decision-making processes of our movement. To accomplish this we ask for your support in organising a group meeting next year so that we may continue our work.

In his address, Peter Tallberg kindly referred to the athletes as a reserve—a hidden treasure. His inclusion into our group could be the key to unlocking the trove.

Finally, I feel that our inclusion in the Congress here in Baden-Baden and the tenacity with which we have grasped our tasks kills if not buries the common misconception that athletes are unthinking robots.

Seb Coe, on behalf of all athletes

✻ ✻ ✻

The speech had now taken flight. Where it would land in the lives of athletes was yet to be seen. We could only hope that our words would resonate: that sports' governing bodies would take action to enforce new rules around doping and protect the integrity of the athlete through more stringent doping measures and controls, that politics would no longer affect the future participation of athletes at the Games, and that more women would participate on the field of play and in the boardroom. That the athlete's voice would continue to influence and have an impact on the sporting world, to protect the athlete.

The athletes' voice in Baden-Baden became a turning point for sport across the globe. With the redrafting of Rule 26, we achieved a wide-reaching effect across all sports, be it Olympic or other, whereby athletes could receive money for their participation.

Our emphasis on gender equality was before our time and opened the door for dialogue towards equal opportunity for women. Today, there is equal participation at the Olympic Games of male and female events and athlete numbers, though there is still a long way to go for equality in the administration of sport.

While doping is still the most serious crime against fair sport, it has been perhaps the most difficult to eradicate. Our statement of a lifetime ban on doping athletes and coaches was not established, for legal reasons. However, the IOC established out-of-competition testing through the creation of the World Anti-Doping Agency (WADA). As an October 1985 press release from the IOC Athletes' Commission stated, "The health of all athletes must remain a primary concern of all partners in the Olympic movement."

Intelligence and evidence gleaned from studying athlete biological passports and through investigation by Canadian lawyer Richard McLaren and the former head of the Russian anti-doping laboratory, Grigory Rodchenkov PhD into allegations of state-sponsored doping in Russia should send a clear message to athletes, sports administrators and political leaders.

The Birth of the IOC Athletes' Commission

In October 1981, just one month following Baden Baden, President Samaranch announced the establishment of a 'Commission for Athletes'. The Commission would initially be composed of the six athletes who presented at the Baden Baden Congress: Thomas Bach (FDG), Sebastian Coe (GBR), Ivar Formo (NOR), Kipchoge Keino (KEN), Svetla Otsetova (BUL) and Vladislav Treytyak (URS).

The Commission was in flux for a few years, with the addition of two representatives from the Organising Committees (winter and summer) appointed in May 1982. In 1985, following the Los Angeles 1984 Olympics, the Athletes' Commission membership represented all continents for the first time.

Michelle Ford (thid left) with Thomas Bach to her left and other athletes representing all continents at the first IOC Athletes Commission at IOC headquarters, Lausanne, 1985.

The formation of the Athletes Commission was one of the most important decisions made from our presentations in Baden-Baden, having far-reaching impact on the IOC and the Olympic movement worldwide. We represented the four corners of the world, each with different ideologies, colour and creed, but we were bound by a common thread: we had surmounted the odds and won Olympic medals. I was honoured to be one of the founding members of the Athletes Commission (1985–1988).

It is extraordinary to consider the list of athletes represented in Baden Baden and those who represented on the first IOC Athletes Commission and realise the impact they have had on world sport. Amongst us was one future IOC President, Thomas Bach, a future chairman of London 2012 and president of World Athletics, Lord Sebastian

Coe, the future president of the Ice Hockey Federation of Russia and Minister of Sport for Russia, Wladislaw Tretyak. In recent years, as a member of the Russian Parliament, Duma, Tretyak was sanctioned by the British Government for voting in favour of military attacks on Ukraine.

Psychology and Sport—LA, Here I Come!

As we left Baden-Baden with a spring in our step on the cusp of autumn in Germany, the summer swim season was not far away back home. I returned to Wollongong University to finish my first year of university, but the scholarship offers from Stanford, UCLA and USC I received following Moscow were tempting. I decided to accept a place at the University of Southern California, the site of the 1984 Olympic swimming competition.

I would be there from northern autumn 1981 through to being awarded my master's in sports psychology in 1985, a year after what I hoped would be a third Olympic campaign.

Chapter 22
When One Door Closes

"When one door closes, another opens; but we often look so long and so regretfully upon the closed door that we do not see the one which has opened for us."
– Alexander Graham Bell

Snap! Pain. Dread. Coach Don Lamont was still barking orders but I could no longer hear him. My head dropped, my hand cradled my shoulder, and the 10kg medicine ball I had just hoisted was now a dead weight on the floor where it had dropped.

I was in the weights room at the University of Southern California's Trojans Heritage Hall. It was November 1983 and I was two years into feeling the benefits of USC's generous athlete program. It had been motivating, invigorating and supportive.

I had been buoyed by the USC's team approach, and it was also having a positive impact in the pool. The American support was unstinting, even though they knew I'd be among their opponents if I achieved my chief goal of representing my country in Los Angeles at the next Olympics. The 1984 Games would be my third, and my first as a defending champion. I was in the fortunate position of being a foreigner with 'hometown advantage' because the pool I trained in was also the Games competition pool.

Things were going really well. I was doing repetitions in training that indicated I was on world-record pace. Physically set, I was also in better mental shape than I had ever been in, with maturity and confidence underpinning my will, power and enthusiasm. At 21, I was in the perfect place for peak performance.

With Australia's Olympic trials approaching, I was coming towards the end of a gruelling winter of work, with gym sessions followed by sets such as 10x200m butterfly.

That was when the trouble started. At first, there was just a slight throbbing in my left shoulder. Pain is a common feeling among swimmers in heavy training and what I felt wasn't enough to keep me from my nine to 10 miles a day. I refused to give in, using heat on my shoulder before workouts and ice afterwards. Tenacity is a tool of champions—and sometimes their greatest risk.

Swimmers are notorious for having shoulder trouble. It's a complicated joint. On a twice-daily basis for months on end, year after year, swimmers take advantage of a range of movement that's close to a full circle. The arm must clear the surface, pull the body forward by dragging water (a heavily resistant element) from the entry of the hand through to the full extension of the arm down the body, and repeat that movement many thousands of times each training session: lift, scoop, grab, push, lift, scoop, grab, push.

I had been doing it regularly for over a decade without a hint of damage. However, the heavy demands of swimming training can come at a high price. Athletes are taught from an early age never to give in. But pain is its own master. It's the body's way of saying, "Stop! Listen! Take advice!"

Desperate to revisit my Olympic heights and relive that thrilling golden moment I had experienced in Moscow, I ignored the red flags until I had no choice. I sat on the end of the bench alongside varsity basketball and football players, waiting for the doctor to call me in. I was numb, the endless aching having deprived me of sleep and my usual ability to concentrate in classes.

The doctor declared, "You've got chronic tendonitis. You have to take two weeks off. It's the only way your shoulders will recover."

Disaster! I was due to travel home for Olympic trials in a matter of weeks.

There was nothing to take for it. I took up running six miles a day in the heat of smog-laden LA and cycled for half an hour afterwards. In the pool, I endured 6km kick sessions and even took up one-armed freestyle, throwing in the odd regular stroke to see how my shoulders felt. The jogging went well until I pulled a tendon in my right ankle.

To make matters worse, the painkillers were playing havoc with my stomach. I couldn't eat. My enthusiasm and energy had been sapped. In short, I was a mess. Weeks had gone by without being able to do any of the sets I should have been doing in the water.

In the lowest of moments, it felt like a curse.

Then, just as I thought the inflammation had eased off after a complete rest, it all flared up again and the stabbing pains returned. The joint swelled to twice its size and I was back outside the doctor's room feeling literally dizzy and metaphorically sick to my stomach with worry. How was I going to manage to race at the Olympic trials?

"The tendonitis is now complicated by inflammation of the joint caused by friction of the tendon as it moves through the shoulder," the doctor said sternly. He picked up a syringe and explained, "I suggest we give you a cortisone injection."

Cortisone injections were a quick fix, but I had heard they could cause more damage in the long term. I shook my head. I had always said that if ever I had to have cortisone, I would quit swimming. I told him that I would have to speak to my parents. Reminding me when his surgery times were, he handed me a box of Butazolidin, a non-steroidal, anti-inflammatory drug to reduce the pain and swelling.

I had known injury before, even in competition, but nothing had been this bad. A girl from the home team at the New Zealand Games in January 1981, my first big international meet after Moscow gold, had accidentally swum into me during warm-up. My nose had swollen up, I was forced to breathe through my mouth, and an x-ray confirmed two small fractures.

Even in those circumstances, I got in and gave it my best, coming out with a 2:13 win in the 200m butterfly, a couple of strokes shy of my Commonwealth record. The story gave Ian Hanson, later to become the media officer for Swimming Australia in the days of Susie O'Neill, Ian Thorpe and Grant Hackett, his first exclusive in the Daily Telegraph as a young reporter.

I told him, *"Who knows what kind of time I would have done under normal circumstances but these days I just don't seem to have normal circumstances."*

A throbbing, frozen shoulder with trials on the horizon was a big impediment. The best of the best of Australia would be in peak form and gunning for me just at the worst possible moment. In late 1983, I had missed about seven weeks of full swimming. Depressed, I returned to the doctor and asked if he could give me that cortisone shot after all.

A retired athlete, he was poised with the syringe hovering over my shoulder when I changed my mind, excused myself and scurried out of the clinic. I was embarrassed, but just couldn't do it.

The Promise

By Christmas, time out had led to a significant improvement in my joint and the pain had subsided. Hope returned and I was happy to be able to start a steady build-up in training. At the same time, I knew that I would not get back to my best in the few weeks I had before heading home for trials.

I consoled myself with the thought that selectors could take three swimmers per event for the Los Angeles Olympics and after trials I would have five months to get my shoulder back to full strength. I very much considered myself a defending champion who would be racing for Olympic gold once more in July 1984.

Worrying over the trials kept me awake at night. I believed I still had career-best swims in me but that wasn't going to happen at trials. In desperation, I rang the Australian Swimming Union, told them about my injury and asked for advice.

"It's okay," I was told. They understood, agreed that there was time after the trials to get back to my best shape and added, "Don't worry. We'll take the injury into consideration, Michelle." What a relief!

In the past, they had taken a holistic view of a swimmer's potential before nominating teams. An athlete's record in major competitions counted. They knew I stepped up on the big occasions. They also knew I had been shy of where I needed to be just four or five weeks out from Moscow but with the right work and determination, in partnership with coach Bill Sweetenham, the result had been gold.

Moreover, had it not been for GDR doping, it would have been three golds, not one. They knew that I was able to meet challenges head-on and thrive.

Olympic Trials 1984

Trials began in Brisbane on February 23. I faced a new crop of swimmers hungry to make the Australian team. On the blocks for my first race, I tried not to let doubts flood in.

"Mind over matter, Michelle," I kept telling myself, but no amount of positivity could negate the challenge of what had become physically impossible and forced so much time out.

I finished third in my two main events and fourth in another. The winner of the 200, 400 and 800m freestyle finals was Anna McVann, who had made good progress but whose 800m time at the trials was two seconds slower per 100m than my Moscow-winning effort. An ocean. My swims were just outside the qualifying time set by the ASU, with my 800m just 0.2 of a second per lap adrift. A puddle.

The federation's promise to consider my injury had led me to believe that all I had to do was finish in the top three and show that I was getting back into form. At the same time, Bill had been quoted in the papers as saying, *"Everyone's been told that they have to meet the qualifying time."* I hadn't been told that. And, it seemed, neither had the selectors.

After the last race of the trials, we all waited for the names of the 1984 Olympic team to be read out. I was feeling uneasy. Then my stomach churned and I wanted to run away and hide as I realised they had left me out.

Confused, upset and accepting but with tears welling, I collected my gear. There was a sense of shock in the air and I felt all eyes were on me. I just needed to melt away and never come back, but suddenly I was surrounded by journalists asking me how I felt.

Robotically, I told them that I had no choice but to accept the decision. I had bounced back from injury and shown them I was on the right track, just as they had asked when they said they would take my injury into consideration. They would have the chance to add me later when the team's fitness-confirmation trials came round, but the chances of that happening looked remote given that they had just broken their promise.

One of the reporters asked, "What do you think of the fact that seven other swimmers who've been accepted on the squad didn't make qualifying standards either?"

What?! That was like a punch to the stomach. It just felt like they were reinforcing one of the biggest mistakes the sport kept on making season after season.

At every level, the message was clear: rules are rules until regulators decide they can be broken.

The media urged me to come with them on a hunt for the selectors. In the dimly lit corridors behind the swim stadium, we had a brief exchange with one of the selectors before I stood behind the reporters as they knocked on the door of the small room where the swimming board was meeting.

No sooner was the door opened than the questions rained in. "Why was Michelle Ford left off?" No answer. "What about your promise to consider her injury?" More silence, other than them squirming in their seats. "Why have you nominated seven others for the Olympic training squad who haven't made qualifying standards?" Awkward looks all round. "Michelle's the defending champion ... why not include her on the team?"

The media were unrelenting, but the blazers were unrepentant. The questions were spot on. Then I ran a quick calculation in my head and realised there was a place on the team that hadn't been filled. For a brief moment, I joined the media throng and called for answers.

The selectors dug their heels in and said they didn't have to justify themselves. A last volley of questions ricocheted off the walls: "What if she beats the best swimmer's times? What if she breaks a world record? Will you add her to the squad then?"

Belligerent faces stared back but those last questions lit a spark in me as I beat a lonely retreat from the pool. Would I ever swim again? Under a flickering streetlight in the car park, I stood with tears streaming down my face, every part of me reeling and my heart beating furiously in frustration.

My mind was racing with questions. Was this because of my decision not to choose the AIS? Was it because I had opted for the USA instead? Had they seen it as betrayal? The same thing had happened the year before when they excluded me from the squad for the World Championships in Ecuador with no explanation. Was there anything that might make them change their minds?

The answer awaited me at home in the very room where decades later I would find the courage to dive deep into the archives to tell my story. All the trophies, Olympic medals and accolades stared back at me from the walls and cabinets.

I was drawn to a forgotten photo on the wall. It was me, aged 13, next to Dick Caine, my old coach and mentor. If anyone could help me now, he could.

Back to the Beginning

A phone call later, I grabbed the keys to my father's car and set off on the two-hour drive south of Sydney to the town of Bomaderry. The whole way, I sang songs like 'To Dream the Impossible Dream', my mood swimming from determination to despair.

Their decision felt personal—a deliberate act they had planned all along. I kept telling myself, "Don't give up; you can do it." I was going to prove them wrong and force a rethink. They would surely have to take the best to the LA Games?

Then again, I reminded myself, these same officials had shown bias in the past. Some on the board were the same people who had banned Dawn Fraser and Murray Rose, two of Australia's greatest swimmers. Now the same people held my fate in their hands.

Seven years had passed since Dick and I had split. He was instrumental in helping to make me the swimmer that I was. Dick had helped many athletes achieve world-champion status in different sports. He had mastered his art but like many coaches in the 1970s and 1980s had never been honoured as a coach on travelling teams or included in Olympic-squad training.

The status quo at the swim federation was solid: athletes and coaches should put up and shut up. Nothing else would be tolerated.

My mind stopped racing as I pulled up outside Bomaderry Pool. The late summer air was beginning to cool, the big gum trees were casting long shadows over the 50-metre outdoor pool and the blue haze of the eucalyptus lent the place a majestic, magical aura.

A lone figure was waiting for me at the end of the pool. After a quick hello, Coach Caine got straight to the point as if our last session together had been earlier that day: "Go and change, get in and do some timed 100s."

Then, after those, it was: "Get out, get changed, then we talk business."

I said nothing. I just did exactly what he asked me to. It was as if I were 13 again. I needed him to say, "You can do this, Michelle." Dick was pensive, silent and I almost thought he was going to say, "The game's up, this isn't going to work." He took a deep breath and said, "Right, Michelle, you are the best swimmer in Australia, and I know you can do this."

The last rays of sun caught his grin but we both knew there wouldn't be much smiling in the months ahead. There was a mountain to climb and limited time to get to the summit. "Listen, Mich," he added. "This is going to be a shit fight. The only way to be selected now is to show them at the confirmation trials and shave seconds off the best time anyone else has managed. If you do that, they'll have to include you. If you're the fastest, they can't afford not to."

I felt a surge of hope. We were back at the beginning—and united for a last stand.

From the day we had first met in 1969 to this day more than 14 years later, we'd lived our fair share of ups and downs. Now, this old coach-swimmer partnership faced a new challenge.

In the weeks ahead, the headlines were stacked with stories like the one by Ian Hanson in the *Daily Telegraph* on February 27 that screamed: *'Shocks in LA Swim Squad and Lisa Going'*. The report noted that sprinter Lisa Curry and six others had been added to the team on the basis that they could swim a relay even though they'd missed the qualification cut in individual events.

To add insult to injury, on February 29, one of the selectors, Geoff Hare, from Victoria, said on radio that Lisa "would get the chance to prove herself for individual events at the Olympics, even though she had only made the selection for relays".

The *Daily Mirror* reported the story and cited coach Brett Sutton, a national team coach, who had worked with Dick and me, as saying, "I have got the interview on tape and couldn't believe my ears when he said it. On that criteria Michelle certainly could have been selected."

At one point, the debate got truly nasty when my teammates, some who had lived through the Moscow Games with me and endured the wrath of those who had not wanted us to represent Australia because of the boycott, were told to appear on television and speak against me.

Some of those I trained with later confirmed that it had been suggested to them that if I had been added to the team, their places would have been put at risk. It was mendacious.

I could relate the details of what happened next in my own words but one of those boxes taken down from the cupboards when I began this writing journey unearthed a note from Coach Caine penned long after I had retired. His recollections brought tears to my eyes and I resolved to let him tell this final passage of our time together in his own words.

"Probably the hardest and worst thing that happened to Michelle and me as a coach, was when they would not put you into the LA Olympic Team. And, even though you swam five seconds faster with no pacemaker or opposition and even when the Prime Minister and leader of the AWU and every poll said you must go into the team, those arrogant sports officials who were in charge of swimming did not put you in the team.

So, we started Michelle and me, in the middle of Australian winter, this massive task with no help, no funding, and no training partners. Mission Impossible. But why Michelle was so great is that once she had her mind set there was only one direction— straight ahead and charge, take no prisoners!

Those arrogant sports officials who were in charge of swimming did not put you in the team.

Every day for six weeks we were front page news. Every day, reporters, photographers and cameras were following us everywhere.

Once even a Channel Nine sport helicopter landed in my back yard. But this time it was going to be different, a lot harder physically and mentally. All of Australia was watching.

The workload became massive. There were plenty of fights. In a way, it was like being a part of an old married couple, but Michelle knew I was there for her. The problem was that Michelle left Australia to complete her studies in America, as a star Olympic gold medallist and came home to jealous officials. Thank god for the Australian attitude toward the underdog. The Australian public, media, and politicians from both sides supported Michelle, and you could start to see the change. Michelle was starting to think Australia does remember, does care.

Now came the hardest and most important part, the quality repeat sessions. Michelle had the pressure of making the times in six weeks. Times that had not been done that year anywhere in the world. Every day the media wanted stories, photos, interviews, etc. and on top of that, I was giving her these intensive, heartbreaking efforts. It was near breaking her. Michelle knew that with me there were no excuses, no missing times. I do not want to know how sick or tired you are, do it! One time we went a 6-miler; she was abusing me every stroke, and if she failed, she has to do it again.

The big night comes at the Sydney University pool. A time-trial for Michelle to swim under the time that the fastest swimmer had done at the trials. There were more spectators than could fill the stands, hundreds in and outside. No more people could fit in the pool complex. Everyone wanted to see if Michelle could do it. Sports officials, including the national Olympic officials, who had said that they would happily put Michelle in the team if the swimming officials put her name up. Media from the most prominent Australian newspapers and every TV and radio station were there. I thought Elvis or the Beatles must be coming.

As always, Michelle sat with me away from the crowds. I never talk to parents, and I never have them near my athletes. Because of the short training time, we had to taper differently. I kept telling Michelle, 'you look good, your skin looks good'. We are in this together, but I am worried sick for her. Every day and night I fight with my wife, nothing matters but Michelle. I tell her that no matter what happens tonight, I will always be there for you. As I talk, the angriness and fear leaves Michelle, she is breathing more relaxed. The officials and timekeepers come forward to take their place behind the starting blocks. The crowd sensing the tensions become silent. Mich and I are standing looking at each other, like the fighter and the old trainer. Three of the leading reporters, all who have supported us, came up to us: 'Look at this crowd for one swimmer. Dick, it feels more like a world heavyweight title fight! Well Dick, what do you think?'

'Boys,' I answered, (Alan Clarkson, Ian Heads and Ian Hanson), 'you cannot go near her.'

'Dick, we know that, do you think under all of this pressure she can do it?'

'Look, this is Michelle Ford. At 13 years old, she made the Olympic team and swam before a crowd of 100s of thousands at the Olympics. She has beaten the East Germans; no other girl has done that. Today, Michelle has more reasons to do this than ever before. This is not just to make the LA team but showing who she really is. A performer, the best in Australia. Someone who can come up to the task and win under pressure. I just hope those bastards see who she really is,' pointing to the Australian swimming mafia and officials.

The time has come. I face Michelle. 'Look at the crowd that is here for you!'

Michelle and the four boys line up to race—because there is not a girl in Australia that can match her. Even though we were happy to challenge the girl selected in the 800 metres for the LA Olympics to race Michelle, they declined. There was no way they would let her race. They knew Michelle would win easily and they do not like being proven wrong even if it means losing gold for Australia.

I have seen many wrongs and spiteful things done by officials in Australian sport but what was to happen next—apart from them putting Dawn [Fraser] out for 25 years—was to top the bill of bastardry. Out walks the referee: 'Michelle cannot have anyone racing her, she must do it alone.' The boys were told to step down, and the place erupted. I thought they might kill the officials. I look at Michelle standing on the blocks alone. She looks straight back at me. I nod my head. She adjusts her goggles. I looked at her—her chest rising and lowering. I knew Michelle was ready.

The low-life officials had done her and me a favour, the tiger was back!

Michelle swims five seconds faster than any Australian girl. The Prime Minister of Australia and the opposition and the Australian Workers Union are all in support of her. A poll run by the Daily Mirror says that 90% of the people want Michelle in the team.

Swimming Australia shows their true colours. They had promised that if she swims faster than the number one girl for the 800m, she would be put into the team for LA.

But Michelle Ford is left out of the Olympic team.

Michelle Ford, one of our greatest distance swimmers, Olympic, world and Commonwealth champion was finished. Australia lost a sure gold medal. In any other country, Michelle would be a hero.

History Repeats

After months of appeals, it was over. I would suffer the same fate as Dawn, Murray and others. I was exhausted and broken. The swimming officials at the ASU had said "no", even though Olympic officials had said "yes", along with Prime Minister Bob Hawke,

Sports Minister John Brown, the Opposition Leader Andrew Peacock, and the public at large. My name was not submitted to the AOC for approval.

The past four months had been a whirlwind—an unrelenting, unforgettable struggle. That lonely time trial would be the last 800m freestyle of my career. It was also the most challenging. I would race butterfly and in relays at international events over the coming year, but my heart wasn't in it.

I could no longer defend my Olympic title. I felt I had been robbed and I was angry. It was hard to forgive the people responsible. Whether officials, coaches or even some athletes, they were not people who placed the athlete first.

Despite being emotionally spent, I could also see the gold in that final quest. I had come full circle. I was back with my first coach, the eccentric 'garbo' who had worn those long white socks and purple suit, and who had driven the car into the pool that day when we youngsters had stood open-mouthed staring at the reason why training got cancelled.

To have had the chance to be back working with Coach Caine as a team once more is something I treasure to this day. The same goes for the Australian fighting spirit it brought to the fore.

The people, the press and even all sides of politics had stood by me. There were thousands of letters from people I didn't know, each telling me that I was their hero and that I should not give in. A *Daily Mirror* headline over a story by Ian Hanson read: *'Michelle Winning Public's Support'.* It noted an *"unbelievable wave of public support for Olympic swimmer Michelle Ford in her desperate plight to convince the Australian Swimming Union she deserves a place on the team for Los Angeles".*

Pledges of financial support were offered to the ASU if they put me on the team. Robie Porter, an Australian pop singer known by many as Rob E. G., hit the headlines when he told the media he was appalled at the way I was being treated. He offered to pay my way to Los Angeles.

Even head coach Bill Sweetenham weighed in for me. He told the ASU that the selectors had broken the rules by taking swimmers who had not swum inside the qualifying target. As such, he added, "It's hard to exclude Michelle from the team. She's a defending champion!"

Nothing moved the ASU. They would rather go without the best if that proved they were the bosses and the only thing that mattered was for them to win, not the athlete or Australia.

I felt for my family. The press had lived outside our door for weeks on end. My mother had written appeals to various authorities day in and day out at a time when my father was also vying for Olympic selection in sailing. It was not fair but it was also their loss as well as mine at a time when 'all for one, one for all' was a motivational boast, not a reality.

After my gold in Moscow, four Olympic cycles (16 years) would go by until Susie O'Neill became the next Australian woman to stand on the top step of the dais in the Olympic pool. Little wonder. However, the program did not get going

Meanwhile, the announcement that the Eastern Bloc would boycott the 1984 Olympics hardly made headlines down under. It was simply accepted. I felt for all the athletes who missed out.

It was time for me to force myself to move on. When one door closes, another opens, as the saying goes. And so it was that I came to announce my retirement from swimming. My statement, made through the LA press club, read:

"Today I announce my retirement from swimming. I would like to thank the members of the Australian press and other media for their tremendous support, and the Minister of Sport, Mr Brown, for all of his efforts on my behalf. And to the people of Australia, my family, my friends who gave me their encouragement. A great big Thank You.

At the invitation of the International Olympic Committee, and the Organizing Committee of the 1984 LA Games, for the first time in history, I have joined the IOC Athletes Commission and will be at the Olympic village throughout the Games to assist athletes from all countries. I would like to take this opportunity to wish all Australian swimmers and all our athletes the very best of luck in Los Angeles. I'll be here cheering for you."

Chapter 23
State Secret Doping Plan 14:25

"They always say time changes things, but you actually have to change them yourself."
– Andy Warhol (April 2020)

The only opponents who finished ahead of me in finals at the Moscow Olympic Games were East Germans fuelled by banned substances.

When the truth was revealed in the 1990s, we learned that the dosages of the male hormone testosterone given to those who beat me were higher than the Canadian sprinter Ben Johnson had taken in the year leading up to his 100m track victory and subsequent disqualification at the Seoul Olympics of 1988.

All five girls ahead of me in Moscow were teenagers who had been through the GDR sports school system and were put on the anabolic steroid Oral Turinabol from as young as 12. The aim was to give them strength, by artificial means, that boys get naturally at puberty.

We've known this for three decades, courtesy of GDR State Security police files saved from the shredders in the year after the fall of the Berlin Wall in late 1989 and the subsequent police investigation.

When officers raided the garage of Dr Lothar Kipke, among the horrors unearthed was clear evidence that all those who finished ahead of me in my three finals at the 1980 Olympics had been doped.

The proof was provided by the positive tests registered at the IOC-accredited laboratory in Saxony. Of course, that evidence not only affected me but every single female swimmer who raced in Moscow and missed a place they deserved in their race.

Kipke's papers confirmed the dosages of male steroids, mainly supplied in 'little blue pills' of Oral Turinabol and given to each of the swimmers in preparation for Moscow: Ines Diers (1,320mg), Sybille Schönrock (1,320mg), Petra Schneider (1,895mg) and Carmela Schmidt (1,725mg), who all finished ahead of me in either the 200m butterfly or 400m freestyle.

The notes found in Kipke's garage in the mid-1990s backed up what we had known since 1991–92 when State Security papers saved from the shredders as the Berlin Wall fell provided proof of cheating that had not only affected me, but every single female who finished behind East Germans in Moscow.

The same was true for all who competed in 1976 at the Montreal Games and Seoul in 1988. And it was also true for all those who were beaten by East Germans at World and European Championships between 1973 and 1989. Los Angeles 1984 was the break in the storm because the GDR was part of the Soviet Bloc boycott.

In all, an estimated 15,000 male and female East German athletes, especially those who competed in sports that required explosive power, were victims and unwitting players in the biggest pharmacological experiment in sports history: State Research Plan 14:25.

The difference in how the drugs morphed the female athletes' performances was more than evident in the medal counts. The GDR men's swimming teams claimed a combined total of eight medals, including two gold, at the Montreal 1976, Moscow 1980 and Seoul 1988 Olympics.

However, the women's rise to dominance was a tidal wave that swept through the international swimming community.

Records 1973–1989

- In 1972, the GDR women's swim team held no individual world records.
- From 1973–1989, GDR women set 110 solo world records and 17 relay world records, including 78 standards in races that were over 100m.
- GDR women set 171 European records (151 solo and 20 relay) from 1973–1989.

Medals

- **Olympic Games, 1976, 1980, 1988:** 66 medals out of a possible 98 went to GDR women, including 32 out of a possible 41 golds.
- **World Championships, 1973, 1975, 1978, 1982, 1986:** GDR women claimed 44 golds from a possible 72, including a sweep of every 100m freestyle title.
- **European Championships, 1973–1989:** in the seven editions of the continental showcase held in that period, GDR women lost only eight races for a tally of 96 out of a possible 104 titles and won more than 92% of all medals.

How They Targeted Women

The rumours of doping began as world records started to tumble to East German women in 1973 at the inaugural World Championships that year.

In their 1997 paper, *Hormonal doping and androgenization of athletes: a secret program of the German Democratic Republic government,* Professor Werner Franke and his wife Brigitte Berendonk (an Olympic discus thrower in 1968 and 1972) wrote:

"Several thousand athletes were treated with androgens every year, including minors of each sex. Special emphasis was placed on administering androgens to women and adolescent girls because this practice proved to be particularly effective for sports performance. Damaging side effects were recorded, some of which required surgical or medical intervention."

The depths of depravity that the communist state sunk to in building a fraudulent medals' machine had been in print since 1991 when Berendonk's book Doping: von der Forschung zum Betrug *(Doping: from Research to Fraud)* was first published.

Franke and Berendonk presented their paper at the Doping in Sport Symposium in Leipzig, Germany where scientists under the state-sponsored Research Institute for Physical Culture and Sports worked out how East Germany was prospering in sport by cheating.

This institute was one of the twin towers of the GDR system. The other was the German-run Central Doping Control Laboratory in Kreischa, Saxony. This was also the IOC-accredited anti-doping facility—its mission was to detect cheating and report back to international authorities.

GDR scientists and doctors were members of expert committees at these two international sports federations and were tasked with keeping abreast of trends and discussions of new rules and testing methods. The GDR machine wanted to stay at least one step ahead of anti-doping developments so the truth of what they were doing remained a secret.

As a result, athletes who tested positive before competitions did not travel. A variety of excuses and explanations were offered in place of the truth. It is estimated that 12,000 secret samples were analysed every year. Not a single one of the many recorded positive tests was ever reported to international authorities.

What the fraud ringleaders had not planned for was the fall of the Berlin Wall that led to the raid of Kipke's residence and the subsequent discovery of damning evidence. That rich archive of classified documents was compiled from the work of those who were unofficial collaborators for the Ministry for State Security (known as the 'Stasi'). It revealed that hundreds of physicians and scientists, including top-ranking professors, performed doping research and administered prescription drugs as well as unapproved experimental drug preparations.

All of these records, and the subsequent work of a special police investigations unit after the German reunification in the 1990s, confirmed the astonishing lengths the state had gone to in its efforts to use sport as propaganda for its political system in the Cold War of East vs West.

The Agent of Success: Androgyny

An even bigger shock was proof that these scientists and architects knew the doping program they were carrying out posed a serious risk of harm to these young athletes. The drug company Jenapharm that developed Oral Turinabol, the most prevalent steroid used in the GDR sports system, noted:

"If the treatment with anabolics is long-term, or at high dosages, real possibility for androgenic side effects exists. Skin conditions such as acne will develop, virilization effects such as deepening of the voice, growth of facial hair, masculine habits, increased sexual appetite, and clitoral hypertrophy will all occur."

However, these warnings were ignored with hostile silence, and data from the 1968–1972 Olympic cycle taught scientists a lot about the most effective dosing amounts and when to best administer drugs to coincide with major competitions. Lesser-performing athletes were used as guinea pigs, receiving experimental dosing amounts and subjected to insane training regimens with hopes of perfecting the scientific experiment on performance enhancement.

According to a 1990s confession from Manfred Höppner, the Deputy Director of the Sports Medical Service and a member of the Medical Commission of the International Amateur Athletics Federation in the GDR era, *"many, if not all, medal-winning GDR athletes in strength-and-speed-dependent events"* had been part of the learning curve with Oral Turinabol in preparation for the 1972 Olympic Games.

However, the program did not get going in earnest until after the 1972 Games when all drugs would officially be referred to as 'Unterstützende Mittel (UM)', or 'supporting means'. Hopper noted: "Under UM, we refer exclusively to anabolic steroids". Franke and Berendonk, who in the early 1990s revealed the nature of what UM really meant (see graphic on opposite page), noted:

"The effects of androgenic hormones were so spectacular, particularly in female athletes ... that few competitors not using the drugs had a chance of winning."

In a summary report to the Stasi on March 3, 1977, Höppner, under his spy code name 'Technik', confirmed:

"At present anabolic steroids are applied in all Olympic sporting events, with the exception of sailing and gymnastics ... and by all national teams ... The positive value of anabolic steroids for the development of a top performance is undoubted.

Remarkable rates of increase in performances were also noted in the swimming events of women. From our experiences made so far it can be concluded that women have the greatest advantage from treatments with anabolic hormones with respect to their performance in sports. Especially high is the performance-supporting effect following the first administration of anabolic hormones, especially with junior athletes."

That last line would cut to the core of Höppner's later conviction for bodily harm to minors during the German doping trials of 1998–2000.

Cheats' Cabinet:

The GDR Cocktail of Banned Substances
Androgenic-anabolic steroids

Oral
Oral-Turinabol (tablets)
Steroid substance 646 [Mestanolone]
Steroid substance XII Steroid substance 482
Steroid substance 648
Dianabol [Methandienone, methandrostenolone]

Injectable
Testosteron-Ampullen [Testosterone propionate]
Testosteron-Depot-Ampullen [Testosterone enanthate]
Testo-Tropin-Ampullen
Turinabol-Ampullen [Nandrolone phenylpropionate, Durabolin]
Turinabol-Depot-Ampullen [Nandrolone decanoate, Deca-Durabolin]

Nasal spray
Testosterone esters
Androstendione

Substances stimulating testosterone synthesis
Gonabion-Ampullen (injectable) [Chorionic gonadotropin (hCG)]
Clomiphen, Clomifen (tablets)

Neuropeptides
Lysine-vasopressin
Oxytocin
Substance P

Stimulants
Amphetamine
Methamphetamine (Pervitin)

Neurotropics, psychotropics
Corticotropin
Piracetam
Nicergolin
Nivalin

Polypeptide hormones
Human growth hormone [Somatotropin]

Source material: Hormonal doping and androgenization of athletes: a secret program of the German Democratic Republic government Werner W. Franke and Brigitte Berendonk (see reference notes 217 & 218)

How They Kept the Secret

The Stasi was established on February 8, 1950. It was the GDR's intelligence agency and crime investigation service, and it thrived on having citizens spy on each others.

Among its 180,000 informers were athletes, coaches, doctors and others working in performance sport. They were known as 'unofficial collaborators' and they travelled with every sports team. Special agents oversaw the doping program overseas during major events under the very noses of event organisers.

Some athletes were sworn to secrecy, while others were kept in the dark along with their parents. Most of those involved in sport were being spied on by teammates, coaches, doctors and in some bizarre cases that involved coercion, parents even shopped their own children to the program.

One of those cases involved Kornelia Ender, the four-time winner of gold at the Montreal Olympics who had cast an enormous shadow over me as a 13-year-old as she walked in front of me to race in the heats of the 200m freestyle at my first Games.

It was revealed by German media in 2015 that Ender and husband Stefan Grummt, a former bobsleigh ace for the GDR, had unsuccessfully tried to flee the country via Hungary to the West with both of their daughters in 1989, five months before the Berlin Wall came down.

When Ender and family arrived at a remote crossing on the Hungarian border, guards were waiting to turn them back. The Hungarians said that they would not report the matter. But when Ender and family completed their vacation and returned home, they faced unexpected interrogation by the Stasi. In the 2015 interview, Ender revealed her own father, Heinz Ender, a colonel in the GDR Army, had heard a whisper in the family about the plot to escape and she believed that he had informed the Stasi.

Ender, who had a reputation on the GDR team for being a rebel, told the authorities in 1989 that she would apply to leave the country through official channels. The paperwork was submitted on November 1, 1989. Just eight days later, the Berlin Wall was opened and the end of the GDR was nigh. Ender and her family moved to the West soon after, unsure whether the political situation would be reversed or not.

In GDR times, those who defied the system or did manage to escape lived in constant fear of what might happen to their families remaining in East Germany. There are many accounts of consequences for the relatives of athletes perceived to have been a threat to the state secret.

Those safest from the long arm of the GDR government were the athletes who obediently complied with the program and asked no questions. In fact, teenage athletes were specifically told not to tell their parents because they didn't need to worry about details of performance sport that they wouldn't understand. That same principle was handed down from the very head of the entire systematic-cheating program.

Manfred Ewald, Minister of Sport from 1961 to 1988 and president of the GDR Olympic Committee between 1973 and 1990, was quoted as having told coaches, "They're still so young and don't have to know everything."

On August 26, 1993, Stasi records were opened as part of legal processes in reunified Germany and details of the abuse were released.

They included a 1975 report by Hans Schuster, head of the Research Institute for Fitness in Sport in Leipzig. He noted that anabolic steroids were prescribed in both combination and pure form. Schuster further confirmed that the drugs led to "considerable improvement in performance" and resulted in "liver damage and changes in physical appearance" among female athletes.

The Truth Will Out

In November 1990, *Stern,* one of the world's leading current-affairs magazines, published a document showing that Kristin Otto, six-time Olympic gold-medal winner of 1988, and three GDR swim teammates had tested positive for anabolic steroids just weeks before they all claimed European titles in 1989.

The damning document was typed up on the headed paper of the GDR's Central Institute of Sports Medicine Services, complete with the address of the IOC-accredited laboratory at Kreischa in Saxony.

It was signed on August 9, 1989 by one of the leading doctors working in the GDR doping program, Claus Clausnitzer. He was the director at the Kreischa laboratory and a senior figure in the doping program; he was also appointed as a member of the IOC's sub-commission on doping and biochemistry of sport.

In 1972, Clausnitzer wrote an article titled *'Influenceability in Anti-Doping Control'.* In 1984, he received his PhD in chemistry and after the collapse of the GDR in 1989, he was among officials who confirmed the use of doping substances by successful athletes, including Kristin Otto.

The clandestine operation at Kreischa continued until the GDR collapsed in late 1989. One of its final acts was recorded in an analysis of test samples on swimmers dated August 7, 1989. Otto's fellow Olympic champions, Heike Friedrich and Daniela Hunger, and GDR swim-team newcomer and future European and Olympic champion Dagmar Hase also tested positive for illegal testosterone levels.

Coaches were informed and doctors instructed to clean the girls up before they contributed to another 14 out of 16 golds for the GDR just a week later at the European Championships in Bonn.

Stern ran the damning laboratory evidence in an eight-page exposé under a banner headline *'How the GDR Made Winners!'* The feature included an interview that amounted to a confession from one of the former heads of the East German

The damning document from the Kreischa laboratory showing the positive tests of GDR swim stars.

doping program, Manfred Höppner.

The top doctor in the doping program, Höppner was one of the three most senior figures in the GDR's fraud. The other two were Erich Honecker, leader of the GDR between 1971 and 1989, and Manfred Ewald, Minister of Sport from 1961 to 1988. All relied on the next tier down, where the likes of Kipke worked directly with athletes and coaches.

Doctor Doping

Kipke was a member of the medical commission of FINA.

A former member of the Nazi party, Kipke was described in the doping trials in 2000 as "the Josef Mengele of GDR sport" (a notorious German SS officer and physician during World War II). He had been damned by Höppner's hand many years before. At the height of my career, Höppner wrote to his Stasi liaison officer:

"In preparation for team travel to the US, Dr Kipke forced ... athletes to be given testosterone injections. Dr Kipke is brutal in giving the injections. He doesn't consider any pain it causes to the athlete and almost rams the syringe into the body."

Such insight was part of a vast body of evidence, including scientific papers, that led to the push for legal action. Armed with an overwhelming amount of evidence that suggested crimes, the Central Investigations Office for Government and Reunification Crimes (ZERV) was established as a special division of the criminal police force in Germany.

Charged with investigating doping crimes, it invited 1,000 athletes to testify. Many did not want the public exposure that was an inevitable part of the process, especially because in some parts of East Germany, athletes who did speak up, like one of my Moscow opponents, Petra Schneider, came home to find "Traitor!" and other insults painted on their front doors.

There were also those, like 1980 Olympic swim champion Caren Metschuk, who did not feel they had suffered at the hands of the GDR regime.

Metschuk told journalist Craig Lord that she was *"always well looked after ... We had doctors who checked us every day and we felt like we were in a safe environment. We were better looked after than almost any other athletes in the world at the time. Those who were taking substances without any medical experts by their side were in a far worse place. I had no health issues."*

A great many others felt quite differently and stepped up to tell their stories of abuse. In the end, around 300 followed the ZERV process all the way to court, testifying against coaches, scientists and others.

Charges were brought and several athletes testified in court against the doctors, trainers and coaches who experimented on them and exploited their talents through illegal means in order to dominate international athletic podiums.

I still feel the sting of injustice in competing as a clean athlete against the stacked odds of the performance-enhanced GDR swimmers. However, age and maturity have softened the bite, and I have a lot of empathy for those young women who unknowingly followed the direction and advice of the people they most trusted.

Franke and Berendonk noted: *"Not only was cheating at the center of the program, but so was the abuse of the athletes' health. Female athletes, including adolescents, experienced virilization symptoms, and possibly as many as 1,000 sportsmen and women suffered serious and lasting physical and psychological damage."*

Many of these athletes have suffered a lifetime of symptoms and treatments for numerous side effects from steroid abuse, including sterilisation, endocrine disease, heart, liver, kidney and gallbladder problems, chronic back and joint pain, tumours and violent mood swings. The link between steroids and certain forms of cancer has also been well established.

All competitors were given birth control, and those who became pregnant were forced to terminate their foetuses. Stasi files stated:

"Should a pregnancy occur while anabolic steroids are being taken, then it is recommended in all cases that an abortion is carried out. Children born to athletes who had taken steroids are to be delivered in a Stasi clinic so that a decision could be taken as to what to do in the event of complications."

The weekly German magazine, Der Spiegel, reported from the trial in 2000 that Kipke had even informed his bosses about the possible effects on embryos from anabolic steroid use. Kipke wrote, *"During pregnancy, transplacental virilization of the female fetus may occur."*

Other victims testified of miscarriages after being released from the doping program, and of severe birth defects in their children. Many of these offspring sat in the courtroom with their mothers as they testified against the government.

The crisis among victims was not only physical, noted Giselher Spitzer, a sports psychologist at the University of Potsdam who attended the trials and would later compile a comprehensive, official and redacted record of the 14:25 doping program for the German state.

"The psychological implications of being doped are immense," the psychologist said during the doping trials. *"These women live with the fact that their successes were a result of having cheated. Their identities are still very much connected with swimming, and they now fear that they are not able to accomplish anything on their own. Added to that is the fact that these drugs were administered along with birth control pills. That can have unbelievable psychological consequences."*

While testifying on his own behalf against charges of supplying drugs, doping and causing bodily harm to 58 swimmers, Dr Kipke told the court he had been unaware that the drugs carried any adverse side effects other than a deepening of the voice.

According to Kipke, as research increased in the 1980s, he began administering the steroids in lower dosages and only in pill form.

Retribution

The heads of GDR doping, Manfred Ewald and Manfred Höppner, faced 142 counts of assisting grievous bodily harm. On grounds of time, presiding Judge Faust heard just 22 cases against them before coming to his conclusion: they were both guilty on all charges.

On July 18, 2000, both were convicted of a combined 142 counts of aiding and abetting bodily harm. However, Ewald was only given a 22-month suspended sentence and Höppner an 18-month suspended sentence. Both were ordered to pay the legal costs of 20 former East German women athletes who jointly sought the prosecution of the officials.

As for Kipke, Judge Peter Faust ruled that he had acted with "willful malevolence" in overseeing doping of the swimmers during his tenure as head of the doping program. He was slapped with only a 15-month suspended jail sentence.

These judgements against the defendants only hurt their victims further. They were not happy with the punishments, feeling all men got away with a mere slap on the wrist.

Among physicians called to court to account for their personal roles in the deception was Dr Dorit Rosler. On hearing the testimony of athletes, she broke down in tears and said, "I should have shown more courage. In Nazi Germany we did what we were told to do. The GDR doping machine was no different; we were just carrying out medical orders ... have we not learned anything?"

After the trials ended, Dr Rosler would go on to set up a surgery centre in Czarnikauer, Strasse in the very offices in which Manfred Höppner had sat at a fold-down table and written his reports to the Stasi spymasters. Her service provided free medical help for all victims of the GDR doping system. She was the only doctor who expressed and showed deep remorse.

There was none of that from Dr Dieter Binus, Dr Ulrich Sunder and Dr Horst Tausch. They all broke both the Hippocratic Oath and the law when they administered drugs to under-age swimmers. They too were convicted of bodily harm, but allowed to continue to practise as doctors.

Among others working in the system was Dr Eberhard Koehler, who sought an injunction to try to prevent publication of a book on GDR doping in which he was named.

There was no hiding after researcher Giselher Spitzer unearthed official documents dated April 23, 1985, that stated, *"The evidence is kept by Gen. Dr. Köhler on open index cards with the names of the athletes, the type and quantity of the preparations issued, the date, the stock held by the respective section doctor and the signature of the section doctor."*

The statute of limitations set for the trials ran out during the Sydney 2000 Olympic Games, preventing the filing of any further litigation. Many eyewitnesses and victims missed this deadline and were not called to account because they lived and worked overseas, some of them as head Olympic coaches for other nations in a variety of sports.

Meanwhile, Kreischa's status and work continues: the site is now called the Institute of Doping Analysis and Sports Biochemistry (IDAS) and remains an IOC-accredited laboratory to this day.

Compensation

Many swimmers were among the 170 ex-GDR athletes awarded €9,250 each in compensation in 2006 from the German Olympic Sports Confederation (DOSB) and the drug company, Jenapharm. The out-of-court settlement was the first of three compensation processes that have paid out more than €28 million to victims so far.

Doping-Opfer-Hilfe (the 'Help for Doping Victims' organisation) was founded in 1999. It drove the process that led to the German Bundestag passing the *Second Doping Victims Assistance Act* in June 2016.

The move established a €13.65 million fund to provide financial assistance to former East Germans who suffered "significant health damage" as a result of the GDR's state doping program. Within half a year, 240 of the 400 athletes had their applications approved for compensation.

No such reparation has ever been offered to the victims of the GDR's athletic victims of a state secret. They are the forgotten generation, the women whose calls for justice, truth and reconciliation have been ignored, and whose names still remain in the columns outside the medal counts.

Between 1991 and 1995, then IOC President Juan Samaranch sent a clear signal on GDR medals in response to media questions: the results would stand as the official record. His words spread to the ranks of IOC members and affiliate federations: a line had been drawn and there would be no further discussion.

As things stand in 2024, East Germany's gruesome success and cheating remains the official record and result of almost 20 years of sport in which the victims of cheating have never been granted the dignity of a reconciliation and justice process.

A spokesman for Germany's Olympic Committee, Michael Schirp, noted that 1980 Olympic swimming champion Petra Schneider had confronted her abusers in court and acknowledged she had been duped by those who had doped her. She went one step further by asking for her world records in the 400m medley to be expunged.

Schirp said that it is "baffling" that the women denied medals by East German doping have not been elevated to their rightful place in Games history.

Chapter 24
In the Mirror

"I ran past the first watchman. Then I was horrified, ran back and
said to the watchman: 'I ran through here while you were looking the other way.'
The watchman gazed ahead of him and said nothing. 'I suppose I really
oughtn't to have done it,' I said. The watchman still said nothing. 'Does your silence
indicate permission to pass?'"
– Franz Kafka, 'The Watchman' (Parables and Paradoxes)

I took my seat next to the first woman to chair the IOC Athletes Commission, Claudia Bokel, the 1996 silver medallist in fencing for Germany. She turned to me and said, "Michelle, do you know what you have just signed? ... That's big, really big."

My signature had just been added to a declaration giving athletes the right to compete at an Olympic Games without political interference.

It was 2015, 35 years after my gold medal swim at the Moscow Olympic Games in 1980. I had been invited back to the Russian capital to join a panel discussion on Women in Sport at the World Olympians Association (WOA) forum.

At the time, I had been helping WOA to build a closer working relationship with the International Olympic Committee. The 2015 forum agreed to a new WOA constitution that committed both organisations to work together.

The global body of Olympians was set up as an independent association. Separate from the IOC, it was established in 1995 by Peter Montgomery, a former water polo player and teammate of mine at the 1976 and 1980 Games (who also competed in 1972 and 1984). He was the founding chair until 1999.

Around the same time as the 2015 forum, I had also been working to create the IOC Athlete Career Program aimed at helping athletes transition to a professional career after sport. My 1984 master's thesis at the University of Southern California was on 'The Retirement of Athletes'.

By 2015, the IOC had a new motto—*'The athletes are the heart of the Olympic movement.'* It was welcome; however, there was a clear line between the active athlete and what I believed was the movement's biggest asset—retired Olympians/alumni.

A more significant milestone was also achieved at the WOA forum. My notes in Baden-Baden and the speech I had written for Kip Keino spelled it out:

- Athletes should not be punished by political decisions.
- Protected from geographical boycotts, athletes need to be chosen solely on their athletic ability.

The declaration was the answer to our call as athletes.

"We pledge to oppose any political or governmental interference in the autonomy of sports organisations which might prevent an athlete from exercising their right to compete in the Olympic Games or other major sporting events which also embody the Olympic spirit."

The declaration was signed by World Olympians Association (WOA) president Joel Bouzou, IOC president Thomas Bach, and WOA patron and IOC member, Prince Albert II of Monaco. There were also signatures from the following Olympians on behalf of all fellow athletes:

- Willie Banks, American Olympian and former world-record holder in triple jump;
- Anastasia Davydova, Russian Olympic Champion in synchronised swimming;
- Hicham El Guerrouj, Moroccan double Olympic champion in middle-distance running;
- Michelle Ford-Eriksson MBE, Australian Olympic champion and former world-record holder in swimming;
- Koji Murofushi, Japanese Olympic champion in hammer throw.

Since the IOC Congress in Baden-Baden in 1981, many of our calls have been answered, but there is still a great deal to be done. I see this from the different levels of sport that I have been involved with from grassroots through to the elite level, and from the boardroom to the field of play.

Four decades after Baden-Baden, doping continues to be the scourge of sport throughout the world. The China crisis of the 1990s and the Russian scandals of the past decade provide proof that the systematic side of cheating survived the collapse of the GDR.

The group's final speech, delivered by Coe, struck a chord. We were polite, but we were resolute.

On doping, we stated, "We consider this to be the most shameful abuse of the Olympic ideal."

Those words were penned and agreed by the pioneers of the Athletes' Voice:

Coe, Thomas Bach, Ivar Formo and myself.

We called for lifetime bans for offending athletes, coaches, doctors and others involved in doping. Emphasis was placed on the unfair nature of laying all blame on the athlete and letting the entourage go free. We stand by that statement today, 43 years on.

The history of anti-doping clearly tells us that many athletes who tested positive for banned substances were teenagers working in circumstances where choice was not an option and coercion was the accepted norm. Nothing demonstrates that more starkly than the GDR doping era. That state may be gone, but the human nature that underpinned its dark part in sport is still present today as was witnessed in Sochi 2014 by the extreme lengths the Russians went with the urine swapping procedures.

FINA had been drawn into doping controversies for decades. The federation was alerted by journalist Craig Lord, writing for *The Times*, to the damage done to female athletes and the sport of swimming by Dr Lothar Kipke. On the fourth time alerting FINA in 2014, Craig asked the FINA Press Commission to put the matter to a vote. It was a unanimous "yes" in favour of asking the board of FINA to consider stripping Kipke, criminally convicted of bodily harm against minors, from its honours list that he had been on since 1986.

The tide started to turn in October 2023 when Craig made his fifth appeal directly to the newly elected president of FINA, Husain Al-Musallam. He asked for details and within a week issued a statement to *The Times* in which he noted: *"FINA understands the concerns of athletes who have competed against others subsequently proved to have cheated. Athletes work their entire lives for a mere chance to compete for a medal, let alone win one. So, when athletes are denied the reward they worked so hard to achieve, FINA must do everything it can to right this wrong."*

Lessons Learned

I was a naive teenager at the Moscow Olympic Games with a determined will to stand at the top of the Olympic award podium in several races. The magnitude of what I achieved by defeating the GDR doping machine in the 800m freestyle did not sink in until many years later when the dreadful details of systematic cheating emerged.

At the time of winning my gold, we may not have known the exact depths to which the East Germans were stooping in order to dominate the sport of swimming, but we were all very aware that every title and medal at those Moscow Games was being targeted by an unnatural presence. This was evidenced by the morphed physical attributes of the athletes, and statistical results on the scoreboards and award podium.

Looking back, I now understand that this era of tainted sport served a much larger purpose than I ever envisioned.

I believe we have the greatest potential to learn the most by studying mistakes of our past, and that was a catalyst for putting my story on paper. When I started this journey I was not a writer or wordsmith, yet I believed it was time to shed light on the past and bring value to those who have also lived it.

My efforts turned into not only the account of a young athlete driven by passion to fulfil a dream, but the story of a dark chapter in history that continues to overshadow sport despite concerted efforts to stay ahead of those who are always trying to cheat.

As I retraced the past, I was reminded of the battles many of us fought to overcome the many injustices of the doping scandals, unfair politics and media, and the cynicism of those who did not understand how our lives were affected.

I now have a different view and appreciation for what I achieved. I also have a newfound empathy for those who share the heartaches and the tears of dreams that we feel were robbed from us, and for those who were denied their freedom to choose what happened with their own bodies. We are all the generation of world-champion athletes whose scars of past abuses remain.

As a young girl, I managed to break through many barriers and achieve so much. I am amazed that I found the energy to believe in myself no matter what was put in front of me. I was blessed that I had the support and today I'm proud that I persevered with my two careers—my education and swimming—both demanding in time and in effort, yet achievable. They are feats that were made possible through the unrelenting support of my team.

Sport is a paradigm of life—one that requires protection if we wish future generations to enjoy its beauty. As this book illustrates, sport is what you make of it. It is about believing in dreams and never giving up despite any odds.

Embrace challenges because you will never know who will win the race. Life in general is not easy. No accomplishment or feat is easy. The truth is in the mirror: you see the person you have become through adversity and can then say, "I am the champion I dreamed to be."

Epilogue

During a late 2009 training, Australian swim coach Ian Pope invited Bill Sweetenham, the master performance strategist who had helped me prepare for my gold-winning finish at the 1980 Moscow Games, to work with some swimmers who had a chance of making the Australian team for the 2010 Commonwealth Games in Delhi, India.

At the end of one session, young swimming sensation Samantha Marshall approached Sweetenham to thank him for his input and guidance. She also said her grandfather was sitting in the stands and would like to speak with him.

Her grandfather was no less than Malcolm Fraser, the former Australian Prime Minister, who had supported the US-led boycott in 1980 and had led the call for the Australian Olympic team not to go to Moscow for the Olympic Games.

In the years since, Mr Fraser had been a constant presence in his granddaughter's life, witnessing her sacrifices in pursuit of a dream, that dream being to represent her country in her sport, which she would fulfil nine months later, winning a silver medal in the 100m breaststroke at the Delhi Commonwealth Games.

While Fraser apologised to Sweetenham that day for his stance on the Olympic boycott, many of the athletes who competed in Moscow feel strongly that no one from the Australian Government or the Australian Olympic Committee has extended that same level of respect to the athletes who competed in Moscow as with all other Olympic teams.

We were mere teenagers, and we were subject to the foulest abuse, labelled as traitors for supporting our athletic dreams while also respecting the decision of the Australian Olympic Council of the day. We were subjected to bullying, ridicule and even death threats simply because we chose to follow a rite of elite athletic passage, the honour of representing our nation at the highest level.

The athletes and coaches on the Moscow Olympic team faced extreme and challenging conditions. Despite the obstacles, we stepped up to win seven medals, two of which were gold. It was against the odds, and our efforts helped turn the tide of opposing opinion in Australia. It also meant the Australian Olympic Committee could forever claim that Australia is one of only five countries that have participated in every summer Olympic Games.

To this day, however, many of us feel we did not count and that our efforts were a historical blip and an embarrassment in a long tradition of Australian excellence at the Olympic Games.

Recognition from our Olympic peers will go a long way in helping many of us find closure and erase the anguish that many have been carrying for over 40 years.

As a representative of the 1980 Olympic athletes, I call on all national sporting federations in Australia and the Australian Olympic Committee to acknowledge and recognise the Moscow Olympic team of 1980. The athletes, coaches and administrators should all be recognised for their unwavering commitment to the Olympic ideals and their resilience in the face of extreme adversity and negative public opinion.

Those who went to Moscow not only kept the torch lit, we ensured the eternal flame continued burning for all future athletes.

As an elite athlete, I believe high-level sportspeople should be role models for future generations.

We are a direct reflection of the Olympic ideals, and we must teach the rules of fair play and respect for all.

The GDR doping scandal was life-changing, especially for thousands of female athletes throughout the 1970s and 1980s. It is disheartening to know that it also sent a message to athletes that if they wanted a chance of winning in international competitions, they would have to cheat.

My intent for this book is to bring attention to this era. But more so, it is my most sincere hope that the IOC and the International Sporting Federations, hopefully led by World Aquatics, acknowledge the injustice done to these women who were mostly innocent victims of a state-sanctioned doping regime that created a playing field which was inconsistent with Olympic ideals.

With the Olympic Games of Paris 2024, Los Angeles 2028 and Brisbane 2032 upon us, I call upon the IOC and the International Sporting Federations to reallocate the medals through the 'Olympic Medal Reallocation program' and re-establish the record books from the Montreal 1976, Moscow 1980, and Seoul 1988 Olympic Games.

Appendix

Achievements

Awards

- Australian Female Athlete of the Year, 1980
- Australian Sports Star of the Year, 1980
- World Trophy for Australasia (Helms Athletic Foundation), 1980
- Australian Sportsperson of the Year, 1981
- The Order of the British Empire - Member (MBE), New Year's Honours list, 1982
- Honouree/Inducted into the Australian Sports Hall of Fame, 1985
- Honouree /inducted into the International Swimming Hall of Fame, 1994
- Three-time Australia's 'Outstanding Swimmer of the Year', 1977, 1978, 1980
- Australian Sports Medal, 2000

Academic Qualifications

- Scholarship holder, University of South California
- Bachelor of Arts, University of Southern California
- Master of Arts, University of Southern California

In the Pool

- Fastest 12-year-old swimmer in the world 100m freestyle
- Olympic Gold Medallist, 800 metres Freestyle, Moscow 1980
- Olympic Bronze Medallist, 200 metres Butterfly, 1980 Moscow
- Olympic Record Holder, 800 metres Freestyle, 1980
- Two-time World record Holder, 800 metres Freestyle, 1977, 1978
- Commonwealth Gold Medallist, 200 metres Butterfly, 1978, 1982
- Commonwealth Record Holder, 200 metres Butterfly, 1978, 1982
- Commonwealth Record Holder, 200 metres Butterfly, 1976-1984
- Commonwealth Record Holder, 400 metres Freestyle, 1977

- Commonwealth Record Holder, 800 metres Freestyle, 1977, 1978
- International representative for Australia in Swimming, 1975-1985
- Youngest swimmer on the 1976 Montreal Olympics team, at 13 years
- Two-time Olympian, 1976 and 1980
- 31 National Australian Records

Acknowledgements

Setting a goal is one thing. Getting it done is another.

I would never have put pen to paper if it wasn't for the enthusiasm of my sons, Michael and Bo. They convinced me my story was worth telling and stood by me with encouragement, tenacity and indulgence. They pushed me to go further than I imagined I could, embracing my story and my achievements. My endless thanks go to both for inspiring me.

My husband, Christian, shouldered me through thick and thin. His calm and generous manner was a tower of strength when my emotions were scrambled while reliving some of the more difficult times.

It is a journey, not a sprint, I was told. How true. It has taken years of research, writing and sifting through the pages to capture the moments and relive the memories. Thank you to my parents, Jan and Ian, who meticulously saved every press clipping and ensured I had a rich archive to turn to, including letters, clippings, memorabilia and much else, no matter how small or insignificant.

My St George Girls High School friends, who wrote me letters throughout my swimming career, revived many memories.

I was blessed to have a support group of extraordinarily talented friends, Claudia Bokel, Elvira Ramini, Tova and Jonathan Grover, and Karen Puels, who gave me perspective and allowed me to see my story from various angles.

Thank you to Jennifer Kremmer and Kirsty Wood for their patience and enthusiasm to help me with the original manuscript and to Heather Lima for her invaluable assistance.

I extend eternal gratitude to my dear friend from the USC swim team, Robin Anderson, née Fiene, for her enthusiasm and the hours spent discussing the different topics. The ultimate 'go-to person' who provided me with the stamina and direction from start to finish. Her connection to this story was through her status as a contender for the US team in 1980 and as a friend who lived through some of my most trying times. From day one, she encouraged me to dig deep and to leave no stone unturned.

Thank you to Anthony Edgar, a friend from Sydney 2000 and later the IOC, who always believed in the idea. I am grateful for his guidance and encouragement.

I was privileged to have a super-talented writer, journalist and expert on GDR doping to support this project. I am deeply grateful to Craig Lord for his deep knowledge of swimming, attention to detail and capacity to put the right words around some of the more delicate passages in this book. His positive attitude and unnerving style was welcomed, especially when working to meet a tight deadline.

Sports photographer Russ McPhedran gave me many of his photos of my career and was one of the few photographers who went to Moscow. Thank you for capturing and sharing the moments.

To my publisher Bonita Mersiades and the team at Fair Play Publishing, who gave this book priority and got me to the finish line. Thank you!

To the many who have helped me along this journey, including Chip Le Grand, Alan Whitiker, Ian Heads, Travis Cranley, Ian Hanson, I trust you will enjoy the read.

A good team is one that guides us, fixes the rudder, trims the sails and reinforces that what you are doing is right. To a great team. Thank you.

Index

MORE REALLY GOOD FOOTBALL BOOKS FROM FAIR PLAY PUBLISHING

FAIRPLAY
PUBLISHING

fairplaypublishing.com.au

Milton Keynes UK
Ingram Content Group UK Ltd.
UKHW050858190824
447094UK00001BA/1